JOHN BALE

Mythmaker for the English Reformation

JOHN
BALE *Mythmaker*
for the English
Reformation

by | Leslie P. Fairfield

1976
Purdue University Press
West Lafayette, Indiana

©1976 by the Purdue Research Foundation

Library of Congress Catalog Number 75-19953

International Standard Book Number 0-911198-42-3

Printed in the United States of America

For Lynnie

Mulierem fortem quis inveniet?

Procul et de ultimis finibus pretium eius.

Confidit in ea cor viri sui.

Contents

Preface

Scholarship some thirty-five years ago came to recognize John Bale as an important early figure in sixteenth-century English drama and in Tudor antiquarian studies. The pioneering work was the monograph by Jesse Harris, *John Bale* (Urbana, Illinois, 1940), which especially treated Bale's work as a playwright in the 1530s. Soon after Harris's work appeared, Honor McCusker's *John Bale: Dramatist and Antiquary* (Bryn Mawr, Pennsylvania, 1942) drew attention to the importance of Bale's bibliographical studies of medieval English literature. McCusker also usefully printed some lengthy excerpts from Bale's extant letters, making use of archival sources in Britain which had been inaccessible to Harris. At about the same time, W. T. Davies published an invaluable bibliography of Bale's works in print and in manuscript (W. T. Davies, "A Bibliography of John Bale," *Oxford Bibliographical Society Proceedings and Papers*, vol. 5, part 4, [1940], pp. 203-279). Drawing on still more manuscript sources than McCusker used, Davies included in his work a rather thorough biographical sketch of the reformer. Thanks to all this spadework in the early 1940s, Bale's reputation as a Protestant star of the second magnitude was firmly established. A more recent work by Thora B. Blatt, *The Plays of John Bale* (Copenhagen, 1968), has tied up some loose ends left by Harris and McCusker regarding Bale's dramatic activity. In addition, a study of John Foxe as a martyrologist (William Haller, *Foxe's Book of Martyrs and the Elect Nation*, [London, 1967]) recently attributed to Bale a significant influence upon Foxe's historical thought, and through

Foxe, upon the national self-consciousness of the Elizabethan age. Haller was interested in Bale only in passing,
however, and did not treat the development of the early
reformer's historical thought for its own sake.

In this study, I have tried to trace and explain the
growth of Bale's historical ideas. I have characterized Bale
as a "mythmaker" because his retelling of English history
supplied his countrymen with a new way of understanding
the meaning of their national experience. Partly drawing
upon historical data, partly inventing it, Bale wove an
explanation of England's past which showed his contemporaries why the Reformation had been necessary and
inevitable. His achievement—fulfilled in the work of John
Foxe—was to supply Protestant Englishmen with a usable
past.

As the genesis of Bale's historical ideas occurred
because specific influences in his environment bore upon
him, I have included a good deal of biographical data (some
of it new, much of it indebted to Davies and McCusker).
My regard for the details of Bale's life has been, however,
secondary and subordinate to my interest in his ideas.

Several individuals have helped measurably in the
course of this study. Professor Wilbur K. Jordan of Harvard
University guided my initial investigations into Bale's
thought. Mr. Peter Clark, the Rev. Dr. Keith J. Egan, O.
Carm., Dr. Alan Kreider, the Rev. Dr. Hughes O. Old, and
Professor Arthur J. Slavin all offered useful counsel and
assistance. Mrs. Joyce Good and the secretaries of the
Department of History at Purdue coped nobly and cheer-
fully with Latin footnotes. The editors of *Renaissance
Quarterly* and *The Journal of Ecclesiastical History* suggested
useful changes in earlier drafts of Chapter 5, parts of which
appeared in article form in those journals. To each my
thanks.

Leslie P. Fairfield
West Lafayette, Indiana

I / *The Carmelite Friar*

John Bale's early life gave no hint that he would become in his forties an arch-Protestant propagandist and historian of the English Reformation. His later notoriety as the anti-papal "Bilious Bale" may tempt one to forget that he spent nearly thirty years as a Carmelite friar. Before the early 1530s, in fact, Bale's piety and values were wholly typical of late medieval religious life in England. Other Englishmen of his generation may have been feeling a restless dissatisfaction with the faith and worship of Catholic England, and may have been finding in Erasmian or Lutheran ideas a new outlook upon life. Not so Friar Bale. Anticlerical, humanist, and Lutheran currents of thought left him untouched until well after his thirty-fifth year.

Bale was born on November 21, 1495, in the little village of Covehithe, a mile or so inland from the coast of Suffolk between Lowestoft and Southwold.[1] The impressive parish church of St. Andrew, built in perpendicular style by a wealthy fifteenth-century incumbent, belied the poverty of the villagers who lived in its shadow. Covehithe lay on a band of sandy and loamy soil extending up and down the coast of Suffolk, where in the late fifteenth century sheep-raising and the cultivation of barley, rye, and wheat formed the basis of the economy. Unfortunately for the peasants of that area, the manorial landlords (or those to whom they leased their manors) had virtually exclusive rights over the pasturage of sheep on the common fields. Not only was the profitable enterprise of sheep-farming effectively closed to the peasants, therefore, but the latter were also forced to adjust their system of cultivation and crop-rotation to fit the lords' rights of pasturage. In the coastal marshes and fens, it is true, peasants were often able to graze dairy cattle and fatten beef for the market, thereby adding to their meager income from the plowland. The village of Covehithe with its nearby streams no doubt offered pasturage of this kind. But the picture of the area as a whole is marked by great disparities in wealth. Throughout the sheep-and-corn regions of Suffolk and Norfolk, the contrast was striking between the nobles and gentry, the large freeholders and leaseholders, and the many who made up the vast peasant majority.[2] There was little likelihood, then, that a child born into a humble family in Covehithe would know anything in a lifetime but labor for little return. Rarely would he or she be able to move up the social ladder, or even to travel much beyond earshot of the bells in St. Andrew's spire (unless of course one took to the sea—an option which evidently never tempted John Bale). The slim prospect of social mobility was made smaller if a family had numerous offspring to provide for, as was the case with Henry and Margaret Bale, John's parents.[3]

One avenue existed, however, whereby a peasant without a rich patron could escape from a lifetime of plowing the Suffolk earth. This was of course the Church— or, more specifically, one of the religious orders which would accept poor youths, and if they were bright, educate them and allow them to rise as far as their abilities and friendships would take them. Henry and Margaret Bale were fortunate to place their eldest son John with the Carmelite friars of Norwich, the most distinguished Carmelite convent in East Anglia, an area where that order had been strong in numbers for a couple of centuries.[4] Young John went up to Norwich when he was a few months past the age of eleven. He was there in 1507 when the great fire of Easter week broke out and nearly destroyed the city.[5]

The order which accepted John Bale at eleven—and into which he was in due course professed—had seen more prosperous days in England, but still appeared to be a relatively durable part of the religious landscape. The Carmelites (the Order of Our Lady of Mount Carmel, or the "White Friars") seem to have sprung from a community of hermits which had coalesced, in the wake of the Crusades, on the slopes of Mount Carmel near Acre in Palestine during the mid-twelfth century. The early leaders (a certain Bertholdus, for instance) and probably most members of the group were Europeans, pilgrims who had chosen to answer their calling to the solitary life in a location so evocative of biblical memories. Albert of Vercelli, patriarch of Jerusalem, gave the community a very strict rule around 1210, stressing silence and solitude. This was hardly the pattern of life which the mendicant orders would later adopt. As it happened, the Moslem counteroffensive drove the proto-Carmelites from their mountainside retreats, and indeed from their eremitical pattern of life altogether. In the 1230s they took refuge abroad, first on the island of Cyprus and then in various parts of Europe. Crusader barons like Richard de Grey first brought Carmelites to England around 1242, and helped them establish hermitages in various wild and deserted parts of Kent and Northumberland. Already, however, the solitary and contemplative impulse among the Carmelites was being weakened by the attraction of the mendicant ideal. The early prestige of the Franciscans and the Dominicans, the manifest need in the European cities and towns for the preaching and teaching ministry they offered, the availability of the universities as training-grounds for this active and engaged life—all of these forces, plus the inappropriateness of the old Carmelite rule in the damp European winters, encouraged a metamorphosis of the order into the Franciscan or Dominican pattern. As early as 1229, in fact, Carmelite emigrants to southern Italy had successfully petitioned Pope Gregory IX to be recognized as mendicants. The issue was officially settled in the 1240s and 1250s, when the eremitical heritage of the order was consciously repudiated. Simon (later surnamed "Stock"), an English hermit elected prior general of the order in 1247, obtained papal approval for a revision of the rule. The Dominican prelates who were appointed to the task not surprisingly molded and shaped the Carmelites in their own order's image. Physical austerity and the rule of silence were mitigated, the obligation to seek out homes in the wilderness was dropped, and in short the Carmelites began to infiltrate the towns and universities of Europe with the other mendicant orders. The English Carmelites established convents about this time in London, at Chesterton near Cambridge, and then at York, Oxford, Bristol, Norwich, and other centers of population. The transformation apparently caused a certain spiritual uneasiness, for throughout the thirteenth century distinguished English Carmelites sporadically renounced the "worldly" mendicant life and retired to lonely hermitages. But the die was cast, and the order (with its revised rule) received final sanction and approval at the Council of Lyons in 1274.

Perhaps it was a residual impulse toward the eremitical life that kept the English Carmelites from making a notable reputation in the universities or the Church at large in the thirteenth century. Perhaps the conflicts with the secular clergy, common to all the friars, had a retarding effect as well. In any case, the Carmelites had been in England for almost a century before they produced a scholar of wide reputation, John Baconthorpe (d. 1346), an Oxford theologian and English prior provincial. The reputation of Baconthorpe for learning and piety and the success of the whole order in preaching and teaching enabled the English province to expand (at its zenith, before the Black Death) to include about eight hundred friars in some thirty-five houses. The recurring outbreaks of plague in 1348 and thereafter do not seem to have harmed the English Carmelites' influence or prestige, though perhaps their numbers dwindled slightly. The Carmelites played a highly visible part in the Church's counterattack on John Wyclif, one of their number (Peter Stokes) winning the equivocal distinction of being labeled "White Dog" by the Oxford heretic. The English Church's definitive reply to Wyclif and to Lollardy was penned by Thomas Netter of Walden, Carmelite prior provincial from 1414 to 1430. After Wyclif the Lollards produced no mind that could cope with the ponderous and thorough arguments of Netter's *Doctrinale*. It is also indicative of Carmelite prestige in the early fifteenth century that Netter and other leaders of the order replaced the Dominicans as royal confessors under Henry IV and Henry V.

After the death of Thomas Netter around 1430, however, the Carmelites entered a slow decline in numbers, prestige, and *esprit de corps*. At Oxford and Cambridge, the growth of colleges in the fifteenth century meant that the mendicants' convents no longer seemed such attractive havens for young scholars. Thus the friars could no longer compete so strongly for the brightest minds in each generation. Indeed, the level of Carmelite learning in England seems to have dropped off noticeably after 1430 or so. Likewise the mitigation of the Carmelite rule granted by Pope Eugenius IV in 1432, which seemed a reasonable enough concession to the pressure of Oxford and Cam-bridge life, did nothing to enhance the order's stature in the eyes of the English laity. Actual rather than intentional poverty seems therefore to have become a real problem to the Carmelites in the later fifteenth century. Making virtue of an uncomfortable necessity, the London White Friars even hauled out the old question of apostolic poverty and attacked the secular Church for its wealth in a series of sermons during 1464 and 1465. This foray gained the order nothing save a three-year spell in the papal dungeon, the Castell' St. Angelo, for Prior Provincial John Milverton. The humiliation involved was aggravated when the order found that it could not even raise the money to buy Milverton's release. Despite periodic crises like this one in the 1460s, however, the English Carmelites had a certain plodding durability at the time when John Bale joined their numbers. Their houses were standing, their libraries were frequently well-stocked, and they could still attract some intelligent young men. There was hardly a suggestion in the air that the order's future would not repeat, more or less, the pattern of the recent past. John Bale certainly never supposed otherwise until the early 1530s.[6]

After Bale had lived and studied for seven years or so in the Norwich convent, the Carmelites sent him up to Cambridge. In one of his later books he recalled that he had gone up to the university town in 1514, though entries in some of his early manuscripts suggest that he may at least have visited Cambridge the previous year. Bale was to spend the next sixteen years of his life in and out of Cambridge, but for a while, at least, he still looked upon the Carmelite house in Norwich as his real home. On the cover of a manuscript which he copied during his early years at the university, Bale referred to himself as "an offspring of the convent in the distinguished city of Norwich."[7]

To a young man coming up from the bustling environment of Norwich, the town of Cambridge may not have seemed overwhelmingly impressive.[8] Its narrow streets are not likely to have smelled much different, and on market days the din was doubtless very familiar. Still the Carmelite convent which was Bale's home[9] had a pleasant situation on the banks of the Cam, just north of Queens' College. Across the river was the garden which Queens' had recently purchased, where the fellows might stroll and converse.[10] Bale never had much to say in later years, however, about the time he had spent at Cambridge; he scarcely mentioned either the town or his formal studies (save to condemn the scholastic nature of the latter). As far as landscape and architecture were concerned, Bale would never demonstrate much sensitivity.[11] Regarding his studies, the Cambridge curriculum seems not to have touched him in the core of his being, where he really lived. Bale's voluminous manuscripts from the Cambridge years (filled with miscellaneous information on Carmelite history) give not the slightest indication that the young friar was pursuing a rather rigorous course of studies.

For the doctorate in divinity—which, as it turned out, was to be Bale's goal—the regulations given to the Carmelite order in 1397 prescribed first of all the usual seven years in the faculty of arts, culminating in the master's degree. For the first two years the young student would study rhetoric and Aristotelian logic, qualifying him in his second year to stand and dispute in the university schools (in Cambridge, the quadrangle constructed mostly in the fifteenth century, ten or fifteen minutes' walk north of the Carmelite house). In the third and fourth years, the undergraduate would come to grips with the "three philosophies" (natural, moral, and mental) of Aristotle, with the dubious assistance of commentaries by Duns Scotus and Alexander Hales. Should the student satisfy the vice-chancellor of his competence in all he had been taught so far, the young man would normally be admitted B.A. towards the end of his fourth year. Then, time and money permitting, there followed three more years for the M.A. (the really significant arts degree): more Aristotle, the sharpening of one's wits and dialectical skill by disputing in the schools, perhaps a bit of lecturing. Ideally, at the end of the seventh academic year in early July, the successful candidates were incepted as masters of arts with considerable pomp. This was roughly the course, for secular and regular undergraduates alike, which the Carmelite seeking the doctorate in divinity must complete first. According to the regulations for the doctorate established in 1397, seven more years of study in the faculty of theology followed the M.A., and then four years of lecturing on the *Sentences* of Peter Lombard and on the Bible. "Whatever else they were," Professor McFarlane remarked of medieval doctors in divinity, "they were not raw."[12] By Bale's day, however, dispensations to friars were frequent, allowing them to reckon time spent at some other university (or in various convents) as counting towards their degrees.[13] Bale's "grace" for the B. D. in 1529 in fact mentioned that his studies in theology had been undertaken partly overseas. In Bale's later autobiographical sketches he named Louvain and Toulouse as other universities where he had studied.[14] There is no surviving Cambridge record of Bale's doctorate, but he was being styled *theologie doctor* by 1534.[15] He probably received the degree within two years or less of proceeding B. D., since he had already spent ten years studying theology, and since (judging from his studies overseas) the university was evidently willing to construe the academic regulations somewhat loosely in his case, anyway.

Meanwhile Bale had often been occupied with other pastimes than reading Aristotle and medieval theology, hearing lectures, and disputing in the Cambridge schools. He was after all not a private or independent student, bound for a career in the royal service or for the pursuit of a rich benefice (or several). A friar as well as a scholar, he was charged with duties within the Carmelite order, and indeed the order continued to spark his enthusiasm and hold his primary loyalty. A note in a manuscript of about 1520 refers to him in somewhat questionable Latin as "brother John Bale, the boys' instructor"[16] so he was probably at some point responsible for the education of novices in the Cambridge convent. During these years as well, Bale took Holy Orders as a matter of course. He was ordained to the diaconate by Bishop West of Ely at Barnwell in 1516;[17] presumably his ordination to the priesthood came in the early 1520s, though record of this has not survived. During the 1520s Bale seems to have spent quite some time away from Cambridge, indulging a passion that now emerges as a central facet of his personality: the study of Carmelite antiquities. Judging from the evidence in his massive notebooks, the history of the Carmelite order now became Bale's first love—not the study of scholastic theology or disputation in the schools at Cambridge.[18] The peripatetic life of a friar allowed him plenty of opportunity to wander from house to house within his order, visiting their libraries and making copious notes on the Carmelite writers whose works he found in manuscript there. One collection of such notes, in Bale's youthful handwriting, seems to date from 1522 or 1523 and shows that he visited various Carmelite convents in the Low Countries, including houses at Bruges, Ghent, Antwerp, and Brussels.[19] Probably on his way to the Continent on this trip, he also stopped at the houses in Maldon, Sandwich, and Calais.[20] (In 1550 he was to remember that twenty-eight years previously he had seen an old chronicle in manuscript at Calais.[21]) Perhaps it was during this trip that Bale spent some time at the University of Louvain.[22] He never said much, either in his notebooks at the time or later, about his stay in this stronghold of traditional Catholicism, and one is at liberty to wonder whether the university there made much impression on him. Back in England, on at least one occasion during the early 1520s he visited his home convent at Norwich and copied some material from a manuscript there about Carmelite opponents of John Wyclif—this manuscript being the famous compilation known as *Fasciculi Zizaniorum,* a goldmine of information on Wyclif and early Lollardy, one copy of which probably rested in the Carmelite library at Norwich.[23] Characteristically, Bale was interested specifically in the Carmelite heroes like Peter ("White Dog") Stokes and Thomas Netter of Walden who had opposed the Lollards; his notes show no interest whatsoever in Wycliffite beliefs, and certainly no hint of approval. They had been foils for the exercise of Carmelite brilliance in theology, but otherwise were without significance.[24]

Bale was certainly in England in 1526 when he wrote an antiphon to the Virgin at a chapter meeting in the convent at Hitchin. It is interesting that in identifying the poem as his own, he refers to himself as "Carmelite of Norwich."[25] Despite the years he must have spent in Cambridge, he evidently never felt that he had put down roots there. Perhaps that helps explain why his experience of the university community in the 1520s (the lingering influence of Erasmus at Queens', the Lutheran preaching of Barnes, Bilney, and Latimer in St. Edward's, and so on) passed him by without touching him deeply. At any rate, he was off again in early 1527 to the Continent for another antiquarian tour. He started a new notebook when he set out from Norwich, and it contains poems and epitaphs, notes on Carmelite dignitaries and chapter meetings, and records of Carmelite authors which Bale collected as he wandered from house to house in France. It was quite a thorough trip. From Calais he made his way to Paris, then south to Orleans and Bourges; then southeast into Savoy; after that, west to the convent at Toulouse, which he used as a base for shorter trips to houses in Provence; then west again to Bordeaux, and finally back to Calais through Poitiers and Paris once more.[26] Whether Bale was undertaking this research as a purely free-lance project, or whether he had some specific commission from the English province to gather data, one cannot tell. He seems to have had considerable autonomy to come and go as he wished, even to stop off and study at a university should the fancy strike him. Bale later described how he had made friends with William Gregory, a Scotsman who was prior of the Carmelite convent at Toulouse, and how Gregory had offered him (on what authority is not clear) a doctorate from the faculty of theology there, if Bale would only stay a year. In his Protestant years Bale liked to think that he had turned the offer down because of Gregory's "idolatrous mass-mongering"—a sentiment wholly out of keeping with the spirit of Bale's notes at the time. The Mass hardly had a pejorative connotation for him, when he could record with approval the story of a Provençal friar who was so filled by the love of God while celebrating Mass that he rose a foot off the ground.[27] Probably Bale's commitment to his antiquarian project was the reason he decided to move on, though his copious notes from Toulouse indicate that he had found a good deal of useful material in the Carmelite library there.[28]

So by the middle of 1528 Bale was back in Cambridge,[29] pulling the strands of his education together and preparing to take his degrees in divinity. What had been the cumulative effect of his university training on him? It is intriguing, for example, to imagine the young Friar Bale living in the Carmelite house just across the narrow lane from Queens' College, where Erasmus had resided during part of his stay in Cambridge. Bale must have heard a good deal about the famous Dutch scholar, who had only just departed when Bale came to stay in 1514. The figure of Erasmus had evidently been a well-known sight as he took his infrequent exercise by riding around Market Hill.[30] Though the great humanist may not indeed have spent the latter part of his Cambridge days in Queens' College, next door to the Carmelite convent, still the Erasmian spirit represented one breeze stirring the community in which Bale lived and studied.

Was the young friar totally oblivious to humanist ideas? One is led to wonder here especially because in Bale's manuscript notebooks from the 1520s there are a good many quotations from the Italian Carmelite humanist, Baptista Mantuanus (1448-1516). Mantuanus had joined the Carmelite order in 1466, after having studied Greek and theology at Mantua and Padua. His classical interests persisted after he became a friar and he continued to write prolifically. He also rose within the order, becoming prior general during the last three years of his life.[31] For this reason, as well as for his literary and scholarly fame, Mantuanus naturally caught Bale's eye. It is interesting to note, though, that the passages which Bale transcribed from Mantuanus's works were all ones which breathed a conventional spirit of late medieval piety. Nothing at Cambridge (or elsewhere) had sensitized Bale to notice or value Mantuanus's intimations of nostalgia for Greek and Roman civilization, the passages in his works which viewed the past as past, or any other expressions of the humanist side to his mentality. Only the Mantuanus who agreed with Bale's own world-view was worth the trouble to record. Bale copied, for example, a sermon which his fellow Carmelite had preached in 1476, demonstrating that by the example of the four winds, the four gospels, and so on, there ought to be four mendicant orders—and that of these the Carmelites were obviously the most venerable since they traced their ancestry all the way back to the prophet Elijah's foundation on Mount Carmel.[32] There was not a lot here of humanist historical criticism or philological scholarship, but a good deal which appealed to Bale's enthusiasm for his order. Another of Bale's transcriptions from Mantuanus described the latter's vocation to the Carmelite life—he had felt a deep sense of sin and a fear of death, and had dedicated himself to the Virgin during a serious illness.[33] Again, there was nothing in this that would conflict with Bale's own piety. Perhaps the most striking example of Bale's lack of empathy with the inner spirit of humanist thought is a short poem which he composed at Toulouse in 1527, and dedicated to St. Joanna:

> *Votum balei ad beatam Johannam virginem*
>
> *Virgo tholosana quam prenutrivit in urbe*
> *Carmelus, sceleri propiciare meo.*
> *Fac placeam christo, fac me servire tonanti*
> *Nec pereat tempus maxima dona dei.*
> *Proficiam scriptis, studio quoque relligione* (sic)
> *Et meritis vitae, diva Johanna fave.*[34]

In form these are quite respectable elegiac couplets, and Bale even uses the classical epithet *tonans* ("the Thunderer") in referring to God. But the motivation and the spirit of the poem are completely traditional. Bale wants the saint to help him be a better friar and win admission to heaven.

Bale seems to have been no more sensitive to the concerns moving the northern humanists in the early sixteenth century than he was aware of the inner spirit of the older Italian movement. No more than he understood the whole of Baptista Mantuanus did he really grasp what Erasmus, Colet, and their allies had been trying to do.

Bale's early manuscripts are notable for the absence of references to the Bible in them—let alone references demonstrating any philological interest or desire to recapture the pure text of Scripture. There is no sign that he ever had any notion of acquiring Greek. Nor is there any evidence that Bale found the ethical inwardness of Erasmus's *Enchiridion* appealing. And in Bale there is certainly nothing of the droll irony toward English piety which provoked Erasmus's lampoon *A Pilgrimage of Pure Devotion*. The shrine of Our Lady at Walsingham was still to Bale an object of veneration. So the Carmelite convent and Queens' College may have been juxtaposed physically in Cambridge, but spiritually and intellectually they were worlds apart. Humanist influences seem to have left Bale's traditional piety quite unscathed.

As for the Cambridge of Robert Barnes, Thomas Bilney, and the Lutheran circle at the White Horse Tavern,[35] there is still less sign that their world impinged on Bale's life. He did recall much later that he had known Barnes during their years at Cambridge (Barnes, Bale said, had got on more quickly in the arts course than he had himself). And Bale had also known Thomas Cranmer while the latter was a fellow of Jesus College. But there is no evidence that Bale himself belonged to Jesus College, rubbing shoulders daily with the future archbishop.[36] And there were any number of the leading first-generation reformers who were at the university in the 1520s, and whom Bale never claimed to have known—Coverdale, Frith, Joye, and Tyndale, for example. All this argues against Bale's having spent much time in "Little Germany," the White Horse Tavern in St. Edward's parish. It is quite clear from Bale's notebooks that during the 1520s he was marching to a traditional drummer, quite out of step with the evangelical circle at the university. Bale was not wholly oblivious to the influx of Lutheran ideas and Lutheran books, to be sure. Despite the formal burning of such books at Cambridge in 1520 and 1521, and despite Bale's obvious distaste for Lutheran literature, he did read a Latin edition of Joachim von Watt's *Vom Alten und Neuen Gott* (which appeared in 1521). However, Bale was interested only in the book's sardonic treatment of Carmelite legends, and he dismissed the author as "impious." In his notes, Bale wrote off the author of another Lutheran book as a "scoundrel."[37] Other references to the progress of the Continental Reformation or its reverberations in England are very scanty among Bale's notes. He did in one place quote a poem against Luther by a Carmelite from Ghent.[38] But on the whole Bale seems to have been neither interested in the beginnings of the Reformation in the fifteen years or so following 1517, nor especially aware of the threat the movement posed to his Carmelite order. That is, unless one assumes that he hurried from convent to convent recording notes on Carmelite history precisely because he sensed the order crumbling around him, and wanted to save what he could. That is possible, but nothing he wrote before 1530 or so suggests this motive. The impression one gets from reading his early notebooks is one of sheer filiopietistic enthusiasm. During his Cambridge years, Bale's traditional Carmelite world-view was evidently not threatened or shaken by the novelties being discussed over at the White Horse Tavern. No more was Bale a part of that environment than he was a citizen of the Cambridge which looked to Erasmus for inspiration.

If Bale's Carmelite upbringing at Norwich kept him effectively insulated from the newer currents of thought when he got to Cambridge, one wonders if for that reason he was more receptive to the traditional curriculum in philosophy and theology which the university offered him. Here one is on rather shaky ground, for the *argumentum a silentio* is dangerous, and none of Bale's notebooks which might have related specifically to his formal studies have survived. Those which do exist represent his extracurricular antiquarian work, and not surprisingly have very little to say about Aristotle, St. Thomas, Duns Scotus, and the like. Nor are Bale's later works much help in revealing the impact of the late-medieval curriculum on his mind in the

1520s. The fact that he later repudiated it all does not prove that he consciously found the curriculum frustrating in the years before 1530. When Bale in his old age said that he had wandered about at Cambridge in "blindness of mind,"[39] he was revealing more about his attitude then than about his thoughts as a young friar. One has therefore rather little of a direct nature to go on from Bale's Cambridge years themselves.

If one admits as evidence the books he published later in his life, however, one can make a few observations about how the university education molded and shaped Bale's mind in the long run. In the first place, it is striking how few references Bale ever made in his later works to Aquinas, Bonaventura, Scotus, Ockham, or other doctors of the medieval Church—save to condemn them *en bloc*. Nor did he use their own ammunition to attack them. Once, he said, he had used a Scotist distinction in an argument with Archbishop Lee of York;[40] but he obviously felt badly about this concession, and blamed Lee for being more impressed, on the whole, by Scotus than by the Bible. Bale's plan of action, after he became a Protestant in the 1530s, was simply to assert the futility of medieval theology, using Scripture and chronicles as evidence. He did not consider it his calling to refute the traditional the-ologians on their own terms, systematically and syllo-gistically. Manifestly, Bale's strong point was not closely-reasoned argument. On the occasions when he attempted it (as for example in his *Apology of Johan Bale agaynste a ranke Papyst*, in 1550 or so) his efforts fell flat. Prob-ably Bale recognized his limitation here. In his Protes-tant pamphlets, he generally found it more congenial to eschew the rapier of dialectic in favor of a blunter in-strument: "Ye fare lyke a gargull in a wall with a spowte in his mouthe, which doth nothynge els but spewe oute water."[41] If it is permissible to read back anything from Bale's later work, one may guess that he failed to find either the content or the method of scholastic theology overwhelmingly appealing. There was to be sure one habit of mind, a by-product of the scholastic method, which Bale evidently did pick up at Cambridge and which he retained all his life: the belief that when an opponent had been refuted *in singulis* he had been dealt with *in toto*. This laborious sentence-by-sentence approach was of course characteristic of most sixteenth-century argumentation. So the plodding, point-by-point construction of Bale's Protestant pamphlets (including those of the very last years of his life)[42] represented one legacy of Bale's training in the Cambridge schools. Apart from this methodological contribution, however, the university does not seem to have supplied the really crucial items of Bale's intellectual furniture, either in the 1520s or after his conversion.

While Bale was still a friar, then, his basic values and beliefs stemmed (not surprisingly) from his Carmelite environment. Here was the matrix in which his early habits of piety had been formed, and here was the focus of his intense loyalty—the enthusiasm which moved him to gather and collect so diligently the records of his order's distinguished past. The piety, first of all, which suffused Bale's early manuscript notebooks is like so much of his character: exaggerated, a bit overdone. His early exuberance in this vein may help explain why he later had to repudiate it all so violently. It is all so conventionally late medieval that one wonders a bit how Bale was able to travel so much and change so little. (The change was the more explosive when it finally came.) Several characteristics of Bale's spiritual life stand out in particular as one reads his notebooks from the years before 1530.

First of all, the Virgin and the saints are the primary objects of Bale's devotion, not the Father or the Son. There is no sign, to be sure, in Bale's manuscripts that the figure of Jesus was a fearsome one for him—the Lord sitting on the rainbow at the Last Day holding the sword of judgment and punishment, as in the popular woodcuts which had terrified Martin Luther.[43] Neither is there any indication in Bale's notebooks that fear of purgatory and its grisly torments preoccupied him especially. He seems to have avoided this pitfall of the late medieval religious imagination.[44] A certain fear of God's wrath may have underlain Bale's devotion to the Virgin and to the approachable saints, as mediators. This was after all one part of the thought-world in which Friar Bale lived. But probably much more influential in shaping his devotional life, more important than *Angst* about his salvation, was the elaborate round of Carmelite offices in honor of the Virgin and the saints, especially those saints whom the order claimed as its own. The Virgin, patron of the Carmelites, was naturally the object of Bale's special veneration.[45]

The earliest existing manuscript in Bale's hand—a collection of Carmelite offices which he made as a young student at Cambridge[46]—contains a service entitled *In festo solempnis commemoracionis beate marie specialis carmelitarum patrone.*[47] The prayers addressed to the Virgin in this office give a useful indication of the Mariolatry which was a central part of Bale's piety. Mary is the channel of grace par excellence ("O Thou Mother, closer to God and swifter than the saints to bestow the gifts of life. . .").[48] She is the trusted patron of the Carmelite friars, who are under her special protection ("O happy Lady and Patron of Carmel, who . . . keeps the enemy from savaging her Carmelite flock . . .").[49] Virginity and purity are among her special characteristics ("O blessed Lady of Heaven, flower among virgins . . . lily of chastity . . .")[50] and by implication the celibate life is particularly pleasing to her, winning her special favor. All of these conventional attitudes toward the Virgin appear later in Bale's notes and in the poems which he wrote in the 1520s. The antiphon which he wrote in the convent at Hitchin in 1526 begins,

> *Ave florens flos Carmeli, pia patris filia*
> *Genetrix emanuelis, felix inter millia* (sic)
> *Virgo tuis da ceu soles, fratribus auxilia . . . .*[51]

Just as Mary could be trusted to help her Carmelites acquire the virtues which would win entrance to Heaven, so also were there many saints who would be happy to share with the friars the treasury of their accumulated merits. In the early manuscript of offices which Bale copied at Cambridge, there is a prayer to St. Cyril asking, "By thy holy merit wipe out our debts . . . ."[52] Bale's poem to St. Joanna of Toulouse, quoted above, expresses the same trust in the intercessory power of the saints and in the availability of their merit for transfer to those who petition for it. It is interesting that in all of Bale's notebooks, before 1530 or so, there is not a hint of doubt or restlessness regarding this traditional piety. The Hitchin antiphon may not have been magnificent poetry, but it came from the heart.

Closely related to Bale's trust in Mary and the saints was his conventional belief that the religious life (and especially life under the Carmelite rule) was particularly pleasing to the hosts of Heaven. Again, not a single murmur of dissatisfaction was heard—at least, none that Bale was prepared to commit to writing. Perhaps his occasional touchiness about attacks on the Carmelite order might seem to betray a certain lack of confidence. In copying from a chronicle which heaped scorn on the Carmelites' claim that Elijah had been their founder, Bale was moved to add in the margin, "These are lies. . . . What a liar!"[53] But this was probably excess of zeal, not lack of conviction. Elsewhere he took it for granted that celibacy was the superior state,[54] that "in the cell you will find what you most often lose outside,"[55] and in particular, that wearing the Carmelite scapular gave the friars a special claim to divine favor.[56] When in the 1530s Bale began to denounce the religious orders as "beastlye bellygoddes" (and worse) he was uprooting an institution that was as deeply planted in his own life as it was in the English past. The fervor of his early commitment to the Carmelite life helps one see why his humor turned so bilious when his first love disappointed him.

While Bale remained a friar, his spiritual life was strongly liturgical—as was appropriate to his religious calling, and as the importance of the Carmelite offices in his devotional life indicates. His piety was also largely formal. Johann Huizinga's comment on popular thought at this time on the Continent could as well apply to Bale: ". . . every notion is strictly defined and limited, isolated, as it were, in a plastic form, and it is this form which is all-important."[57] The visible and tangible Carmelite scapular, for instance, took on an almost independent potency and drew the mind of the friar away from the inner, ethical attitude which the yoke-like garment symbolized.[58] Young Bale therefore by no means escaped the materialist or *ex opere operato* frame of mind which was so widespread in late medieval Christianity. There is no hint in his notebooks that he found the spirituality of great fourteenth century mystics like Richard Rolle or Walter Hilton attractive, nor is there any suggestion that in his wanderings on the Continent he had discovered the inner life—the quiet *imitatio Christi*—which the Brethren of the Common Life cultivated. One feature of Bale's devotion in these years did raise it out of the ordinary, however. This was its scholarly bent. Collecting scraps of information, bit by bit, on Carmelite saints, leaders, and authors was as real an expression of piety as any pilgrimage—which, in a way, Bale's wandering was. His veneration for the Carmelite past no doubt cost him a good many cold nights sleeping by the wayside, and—whatever Bale thought later of his years as a friar—this devotion was not unimpressive.

So the Christianity which one finds expressed in Bale's notebooks was hagiographic, liturgical, formal, and scholarly. It was also supernaturalist. Bale lived in the expectation that divine power typically and normally operated in the physical world, in a man's body, his home, his fields, and so on, and not merely in the hidden depths of his heart. God's power (usually channelled through the saints, to be sure) was for Bale, as for the popular religious mentality, something very practical, very down to earth. God's care extended to a man's health, the feeding of his family, the well-being of his cattle, and not merely to the inner condition of his soul or his future status before the throne of judgment. Bale, in other words, shared the conception of religion which was widespread in pre-Reformation England, which expected God's intervention in man's whole environment—spiritual, psychological, and material.[59] There are stories like the following scattered all through Bale's early notebooks—stories which he heard or read as he traveled from convent to convent, and recorded as useful and edifying. "A certain other woman was obsessed by an evil spirit. Her friends made a vow that they would visit the tomb of this holy man with the woman and with a candle weighing twelve pounds.[60] When they did this, the woman was freed at once."[61] The story of course makes clear as well the late medieval preoccupation with the physical object as the locus of supernatural power, the belief in the efficacy of vows, and the recognition that there were other spiritual forces at large than divine ones. Bale's notebooks from the years before 1530 are filled with notes of this kind and represent again part of the heritage which he would repudiate so violently when he converted to Protestant beliefs.[62] He would come to see God's power at work less in the physical environment, more in the human heart, and perhaps most of all in the dimension of time and of history.

One final facet of Bale's devotional life—a mild counterforce to the optimistic spirit which expected divine power to intervene in daily life—was the preoccupation with mortality and death which one finds here and there in the pages of his notebooks. This was no obsession with Bale. There was with him no fascination with the physical signs of death or with the stench of decay, as in the "Dance of Death" illustrations of the period. But one is struck nevertheless with the number of epitaphs he collected and recorded. It was not merely because the epitaphs supplied facts about otherwise dimly remembered Carmelite friars. Often they did not, in fact—frequently one finds only a few conventional sentiments about the piety of the deceased and about the transitory quality of life. One has the sense that in the epitaphs which Bale copied and in the ones he wrote,[63] he was expressing a wistful sense of *où sont les neiges d'antan*, that he was verbalizing the feeling for human fragility which he shared with his age. Pessimism was not a dominant motif with Bale, now or later; he was too robust and vigorous to dwell too long on a note of *contemptus mundi*. But it was evidently a mood to which he was now and then prone.

When one turns from Bale's devotional attitudes as a Carmelite friar to consider his writing and antiquarian efforts during the years before 1530, one finds (not surprisingly) the same conservative mind-set. The distinction between piety and scholarship was of course not one which Bale would have made himself. The two literary forms, apart from religious poetry, with which Bale experimented during his Cambridge years were the saint's life and the chronicle—both of which were vehicles for praising and venerating the heroes of the Carmelite order as well. Bale's notebooks contain several early attempts in each genre. They are interesting not only for what they reveal about his thought-patterns in the first half of his life, but also because they supply an indispensable background for understanding what Bale wrote after he became a Protestant.

Ever since the earliest days of the Christian Church, saints' lives—especially records of their interrogation and martyrdom—had been closely bound up with the liturgies which honored them on their festal days. In the course of the Middle Ages, to be sure, saints' lives had often been detached from their liturgical matrix and circulated separately—in collected martyrologies which could be as massive as Voragine's *Legenda Aurea*, or as small as single lives like Eadmer's biography of St. Anselm.[64] With the advent of printing in the late fifteenth century, these popular saints' lives formed one staple of the early book trade.[65] People in religious orders, however, continued to read and hear the lives of the saints in a liturgical setting. And so Bale's early experiments in hagiography embodied not merely the traditional values and attitudes of medieval saints' lives in general, but much of the liturgical frame-work which had characterized monastic *legenda* in par-ticular. This was obviously true of Bale's very earliest Cambridge manuscript[66] and remained so of other Car-melite lives which he compiled—a collection, for example, in a manuscript codex of Bale's now in the Bodleian Library. Dating from the years 1515 to 1520 or so, this little work contains twenty-four leaves filled with short lives of various Carmelite saints, with prayers addressed to each of them.[67] Bale evidently meant this manuscript to be something between a formal book of offices and a collection of saints' lives for the Cambridge friars to read privately. Since he later claimed credit for com-piling these lives, at least,[68] and since they embody so clearly his beliefs and method at the time, they are worth a brief look.

The saints whom Bale described in this manuscript (and they reached back as far as Elijah, the order's supposed founder) represented all the qualities valued in traditional monastic hagiography: ascetic life, miraculous powers over nature, devotion to the sacraments, and so on. And just as Bale's actual words were quite unoriginal (in whatever sense the lives may have been his own, he copied extensively from previous works),[69] so also the pictures which he drew of the saints were quite lacking in individuality. Whatever quirks and foibles they might have had, in Bale's description the saints were scrubbed clean and emerged as examples of all the standard monastic virtues. Likewise, they were forever enacting the standard gestures which saints in the Bible were wont to make, and doing the same miracles. Bale's St. Andrea Corsinus healed sick people by washing their feet, St. Cyril the Confessor restored a blind man to sight, and so on.[70] Standard patterns recurred with regularity. This assimilation of the saint's story to a standard type was of course a nearly universal phenomenon in medieval hagiography (indeed, in the folk literature of almost all ages and cultures). And there were several reasons for this preoccupation with the typical, which characterized Bale's thinking in general during his Carmelite years and indeed after he became a Protestant as well.

One fundamental influence on Bale's thought was the pronounced "realism" (or "idealism" in the Platonic sense) of the early European folk-mind in general, which considered transcendent archetypes more "real" than their particular embodiments within space and time. One finds a concise description of this attitude in Johann Huizinga's study of France and the Low Countries in the late Middle Ages, and Huizinga's words could as well apply to the English environment in which Bale grew up:

> Whatever the faculty of seeing specific traits may have been in the Middle Ages, it must be noted that men disregarded the individual qualities and fine distinctions of things, deliberately and of set purpose, in order always to bring them under some general principle. This mental tendency is a result of their profound idealism. People feel an imperious need of always and especially seeing the general sense, the connection with the absolute, the moral ideality, the ultimate significance of a thing. What is important is the impersonal. The mind is not in search of individual realities, but of models, examples, norms.[71]

The popular memory in traditional Europe, for instance, would seem to have fixed most readily upon the traits which individual saints, kings, and other heroes shared with others of their kind—and especially with the accepted prototype, the ideal martyr, hermit, monk, bishop, king, or the like. What made one particular monk different from all the rest, how one mighty king managed to win a particular battle—this kind of detail would often fade rather quickly, sometimes in a generation or two, and the individual figure or event would absorb mythical or typical features. The assumption was that if so-and-so really had been a godly king, virgin martyr, or whatnot, he or she obviously must have shared all the qualities and powers appropriate to that status. So if a miraculous birth, a battle with a monster, or whatever, had to be "discovered," this posed no insuperable problem.[72] (The assumption that the typical outweighed the individual in importance, and was more real, naturally meant that the traditional mentality in Europe approached the problem of evidence with assumptions different from those of modern scholarship.) Now this need to grasp and cling mentally to the dependable, stable type may have gained urgency from the psycho-social upheavals attendant on the Black Death, the Great Schism, and the Hundred Years' War. In any case, this "realism" was part of the mental vocabulary of the age to which John Bale belonged—an age which was drawing slowly to a close in England (as it had elsewhere) but whose assumptions were as yet scarcely challenged at court and university, and not at all in the countryside. The prevailing realist mind-set of Bale's early environment represents one reason for the stereotyped nature of the saints whose portraits the young friar sketched.

On a rather more academic level, another strand of traditional thought in Europe colored Bale's saints' lives and partly explains their standardized nature. This was typology and the typological exegesis of the Bible. Typology had been fundamental to the way in which the early Church had understood history. God, directing all events and actions toward a single goal, sometimes had given signs and promises, foreshadowing as it were His more perfect self-revelation later on. The early Church understood the Old Testament in this fashion. In Adam, Melchizedek, Moses, and others, Christ had been prefigured. Yet the Incarnation had not wholly or exhaustively fulfilled these *figurae* or types, these prefigurations of Christ in Israel's past. The tension between "already" and "not yet" (the hour is coming, and now is . . .) in the eschatological awareness of Jesus and of the early Church had pointed forward again to the *Parousia*, the ultimate fulfillment of God's plan. As the young Church groped toward an understanding of God's action in history, then, a progression composed of three "moments" appeared quite early, in the Gospel of St. John—the Old Testament *figura*, the fulfillment of the *figura* in Jesus, and a continuing operation of God's grace in the Church, through the sacraments, until the *Parousia*.[73] The progression from the Passover meal to the Last Supper to the Eucharist offered one example of this pattern.

The sense of history implicit here—a mighty view of God's providential action which knit past, present, and future all together—became an integral feature of Western Christianity. The Church presented the Old Testament to the barbarian peoples of Western Europe as a book of figures and prophecies, pointing toward the full revelation of God in Jesus Christ. Indeed, the Old Testament was comprehensible to these peoples only in such a fashion; the sense of historical perspective needed to appreciate its character as a book of Jewish law and history would have seemed both irrelevant and impious. The repetitive celebration of the Mass, finally, brought the process up to date, as it were, forging the link which connected the past with the present.[74] Now the view of history implicit in the New Testament did not deny the historical reality of type, fulfillment, or continuation of any of the three "moments." It presupposed, in fact, that all were firmly rooted within time and space—that each individual or event had a concreteness and individuality guaranteed by God, who used the raw material of history to work out His purposes. The figural view of history might well have encouraged an interest in the individual and particular on the part of Christian thinkers. But the influx of Greek concepts and assumptions into Christian thought blunted the force of this possibility very early.[75] The distinction between time and eternity, the belief that God existed outside of time and space, the sense that to Him all time was present—these ideas implied that each "moment" in a figural progression, being a stage of God's plan in His timeless mind, had a static and eternal quality too.[76] Thus the reality prefigured by Abraham, fulfilled in the men of faith of the early Church, and continued in the community of the faithful thereafter, came to be seen as a timeless, exemplary model in the mind of God, a pattern after which each Christian's life ought to be shaped.

It is easy to see how this viewpoint *sub specie aeternitatis* could erase the interest in individual human traits and characteristics which the original figural view of history might have fostered.[77] The influence of these Greek conceptions on Christian hagiography were what one might expect. The individuating features of the saints were de-emphasized, and in the majority of cases their legends were assimilated to the appropriate ideal pattern—of martyr, confessor, virgin, bishop, or whatever, with virtues and deeds drawn from saints in the Bible or indeed from the folk-world of myth and legend. It was no wonder, then, that the traditions of typology in hagiography which Bale inherited encouraged him to compile the kind of scissors-and-paste lives which one sees in the Bodleian manuscript. The people whom he described had obviously (in the Carmelites' eyes, anyway) been saints, and so they must have said and done the sorts of things that one expected of saints.[78] Even if trustworthy information about the personalities and historical deeds of these men had been available, the reality for Bale would still have been the ideal type and the way each saint had embodied it.

Mention of biographical information and its availability suggests two final considerations, on a more practical level, which influenced the standardized nature of Bale's Carmelite saints' lives. One problem arose from the liturgical framework mentioned above, in which much of monastic hagiography was cast. Every saint had his day; and *legenda* were necessary if this office were to be celebrated properly. In many cases, however, there simply was no information at hand about the holy person. Descriptive material therefore had to be borrowed or made up, and this naturally encouraged the repetition of stock incidents and exemplary characteristics.[79] The practical purpose of hagiography was the second consideration, and this too was related to the liturgical framework. The legends were composed in order to glorify God and to edify the worshippers—though this purpose scarcely diminished in importance when saints' lives were detached from their liturgical context and read separately. Therefore as Père Delehaye has observed, the hagiographer was likely to dwell upon the failings or weaknesses of his hero only if he believed that these showed off the power of God to better advantage.[80] Most often it was safer to accentuate the positive—to show what had made the saint a saint, not what had kept him a man. So the purpose of glorifying God and edifying the reader lay behind the stereotyped quality of Bale's Carmelite saints' lives as well.

It would be quite anachronistic (and hardly charitable) to expect post-Renaissance biography from Friar Bale, writing saints' lives for his Carmelite brothers in the 1520s. It would be equally inappropriate to judge his nascent Carmelite chronicles either—the second literary genre one finds in his early notebooks—by any other standards than ones which he would accept. Just what those standards were, however, is not altogether easy to specify. Bale would presumably have agreed that "truth" was one criterion by which his rough notes on Carmelite history could be weighed. But this was an ancient, commonplace, and rather vague sentiment;[81] and truth for Bale was something *a priori* and "given," not a body of information or conclusions which one reached only after inductive research. Thus the postulate that the Carmelite order stemmed from the prophet Elijah was a "given"; so was the principle that the Carmelites outranked the three other mendicant orders in age and sanctity, and so on. (Clearly a Grey Friar or a Friar Preacher would have defined truth in this area a bit differently.)[82] Were histories therefore to be judged purely on literary or rhetorical grounds, according to the persuasiveness and copious detail with which they illustrated already-established truth? Bale never said so, in his early notebooks.[83] All this is not to fault Bale for a lack of clarity on a philosophical question which took centuries to settle. It is simply to point out that he never—then or later—approached historical research or writing in a spirit of calm disinterest. Antiquary he was, but one passionately engaged in demonstrating the truth which he knew before he began.[84]

Bale's early experiments in the chronicle genre may be summarized briefly. His most elaborate attempt in the period before 1530 was actually not so much a chronicle (though he called it *Chronica seu fasciculus temporum ordinis Carmelitarum*) as a systematic collection of notes, the spadework for a full-scale history of the Carmelite order.[85] As Bale went from convent to convent in England and on the Continent during the 1520s, he evidently carried this notebook with him and entered in it useful information as he found it. Some of this came from earlier Carmelite chronicles, some from the *Fasti* of Baptista Mantuanus, and some from non-Carmelite works such as the *Speculum Historiale* of Vincent of Beauvais.[86] All his notes were chosen to illustrate the pattern of Carmelite history which Bale had first learned as a small boy, through the yearly round of offices at the Norwich house. Bale began this *Chronica*, as he called it, with Elijah and the first community of hermits on Mount Carmel. Scarcely an important Old Testament figure thereafter was excluded from the list which gave the "heads" of the early "order": Elisha, Jonah, Isaiah, and so on were incorporated. Clearly the mythical history of the Carmelites was the main strand around which Bale wove his understanding of the Old Testament. The New Testament and the early Church fitted easily into this pattern as well. John the Baptist was a Carmelite, for example. Later, St. Anthony the hermit was, too.

After the fourth century Bale's sources dried up, and his notebook has a good many blank pages. In the twelfth century, with "St." Bertholdus and his companions, Bale was on firmer ground again. His notes expanded in quantity, and likewise he had enough information to be able to sift conflicting reports, and begin to criticize them: "According to some, the Carmelite friars entered England in 1212; according to others, in 1220; but more truly, in 1240."[87] For the fourteenth and fifteenth centuries, when the Carmelites began to frequent the universities and produce literary works, Bale's information was most copious of all (and from the modern viewpoint, most useful). Thanks to the copy of *Fasciculi Zizaniorum* at Norwich, for instance, Bale had a pretty clear idea of who Wyclif's Carmelite opponents had been, and what they had written.[88] But there is no sign that he made a distinction in value between the later, more documented parts of his chronicle and the early sections where he drew on pious folklore. The possibility of criticizing several sources for the period 1200 to 1500 did not mean for Bale that his account of that age was any truer. All of this is quite unsurprising, given who Bale was and the audience for whom he was writing. The one striking feature of Bale's *Chronica* is its organization, the methodical patience with which Bale copied his information into neat boxes and circles on each page. Giving historical data a shape, a manifest structure, was evidently a passion with Bale as early as the 1520s.

The figure who emerges from these notebooks, then, strikes one as a traditionalist English friar, wholly accepting the piety of his order, but distinguishable from his brothers by his energy and antiquarian enthusiasm. One facet of his life is wholly absent from the notebooks—his preaching. Though he apparently was sent by his order to preach against Lutheran ideas in Suffolk about the time that Latimer began to preach in Cambridge (the mid-1520s), and though his "grace" from the university in 1529 says he was to have preached at Paul's Cross in London,[89] this side of his life as a friar has left no trace. One cannot tell if Bale fulminated from the pulpit in support of the old faith as vigorously as he would later for the new. But though this part of Bale's personality remains a blank in the years before the Reformation, his historical consciousness as a hagiographer and chronicler appears plainly. Within the broad sweep of God's plan for history, Bale saw (not surprisingly) the Carmelite order playing a central role. There was little sense of movement or of change, though, in his grasp of history. In every age the Carmelite friars had embodied (some more, some less) the ideal model of the saint, that static example in the mind of God. In the

1520s, Bale still lived in that traditionalist world in which change seemed insignificant. Even the sense of degeneration (that one guise under which the archaic mind could grasp the fact of change) was apparently weak in Bale. He did not yet feel acutely, as he would in the 1530s, that the English province of the Carmelites was in the course of an irrevocable decline. But his world (and the world of so many Englishmen) began in fact to crack and shatter perceptibly the year that Henry VIII gave anticlerical forces a freer rein, in 1529 when Friar Bale was thirty-four years old.

II / *Conversion*

Bale received his bachelor's degree in divinity from Cambridge in 1529, and the doctorate probably within two or three years thereafter. He now enjoyed a moderate status within the order, and his feet were on the ladder of promotion. About 1530 Bale went down from Cambridge to be prior of the White Friars' convent in the little port town of Maldon in Essex, some forty miles northeast of London. He was licensed to preach in the London diocese by Bishop John Stokesley on February 16, 1531.[1] Nothing much is known of what Bale did at Maldon besides preach and supervise the training of the younger friars there. It does seem that later in the decade the citizens of Maldon were enjoying plays depicting the life of Christ, which were put on at the White Friars' former house. This may have been a tradition which Bale started, and which survived the dissolution of the mendicant orders.[2] Bale was certainly writing plays in the mid-1530s. Neither Bale's studies in divinity at Cambridge nor his antiquarian labors in Carmelite history had effaced a facet of his personality which his writing began to reveal in the 1530s—a common touch, an urge to communicate in the earthy language of peasants and fishermen as well as in the Latin of the schools. So the town of Maldon may have had an early taste of Bale's racy verse-plays.

Bale stayed at Maldon only two or three years. About 1533 he moved back to his native Suffolk to take charge of the Carmelite convent at Ipswich.[3] Bale never indicated whether he had sought this transfer or whether the provincial authorities had moved him. The convent at Maldon was evidently a rather small one,[4] and the removal to Ipswich probably represented a promotion. Bale showed a certain restlessness in his new position as well, however. He did make a sufficiently strong impact upon at least one man to be remembered forty years later as the former prior of the Ipswich Carmelites,[5] but he was on his way again after not much more than a year. This time he moved to Doncaster in Yorkshire, where Bale was evidently prior by July of 1534 (at which time Archbishop Lee licensed him to preach in York diocese).[6] Bale's transfer this time may have been connected with his antiquarian studies. He later recalled that in 1533 he had foreseen the storm which would blow down the monastic life in England, and that he had therefore spent the next three years trying to salvage what he could in the way of bibliographical information from the libraries of the Carmelites and the Austin Friars. He had traveled around, he said, writing down the names of medieval English writers and the titles of their works. If the Franciscans and Dominicans and others had been more hospitable, Bale said, he would have searched their libraries too.[7] Bale's recollection—he was writing in 1548—was tinged with the wisdom of hindsight, and in 1533 he may not have foreseen the ruin of English monastic libraries quite so clearly. There is no reason to doubt that Henry VIII's breach with Rome may well have filled him with a general sense of urgency, however, which could have encouraged a removal to Doncaster. There were not all that many houses of friars in the north of England,[8] but it was a region whose libraries Bale had never searched.

By the time Bale got to Doncaster, his friar's robe was concealing a hot-headed Protestant. Probably the movement of his mind away from traditional Carmelite values had begun back while he was prior at Maldon, though his manuscript notebooks do not reveal anything of the sort.

He later claimed (in 1543) that Bishop Stokesley had suspended him in 1531 from preaching in the diocese of London because he would not "leave the Gospel" and swear to publicize an anti-Lutheran tract by the future bishop William Barlow.[9] Reminiscences after the fact are tricky, though. Bale may not have been telling the whole story about his suspension by Stokesley, and may have been unconsciously retrojecting his post-conversion beliefs. Certainly his notebooks from as late as 1532 show no deviation from a spirit of Carmelite piety.[10] But the notebooks do not tell the whole story. By and large they recorded his thoughts before his conversion, and then afterwards, but not during. While his mind was in flux theologically, he was perfectly capable of recording Carmelite information in conventionally pious phraseology. Only when the revolution in his devotional life was complete, after 1536 or so, did the new theology alter the habitual way in which he wrote about his order. So the notebooks are not much help in providing a window into Bale's mind while he was at Maldon. All one can do is to consider his outward circumstances.

It was probably significant for his change of heart that during 1531 and 1532 he happened to be living in London diocese, and not so very far from the metropolis. The impleading of the whole English clergy for a *praemunire* offense in late 1530, the concession of Henry VIII's headship "as far as the Law of Christ allows" in early 1531, the decisive collapse of the Church's resistance in May of 1532—all of these gave ample warning that the future might be bleak for an independent Carmelite order in England, owing obedience directly to Rome. The foundations of Bale's world were beginning to crack while he was at Maldon, and he was certainly close enough to London to have been acutely aware of it. But the real break with his past, the conscious conversion to Protestant theology, probably came in 1533 while he was prior of the White Friars at Ipswich.

Bale later attributed his conversion to two causes. One was the persuasion of Thomas, Lord Wentworth of

Nettlestead in Suffolk, which was about five miles outside of Ipswich. Wentworth was a Protestant courtier, ally of the Boleyns and cousin of the future Protector Somerset—apparently one of the first of the major figures at court to embrace Lutheran ideas with vigor.[11] Wentworth stood out among other Protestant noblemen in the 1530s by his active patronage of young intellectual reformers. In 1538 he would present Thomas Becon (the future author of Protestant primers and devotional books) to the chantry of St. Thomas Martyr in the church of St. Lawrence, Ipswich—a humorous thought, young Becon appointed to say masses for the repose of Thomas Becket's soul in the year Cromwell had the shrine at Canterbury pulled down. No doubt Wentworth had in mind merely giving Becon a sinecure, and there is no sign that the latter actually served as chantry priest there.[12] Wentworth also subsidized the Cambridge education of William Turner, who would later join Bale in writing Protestant propaganda on the Continent, help lay the foundation of modern botanical studies in England, and as Elizabethan dean of Wells train his dog to leap and remove the square caps from conservative prelates' heads.[13] The irenic spirit of Wentworth's protegés might have been more striking. For Bale was among them, too; he received, if not financial support, at least the attentions of the nobleman, and this must have been flattering.

What Wentworth said to Bale, what specific beliefs he urged upon him, one has no way of knowing. Judging from Bale's attacks on the Mass and on the veneration of saints, within a few years, one might guess that these volatile and controversial topics arose in their discussions. In any case, Bale would later cite Wentworth's persuasion as the efficient cause of his conversion,[14] which most likely happened while Bale was prior of the Ipswich Carmelites around 1533. It is not really surprising that he remained a friar even while repudiating the Mass and the cult of saints, two main preoccupations of his former devotional life. He had been in the order for two-thirds of his life; the inconsistency of religious vows with Protestant theology was not yet clear to him, and he no doubt thought that he could use his position in the order (and his access to the pulpit) to spread the Gospel. In his next priorate, at Doncaster, he certainly had a go at it.

In the meantime a second influence had been reinforcing Bale's conversion. Later in his life, writing about Henry VIII, Bale said it was "through his ministration that I am (as I hope) a partaker in God's Gospel kingdom, for before his edict against the Roman Pontiff, I was a very obstinate papist."[15] Bale was not naming Henry as an immediate or efficient cause of his conversion, nor (certainly) implying that Henry would have approved of the beliefs which Bale trumpeted from the mid-1530s onward. Henry's "edict" (presumably the series of acts establishing the royal supremacy in 1533 and 1534) hardly gave aid and comfort to those attacking traditional piety. But for the friars in England, the breach with Rome was more than merely a political or diplomatic formality, occurring in a region far above the rut of daily life. The exile of papal authority from England called the whole existence of the mendicant orders into question, for the pope had been their ultimate jurisdictional head. And indeed, the crown was applying considerable psychological pressure to the friars as early as 1534, to which Bale was evidently sensitive.[16] The special attention given the friars (as preachers and molders of public opinion) when the Oath of Succession was administered in 1534 also drove home the point that the mendicant orders were under Henry's (or at least Cromwell's) watchful eye, and existed on sufferance.[17] The impact of all this on Bale was to shatter his confidence in the order's future, and to sensitize him to the spiritual and educational torpor of the English province. When it had seemed as though a calm and serene future stretched forward indefinitely for the Carmelites in England, the mild depression in energy since the mid-fifteenth century had evidently not seemed too worrisome, and before 1533 Bale never explicitly compared the present unfavorably with the past. The upheavals of 1533 and 1534 revealed the Carmelites' weaknesses to Bale very plainly.[18] So, indirectly, Henry VIII did play a major role in Bale's conversion, by shaking him loose from twenty-five years' accumulated habits of piety. On whichever side of the fence he happened to be, Bale was (and he had the grace to admit it) "very obstinate." In 1533 and 1534 it was beginning to seem as though the Carmelite order was no longer a worthy recipient of total devotion, and Bale was open to alternative suggestions from Lord Wentworth. By the middle of 1534 he had taken these to heart completely.[19]

On July 24, 1534, Archbishop Lee licensed, among others, "Johannes Baille, doctor of Theology and prior of the Carmelite convent at Doncaster" to preach throughout the Diocese of York.[20] The official propaganda campaign to support the royal supremacy was underway, and Lee needed to muster his forces for the offensive. In Bale he found an apt instrument for this purpose,[21] but unfortunately he got a bit more as well. Scarcely a week after licensing Bale to preach, Lee had a problem on his hands at Doncaster. Bale and Dr. Thomas Kirkby (warden of the Franciscans in that town) had been railing at each other from their respective pulpits, and their deviations from fraternal charity were creating a notorious scandal. Kirkby was a theological conservative, an Oxford D.D. in 1527, and a former opponent of Henry's divorce. It was a classic case of Franciscan vs. Carmelite, Oxford vs. Cambridge, traditionalist vs. radical. Kirkby and Bale must have been giving the citizens of Doncaster a good deal to think about. So on August 1 the archbishop commissioned four dignitaries of the diocese to look into the matter and report back.[22] Nothing in the archiepiscopal register indicates what the specific points of difference between Kirkby and Bale had been; one purpose of the commission, after all, was to find out. Nor is it clear how the controversy was finally pacified. If Bale had in fact been preaching the royal supremacy stoutly (half-heartedness not being one of his signal characteristics) and if Lee was as short of good preachers as he said he was,[23] Bale probably escaped with a scolding.

A year and a half later another uproar occurred at Doncaster, and although Bale was not specifically named as the center of the storm, there is every likelihood that it was he. In a letter dated "24 January" (which A. G. Dickens credibly assigns to 1536)[24] Archbishop Lee reported to Cromwell that a "light fryer" had been having a running battle with the vicar of Doncaster.[25] The Carmelite, and probably the vicar, too, had been preaching on matters forbidden by the crown back in 1534 (which had included the doctrine of purgatory, the veneration of saints, clerical marriage, justification by faith, pilgrimages, and false miracles).[26] Lee said that he had warned both the friar and the vicar not to venture into this forbidden territory, but that in the meantime the vicar and certain parishoners had laid articles against the Carmelite, listing the objectionable points he had made in preaching. A "gentle lettre" from Lee summoning the friar had failed to produce him (he had replied tartly that he was going to London for counsel). Upon his return he had been formally cited; still no response. Lee concluded that he had now appointed a commission to examine the articles, and that because the friar had been preaching "mutche slawnderouslie," Lee would revoke his license. At this point information about the affair fades out. Lee's records do not reveal the name of the offending friar, or indicate that he received any punishment other than the exile from the pulpit mentioned in the letter. The "light fryer" certainly sounds like John Bale. Of the Carmelites whom Lee had licensed to preach in York diocese back in July 1534, Bale was the most notoriously radical[27]—though the list of licensed preachers may have been out of date by January 1536. More to the point, Bale later recalled that Archbishop Lee had examined him on one occasion "upon the artycle of honourynge and prayenge to the sayntes, devyded into xvii artycles." This reminiscence occurred in a book which Bale published at Antwerp in 1543, and Bale recalled that the incident had taken place "viii years a go."[28] If Bale wrote this toward the end of 1543, and rounded off his numbers a bit, he could have been referring to an interview with Lee in early 1536, assuming that Lee finally managed to force the "light fryer" to appear. It makes more sense to accept this possibility than to conclude that Bale's anecdote refers to an examination growing out of the altercation with Friar Kirkby in the summer of 1534. In the case of the Kirkby affray, there is no indication that extensive "artycles" had been laid against Bale, while in 1536 against the "light fryer" there were such. Likewise, Bale later said that Thomas Cromwell had intervened to save him from Lee on one occasion "because of the comedies (I had) written."[29] Whatever Cromwell really thought of Bale's Protestant verse-plays,[30] it is more likely that Bale should have had a stack of them to show him in 1536 than in 1534, only a year or so after his conversion. So it sounds as though Bale's examination before Lee (where Bale confuted an "olde dottynge doctor dodypoll" on the matter of saint-worship, and Bale's Cambridge mentor Geoffrey Downes stood by and smiled)[31] took place in 1536, and that the Doncaster "light fryer" probably was Bale. The metamorphosis of the traditionalist Carmelite into the bilious reformer was quite manifest by this time.

Besides preaching against the veneration of saints—uprooting his own past with vengeance—Bale seems to have been arousing his Yorkshire audiences with thinly-veiled attacks on the doctrine of transubstantiation as well. This seems to be the drift of the teaching attributed to him by an irritated traditionalist named William Broman, who testified in 1538 or 1539 that ". . . one Bale a whyte frere sumtyme prior of Doncaster taught him about a iiii yeres ago that Criste wolde dwell in no churche that was made of lyme and stone by mannes hands but onlie in heaven above and in mannes herte in yerthe. . . ."[32] The implicit denial of Christ's corporeal presence in the elements (by reference to Acts 7:48), together with Bale's attacks on prayers to the saints, might suggest Lollard influence on his thinking in the mid-1530s. There were after all "Dowchmen" at Worksop, only fifteen miles south of Doncaster, who were teaching in 1533 and 1534 (among other heresies alleged) that God does not reside in churches made by men's hands, but rather in the body and soul of the true Christian, and that prayers to the saints are useless. The beliefs of these Dutchmen (which touched on a wide range of topics) were characteristically Lollard, Professor Dickens argues, and were probably acquired in England rather than on the Continent.[33]

But the case for Lollard influences on Bale in the early 1530s is not a strong one, despite his similar views regarding the two doctrines mentioned. The people who apparently influenced Bale the most at this time were unlikely to have come to Protestant beliefs via Lollardy themselves. Thomas, Lord Wentworth came from quite the wrong social and educational milieu to have been touched by Lollardy. And the closest friend Bale had in the Carmelite order at the time was evidently John Barret, a native of King's Lynn in Norfolk. Barret had taken his B.D. at Cambridge with Bale in 1529, been prior of the Cambridge Carmelites in 1532-1534, and proceded D.D. at some point in the early 1530s. "He has been bound to me," Bale later wrote, "by the closest bonds of friendship ever since [his] youth."[34] Now the same William Broman who had accused Bale of heresy also said concerning Barret that ". . . he (Broman) hathe lerned by the teaching and doctrine of one doctor Barret sumtyme a whyte fryer of Gipswiche aboute iii or iiii yeres past that the blessed sacrament of the alter is but a figure and a remembrance of the passion of Criste. . . ."[35] which sounds more Zwinglian than Lollard, as one might expect of a Cambridge D.D. So the influence of Wentworth and Barret on Bale and the critical attitude Bale maintained toward the early Lollards as late as 1536[36] make one hesitate to suggest a Lollard influence on Bale's thinking at this time. Later on the Lollards would bulk large in his vision of the English past,

but by the mid-1530s he was scarcely aware of their importance as "morning stars" of the faith he had recently adopted.

Sometime in the early part of 1536 all the changes in
Bale's beliefs crystallized in a series of decisions. First of all
he left the Carmelite house at Doncaster (where later that
year, in December, the Duke of Norfolk would face the
men who led the Pilgrimage of Grace)[37] and his respon-
sibilities as prior there. Leaving the north of England for
good, he made his way to London and to the royal court
at Greenwich.[38] If Bale had indeed been Archbishop Lee's
"light fryer," then the suspension from preaching may have
been the last straw. Probably the thought of leaving the
Carmelite order now bulked large in his mind. His friends
John Barret and Thomas Giles had already done so;[39] both
the liberty of the Gospel and the threat of suppression
hanging over the friars would have encouraged Bale to
consider it himself. But the decision came painfully. Almost
thirty years of commitment could not be repudiated in an
afternoon. And for a friar without a wealthy patron, and
who contemplated the employment possibilities outside his
order, the future might have seemed a little bleak. Most
likely Bale was looking for patronage when he went to
London and Greenwich. He was not enormously successful.[40] Summer found him back at Ipswich where he
had been prior three years before. Still without a post
outside the order, he spent two months or so writing a
history of the English Carmelites (his *Anglorum Heliades*)
for the antiquary John Leland. Leland had received royal
patronage for his studies two years previously, and judging
from the tone of Bale's introduction to the little chronicle,
he hoped very much that Leland would put in a good word
for him.[41] Nothing was immediately forthcoming, however,
and in the fall of 1536 Bale had to settle for the best he
could get, a post as stipendiary priest in the little parish of
Thorndon in Suffolk (some sixteen miles north of Ipswich).
It was at this point that he turned his back once and for all,
emotionally as well as administratively, on the Carmelite
order.[42]

The environment at Thorndon into which Bale intruded in the autumn of 1536 was a very inflammable one. East Anglian society in general during the early sixteenth century seems to have been fraught with social and economic tensions, more so than in many other parts of England. The marked social disparities within the sheep-raising and corn-growing areas and the danger of grain shortage in the dairying regions may have contributed to the undercurrents of dissatisfaction.[43] These problems, compounded by Protestant ideas and anticlerical grievances, were to come to a head in 1549 with Ket's Rebellion. Whatever the socio-economic problems were in the area of Thorndon when Bale moved there in 1536, it is apparent from the records which his brief tenure as parish priest produced that religious feelings were already running high both on the conservative and the radical sides.[44] The Ten Articles subscribed to by Convocation in July of 1536 had not gone down well among the traditionalists in Thorndon, nor had Thomas Cromwell's subsequent Injunctions. By the end of October there was a substantial faction in the village which applauded the conservative rising in Lincolnshire, just to the north. In this volatile environment Bale's irascible Protestantism inevitably caused a stir. Although he won at least a few followers, Bale made an important enemy in William Kyrke, bailiff of Thorndon manor, who saw to it that Bale's tenure as parish priest was short.

On January 7, 1537, Kyrke paid a visit to Sir Humphrey Wingfield, a local landowner who had been speaker of the House of Commons for the past three years. Kyrke told Wingfield that Bale had gathered a group of followers who were meeting daily to hear his teaching, and that he had "lured much people to his doctrine." The bailiff convinced Wingfield that out of these assemblies some "inconvenience" was likely to arise. The next day Wingfield wrote to the Duke of Suffolk for advice, sending along a list of articles said to have been collected from Bale's preaching.[45] Perhaps this collection of articles was becoming a familiar procedure with Bale. As a matter of fact, the nobility and gentry in Suffolk could not be too careful about troublemakers in early 1537. The hopes and fears aroused by the Pilgrimage of Grace had by no means been pacified, and those responsible for order were well aware of the potentially explosive conservative feelings among the peasantry. There was, in fact, an uproar in the village of Thwaite, two miles southwest of Thorndon, only two months later, on March 11. The rector and one of his parishoners tore down the brackets holding votive candles in the church and in derision turned a picture of St. Erasmus to face the wall "against the King's peace."[46] Preachers of radical temperament were a clear and present threat to public order in East Anglia, and neither Wingfield nor Suffolk was likely to prefer the propagation of reformist ideas to the maintenance of the peace.[47] So by January 25 Bale found himself in custody in the porter's ward at Greenwich, waiting for Cromwell and the Privy Council to make up their minds as to what to do with him. Bale took his mind off the "vileness, stink, penury, cold" and other discomforts of prison by writing a point-by-point defense against the articles alleged against his preaching.[48] As a window into Bale's mind in early 1537 this "Answer of John Bale, priest" has its drawbacks,[49] since it is anything but exhaustive or systematic, its content being determined by what the conservatives at Thorndon had remembered as being offensive. Yet it does indicate how far Bale's theology and piety had changed since his Carmelite years, however little his energetic, preaching friar's temperament had altered.[50]

One notices first of all the Christocentricity of Bale's thought. At one point he recalled that he had preached at Thorndon on the spiritual marriage which God the Father had effected between Christ and man's soul (the Gospel for the day being from Matthew 22, the parable of the king who gave a marriage feast for his son). There may have been an autobiographical echo in this; certainly Jesus had wholly replaced the Virgin and the saints as the object of Bale's devotion.[51] The saints, Bale said, were "canonized in

Christ's blood" alone and had no other claim to be called saints. Indeed, any Christian dying with faith in his heart and testimony on his lips was equally canonized by the merits of Christ's sacrifice.[52] Just as Bale had redefined the nature of sainthood to include all faithful Christian people, so also he repudiated the whole cultus of the saints as intercessors (this rejection having meant, no doubt, a greater wrench for him than for most Englishmen without his particular background). Actually Bale said here only that he thought "neither our Lady nor the saints contented with the superstitions which many do use when they pray to our Lady and (the) saints."[53] But his implication was clear throughout that prayer itself (and not only super-stitious prayer) to the saints was misdirected. Bale's words were slightly more radical than the tenor of the Ten Articles the previous July, which had permitted Christians to consider the saints "the advancers of our prayers and demands unto Christ."[54] Bale might have justified his words by reference to Cromwell's Injunctions, which (albeit in reference to pilgrimages, not prayers to the saints) had said, ". . .as though it were proper or peculiar to that saint to give this commodity or that, seeing all goodness, health and grace ought to be both asked and looked for only of God, as of the very author of the same, and of none other, for without Him that cannot be given. . . ."[55] Still, it does sound as though Bale were a bit in advance of royal policy—even judging from his "Answer," on which his future (if not his life) hung and in which one would have expected him to trim his sails as much as possible. But prudence was not really Bale's long suit. Quite likely his actual preaching about the saints (at Thorndon as well as at Doncaster) had been more radical still.

A related matter on which Bale was out ahead of official theology was the doctrine of purgatory. The Ten Articles had asserted the existence of purgatory, though declining to specify its location or the nature of the punishments suffered there. Now the complex of ideas relating to purgatory does not seem to have bulked large in Bale's thinking during his Carmelite years, nor, as a reformer, was he ever moved to single the doctrine of purgatory out for special attack (it provoked his bile far less than matters such as clerical celibacy). But by 1537 he clearly disbelieved in it, as incompatible with the all-sufficiency of Christ's sacrifice. In his "Answer" he denied that he had ever spoken against the Pater Noster for souls departed (that is, in hopes of shortening their punishment). But he went on to admit that he felt the Lord's Prayer appropriate to be said rather for the living than for the dead, for as he defined the state of the faithful departed, the latter were already in such bliss that they needed none of the things the prayer asked for: ". . . the souls departed do so praise God, that they can do none otherwise. They are so satisfied by the name of God that they can be none otherwise but holy. They are so of the kingdom of God that they can not be separate from it. . . ."[56] For one who considered the faithful to have been "canonized in Christ's blood" and not through any acquisition of merit (or purging of sin), gradually and with their own cooperation, belief in purgatory was out of the question. Bale clearly sided with George Joye here, and against William Tyndale, on the question of the state of faithful souls departed, before the general resurrection. There is no way of knowing why Bale found Joye's position the more convincing, except perhaps that the weightier Continental reformers seemed to support Joye.[57] In any case, by 1537 Bale had certainly accepted that *Christus solus* meant the end of purgatory, and was preaching as much.

Just as Bale's Carmelite hagiolatry had given way to a piety focused on the person of Christ, the Incarnate Word, so also for him the traditional sources of authority (Scripture, tradition, the pronouncements of the Church) had been narrowed to one, the written Word: *sola scriptura*.[58] Bale could scarcely have been more explicit on this point: "As touching the fourth article, I said that no man ought necessarily to believe any thing for an infallible or grounded truth but that which is plainly expressed in the sacred scripture of God. Nor none other truth ought to be preached than that which is in the scripture."[59] Accepting this principle naturally meant that Bale had had to reject in large quantity the mental furniture of his Carmelite past. Ceremonies, for one thing, had to be re-evaluated. Though Bale conceded that the liturgy as prescribed by the Ten Articles and Cromwell's Injunctions was "laudable . . . meet and convenient evermore to be observed for a decent order"[60] in the Church, he felt, nevertheless, that the Bible alone should "ground goodness in the ceremonies."[61] A pregnant phrase. Bale (wisely) did not go on in his "Answer" to make a case for the abolition of all non-scriptural ceremonies and usages. Even he knew better than to try to argue his way out of the porter's ward at Greenwich by doing that. He confined himself for the moment to arguing that when preaching of the Word was neglected, and the spiritual meaning of the ceremonies not made clear, the common people would continue to worship superstitiously. This of course was quite consistent with Cromwell's Injunctions. But the germ of Bale's later frenzied attitude toward "popish baggage" was already present at this early date.[62]

On the more positive side, *sola scriptura* meant a new vocabulary for Bale, one thoroughly infused with biblical imagery (often of the most vivid and graphic kind).[63] Without samples of Bale's pre-conversion preaching to compare with the "Answer," it is hard to be sure that the heavily scriptural flavor of Bale's homiletical language at Thorndon was new, but judging from the spirit of his Carmelite notebooks, one can be pretty sure that it was. More important, the new commitment to the exclusive authority of the Word implied for Bale a new purpose in preaching as well: to bring his listeners to respond to the message of the Bible (understood Christocentrically) with a radical change of heart. It is true that Bale hardly shrank from attacking specific vices (like the sin of rebellion) among his flock at Thorndon—that was partly why bailiff Kyrke and his group were so upset. But Bale's attitude differed from that of the late medieval preacher in that he did not presuppose that his listeners were already aboard the ark of salvation and needed only to have residual vices scrubbed away—he saw his task, really, as that of an evangelist.[64] Purely formal, sacramental initiation was not enough. Bale observed at one point that ". . . who so ever is not in true faith but a continual blasphemer of God and His word, and is never in love of God and his neighbor, he is not of the Church Militant but of the Church Malignant, of which speaketh David: *Odivi ecclesiam malignancium, et cum impiis non sedebo.*"[65] The criterion for inclusion in the true Church was, in other words, not so much outward (the performance of certain deeds, the avoidance of others) as an inner posture of dependence and obedience *coram Deo*. And this reorientation came initially from hearing the Bible expounded and preached in the mother tongue: *fides ex auditu*.

The need for understanding in the mind and the heart naturally had consequences for the liturgy and for private devotion also—as indeed Cromwell's Injunctions had specified. Bale recalled having taken the latter to heart: ". . . I exhorted the people to learn the Pater Noster, Creed and Ten Commandments in English according to the King's precept in the Injunctions, and showed them what godly understanding and remembrance they might have in that being in English, which they could never have by the Latin. And that where as no understanding was, nothing could be asked in faith, and that (which) rose not of faith was sin after St. Paul."[66] All of which was characteristically Lutheran (as well as Erasmian) and in particular would characterize the "puritan" frame of mind in England for generations.[67] Bale made this break with his past more explicit by using his own former materialistic thought-patterns as a negative example. While preaching on the article *descendit ad inferna* in the Creed, he cautioned his flock at Thorndon against fascination with the image of Christ fighting with devils "as they see it set forth in painted cloths, or in glass windows, or like as myself had before time set it forth in the country there in a certain play,"[68] for this missed the spiritual significance of the doctrine. Bale continued to write plays, of course, but now they were designed to evoke scorn for the old image-centered piety of his Carmelite past, and teach the new religion of the word and the Book. The old ways of thought were still fresh in Bale's own memory, though, which is perhaps one reason why he had to attack them so violently at Thorndon—and why the villagers obviously hurt him when they called him a "friar": "And whereas in your unadvised fury ye have called me friar, I am neither discontented nor ashamed of it, no more than St. Paul was, when he reported himself sometime to be a pharisee and a persecutor of the Christian sort. But whereas ye curse me, I shall with St. Paul bless you. And whereas ye say ill of me, I will say well of you, and ever be ready to do your good to my power."[69] This statement was a bit lame, for Bale of course had considerable "ill" to say of his erstwhile parishioners, but it was hard to be taunted with the title he had so recently renounced.

It is difficult to be very sure about the sources of Bale's theology as one sees it expressed in the "Answer"; his comments are of course unsystematic and incomplete. He wisely omitted reference to one topic—the Mass—which might have led him to reveal his theological mentors more clearly.[70] Certainly much of what he said was consistent with the Erasmian spirit of reform—his emphasis on understanding the faith, his stress on biblical preaching and on liturgy in the vernacular, his opposition to the cult of saints, and so on. Bale's acquaintance with courtiers like Lord Wentworth or John de Vere, Earl of Oxford (for whom Bale wrote some of his verse-plays, he said),[71] might have exposed him to humanist ideals. He may have read a good many of Erasmus's own works as well. He was familiar enough with the latter's exposition of the Creed (published in English in 1533) to cite it in his "Answer."[72] But of course on many theological matters Bale went far beyond the position of the Erasmian reformers—his belief in the exclusive authority of the Bible, for example.[75] On this and other points, such as the nature of the Eucharist or the doctrine of purgatory, Bale's words in the "Answer" are not so precise that one can point to this or that reformer as his principal guide. But all his specifically Lutheran or Zwinglian ideas can be found also in the printed works of English reformers like Frith, Joye, and Tyndale, which were in circulation in the mid-1530s and were common coin among English Protestants.[74] Theological precision would never be Bale's forte,[75] but his "Answer" does at least allow one to gauge the zeal with which he had embraced many of the more radical beliefs of the early English reformers by the time of his curacy at Thorndon in the fall of 1536.

Bale was not forced for long to savor the vileness and stink which his accommodations at Greenwich afforded. One of his brothers mobilized John Leland the antiquary to write a testimonial to Bale's qualities and send it to Cromwell, and Bale himself wrote to the minister, conceding that he might have "for want of counsel or due circumspection taken too much upon me in God's cause and my Prince's," and offering in the future to bear himself with "more soberness."[76] Whether or not Cromwell found the latter promise credible, he seemed satisfied with Bale's "Answer" and saw a use for his "comedies." So Cromwell rescued Bale from the clutches of the conservative Bishop Stokesley (who was evidently out to get him) and set him to work, if not as his "official playwright" at least as one small pawn in the propaganda offensive against the Bishop of Rome.[77] About the same time Bale sealed his departure from the Carmelite order with a vengeance by marrying a woman named Dorothy,[78] whose optimism in accepting such a husband and later patience in remaining faithful to him have led A. G. Dickens to place her "among the unsung heroines of the English Reformation."[79] The story of Bale's work as a playwright in the years 1537 to 1540 has often been told, and needs no repetition.[80] Those peripatetic years were significant for Bale's intellectual growth in another way as well, though. As the gravity of what he had done in leaving the Carmelite order sank in, as his Protestant convictions deepened, and as (most likely) he ran into opposition from conservative Englishmen in the country churchyards and borough halls where he must have performed his plays, Bale tried to understand the Reformation historically, in part to justify it to himself. As a Carmelite friar he had been concerned with the past and had viewed the past from a Carmelite perspective. He had seen history as an unbroken chain (at least since the time of Elijah) of Carmelite achievements, a succession of distinguished saints and leaders whom the order had boasted. Now in the late 1530s Bale's loyalties had shifted; or more precisely, since he had found membership in the Carmelite order untenable, his enormous capacity for self-giving devotion was seeking a new object. As his new heroes and new loyalties became clear to him, his perspective on the past naturally changed. It took Bale six or seven years from the time he left the Carmelites to evolve a new understanding of God's plan for history. In the late 1530s his historical thinking was a bit tentative and confused, as compared with the clarity of the scheme which took shape in his mind in the Low Countries, to which he fled in 1540. But it was an enormous task to re-evaluate the Carmelite past in the light of the Reformation, and then to reconsider both the whole history of Christendom and England's place within it. The striking fact is that Bale accomplished the job at all.

III / A Pattern for Church History

To understand the evolution of Bale's historical thinking after his conversion, one needs to go back two or three
months before the episode at Thorndon and consider the
brief history of the English Carmelites he wrote while at
Ipswich during the summer of 1536.[1] This *Anglorum
Heliades*, which Bale dedicated optimistically to John
Leland, was a much more finished piece of work than the
Chronica seu fasciculus temporum ordinis Carmelitarum on
which Bale had worked in the 1520s and early 1530s. The
florid, ornate Latin style of *Anglorum Heliades* was perhaps
calculated to impress Leland, and certainly the concentration on the English province of the order appealed to
the antiquary's vocal patriotism. Bale was not feigning an
emotion when he sang England's praises in the preface;[2]
already his *patria* was assimilating some of the devotion that
he had formerly felt for the Carmelite order. But Bale was by
no means liberated completely from his old thought-patterns.
One is struck in reading *Anglorum Heliades* by the weight
of convention under which Bale was struggling. Already a
radical reformer, a preacher fulminating against the Mass
and the cult of saints, Bale nevertheless repeated here with
no visible embarrassment the traditional legends about the
early Carmelites with which his manuscript notebooks had
been filled. That was simply how one wrote about the early

order, the period for which there were few if any existing records. The new wine of Bale's radical theology had not yet burst these old wineskins of convention. And yet one is still surprised to read in *Anglorum Heliades* his story of Simon Stock turning water into wine in order to celebrate Mass in the wilderness.[3] The habit of seeing contemporary men and women as fulfillments of biblical types (here, the references naturally being to the Wedding at Cana) would of course be characteristic of Protestant thought for some time,[4] but Bale's unblushing reference to the Mass is a bit jarring. So is his story of how the Virgin intervened to protect the Carmelite order against hostile prelates in the mid-thirteenth century;[5] it seems rather incongruous in light of the scorn Bale already felt for the cult of the saints. Finally, one finds Bale's continued lack of sympathy for Wyclif and the early Lollards somewhat unexpected. It is hard to say whether Bale felt this way because he was simply unaware of the tentative attempts to rehabilitate the reputation of Lollardy which Tyndale and his circle of exiles had made, and of Lollard tracts which they had reprinted,[6] or whether from force of habit the conventional praises Bale had always lavished on Thomas Netter of Walden (and repeated here in *Anglorum Heliades*)[7] kept him from seeing the Lollards as kindred spirits. In any case, in 1536 Bale still wrote of Wyclif as a benighted heretic and not as the "morning star of the Reformation."[8]

Though many of Bale's sentiments in *Anglorum Heliades* remained quite traditional, the events at London and Westminster in the past three years had of course made one great impact on his attitude toward the Carmelite order: he was now sensitive to its present decay. A feeling of bitterness and dissatisfaction about the Carmelites' loss of literary energy, their laziness (as he now saw it) and pursuit of wealth, the crumbling of their prestige in laymen's eyes—all of this was a change from his untroubled optimism of the 1520s.[9] It was not so much that the order itself had rapidly decayed (literary torpor, for one thing, had been as characteristic of the Carmelites in 1526 as it was ten years later) but that Bale now noticed its weaknesses. His conversion also, as well as the sight of the government's attack on the Church, had naturally influenced his feelings about the order. He now deplored the vast number of saints' offices which the friars celebrated, "as though the worship of God consisted in these things and not in the freedom of the Spirit alone."[10] He regretted the superstitions connected with the practice of burying laymen in the habit of the order, which implied that their assurance of salvation through Jesus was insufficient and needed reinforcement.[11] But Bale saw these practices as aspects of the order's decline since the thirteenth century—not as deeply-rooted customs, intrinsic to the mendicant life. Above all, he did not yet express a belief that the ideal of the separate religious life was cankered at its very root by egocentricity and work-righteousness. He could still view the mythical pre-history of the order, before the thirteenth century, as a golden age of poverty, asceticism, and the eremitical contemplative life. In fact, he rejoiced that the first Carmelites in England had retained something of that early spirit. (One hears an echo here of the longing for the desert which the friars of Simon Stock's generation had felt—revealing perhaps a need for rigor, for harsh discipline, in Bale's own character.) For lack of much evidence one way or the other, he was able to picture the early Carmelites as fulfillments of the godly type prefigured, according to the Epistle to the Hebrews, in the Old Testament faithful: "Especially, these (early friars) were not unlike the ones whom Paul speaks of. 'They wandered about in sheepskins and goatskins; being destitute, afflicted, tormented (of whom the world was not worthy); they wandered in deserts, and in mountains, and in dens and caves of the earth. . . .' "[12]

So the implications of Reformation theology for the regular life were not yet very clear for Bale. Indeed, it sounds (from what he said in *Anglorum Heliades*) as though in the summer of 1536 he were still hesitating on the brink of leaving the Carmelites, not sure whether the Gospel and the vows he had taken were compatible or not. The decay he sensed appeared therefore as a local phenomenon, peculiar to the Carmelite order (though no doubt Bale would graciously have extended his adverse judgment to include the other mendicants as well). It was not as yet something that he perceived in the Church as a whole, stemming from legalism and a belief in man's power to earn his salvation. But at least in *Anglorum Heliades* Bale sensed that for the Carmelites the present and the past were discontinuous: that between the 1530s and a bygone, mythical golden age (however defined) there intervened a period of superstitious darkness and moral decay. This perception—as old as the human race and at the heart of the historical awareness among both humanists and reformers—was virtually a platitude by the 1530s when it entered Bale's consciousness. But like a terrier he began to worry this idea tenaciously, and got more marrow from it than any other historical thinker the Reformation had yet produced.

After Bale had put off his friar's robe and married the patient Dorothy, he began to argue (not surprisingly) that vows of celibacy were contrary to God's will. They created a clerical caste, smacked of legalism and work-righteousness, stifled the liberty of a Christian, and had deplorable ethical results. Therefore after 1536 Bale came to see the decline of the Carmelite order not merely as a phenomenon of the last two centuries or so, but as inevitable and intrinsic from the very moment the order adopted the three-fold vow. What was true for the White Friars applied also to the other regular orders, of course, and indeed to the secular priesthood as well, beginning back when the popes had begun to enforce clerical celibacy. So Bale had good reason now to take a more radical view of corruption in the Church—it was a matter of doctrine, not just of practice; it was more widespread and it went back farther in time than he evidently had been aware when he wrote *Anglorum Heliades*. Whether Bale's marriage was the main cause pushing his thinking in this direction is a moot point.

Plenty of reformers (Barnes, Frith, and Tyndale, to name only the most obvious Englishmen) had said as much without benefit of wedlock. All these ideas were implicit in what Bale had been preaching at Doncaster and Thorndon. The immobility of thought-patterns fixed during nearly thirty years as a friar meant that Bale had perhaps been a bit slow to grasp and assimilate all that his new theology meant in practical terms. But his mind was on the move in the 1530s, and the fact of his marriage most probably speeded the process up (and, no doubt, later encouraged him to justify his action by spreading tales of monastic vice à la Cromwell's *comperta*).

In any case, his new attitude toward vows of celibacy appeared strikingly in a biographical history of the early Carmelites which Bale produced around 1539, a little work called *scriptorum ab helia ... Cathalogus*.[13] Here again, as in *Anglorum Heliades*, Bale accepted *in toto* the traditional legends about the foundation of the community on Mount Carmel by Elijah, the identification of John the Baptist and the Essenes with the Carmelite hermits, and so on. Neither the Gospel nor marriage had had any effect on Bale's convictions along these lines. What Bale did argue in this little *Cathalogus*, however, was that before the time of their leader Bertholdus in the twelfth century, the Carmelites "were not so atrociously bound by those popish monastic vows, which (nowadays) make them hate holy matrimony so much ... and feel so sickened (at the thought of) obedience to parents and rulers."[14] Rather, they had lived a life of voluntary asceticism, compatible with the liberty of the Gospel and avoiding the unhappy moral consequences of enforced celibacy. Therefore, among the "Carmelites" of the first century A.D., Bale said, "monasteries were not then the way they are now, brothels full of lazy soundrels."[15] This begins to sound like the mature bilious Bale. The point is, however, that this idea gave Bale the rudiments of a new periodization for Church history: before vows of celibacy, clerical and monastic life had been relatively honest and worthy. Afterwards, not so.

This was hardly a sophisticated or original insight, but in Bale's case it supplied one peg on which to hang further thinking about the history of the Church.

Bale's works on Carmelite history, however, like this little *Cathalogus*, give an unrealistically conservative picture of his historical thinking in the later 1530s. When one turns to consider the verse-plays which he wrote as part of Cromwell's campaign against superstition and the papal supremacy, one realizes that his ideas on the decay of the Church were much more advanced and complex than the Carmelite works reveal. Two plays in particular, *Kynge Johan* and *A Comedy concernynge thre lawes*, show that Bale was highly receptive to certain ideas about the corruption of the Roman Church which had been current among both English and Continental reformers for a decade and more. When free from Carmelite conventions, as in the "Answer" defending his preaching at Thorndon, Bale could fly his radical colors with gusto. His well-known *Kynge Johan* (of which he composed the first draft in 1538 or so)[16] shows he had taken to heart the theme of clerical subversion which was by now a commonplace of Reformation polemic. Bale had his personification of Sedition say:

> I hold upp the pope, as in other places many,
> For his ambassador, I am contynwally
> In Sycell, in Naples, in Venys and Ytalye. . . .
> In Yngland, in Scotland and in other regyons elles.
> For his holy cawse, I mayntayne traytors
>   and rebelles . . . .[17]

King John appeared as an earnest, pious, and divinely-appointed monarch who had been undermined by an international Romish conspiracy masterminded by the Legate Pandulph and who had finally been poisoned by the wicked monk, Simon of Swinstead. Some modern scholars have argued that Bale's refurbished image of the legendary "bad King John" came more or less directly from William Tyndale,[18] but this is probably taking too narrow a view of the influences on Bale. Many of the exiles in Tyndale's circle from the late 1520s onward had picked up the theme of clerical subversion and were wielding it as a polemical shillelagh, and not a few of them had mentioned King John. Simon Fish did so in his *A supplicacyon for the beggers* about 1528; so did the anonymous *A proper dyaloge betwene a Gentillman and an Husbandman* around 1529.[19] Robert Barnes was another reformer, and one not so closely linked with Tyndale, who had adopted the story of King John and used it to show that the pope was the English monarchy's worst enemy.[20] So Bale was simply developing and broadcasting a theme which he could hardly have missed, if (as was probably the case) he had been paying any attention at all to what the elder English reformers had been saying about the papacy and the English past. Bale did, to be sure, improve on earlier "reconstructed" treatments of King John by making the monarch a proto-Protestant—putting into his mouth harsh words against relics, ear-confession, trental masses, and the like.[21] If John had indeed fulfilled the type of godly ruler established in the Old Testament (and of course he had) then he would naturally have been right-minded concerning Romish baggage. Apart from this hagiographical flourish, however, *Kynge Johan* drew mainly on the earlier English reformers for its reconstruction of the story.[22]

Kynge Johan saw Bale engaged in that typical activity of the early Reformation, the search for historical precedents. Under the aegis of his mentor Cromwell, Bale was trying to show that Henry VIII's breach with the papacy was nothing new, and that in fact over three hundred years earlier, the unhappy John had at least sought a similar independence. It was one thing, however, to follow reformers like Tyndale in pointing to specific instances in which rulers had resisted Rome. It would be quite another matter to offer a systematic explanation of how this resistance had come to be necessary: how (and in what stages) the threat posed by Rome's worldly ambitions had reached the intensity apparent in the time of King

John. This was a much harder task than the search for isolated precedents supporting the breach with Rome. On a slightly different topic, Robert Barnes (the former prior of the Austin Friars at Cambridge and Bale's old neighbor there) had already broken the ground. His *Vitae Pontificum Romanorum* (published at Wittenberg in 1536) had attempted to date the precise origins of various Roman traditions which the reformers had repudiated, and to make patent their post-scriptural character. But Barnes's work had had no particular structure—it was more or less a chronological list, with little in the way of interpretation. He had made no attempt to offer a framework of periodization for the data he presented. It was this latter task which Bale essayed in *A Comedy concernynge thre lawes*, which he wrote at about the same time as *Kynge Johan*, in 1538.[13] The three laws of Nature, Moses, and Christ, Bale wrote, had been corrupted in turn by "infidelity" in various guises. Bale made it clear in his stage directions that his allegorical vices were meant to have a very contemporary sting: "Let Idolatry be decked like an old witch, Sodomy like a monk of all sects, Ambition like a bishop, Covetousness like a pharisee or spiritual lawyer, False Doctrine like a Popish doctor, and Hypocrisy like a grey friar."[24] While *Kynge Johan* had concentrated more on the theme of political subversion by the papacy, *thre lawes* dealt more with the spiritual and moral corruption into which the Roman Church had beguiled Christendom.

Apart from the earthy satire, the most interesting features of the play are its periodic structure and its apocalyptic conclusion. Bale was searching for some way to understand, to view in historical perspective, the attacks by conservatives in England on the Cromwellian Reformation. He needed to see that it had all happened before, and that nevertheless the true faith had persisted. The pattern he chose for illustrating this in *thre lawes* was the ancient division of history into three ages: before the Mosaic Law, the Age of Nature; then the period under the Law; and after Christ, the Age of Grace. St. Paul had assumed this scheme in the fifth chapter of Romans; St. Augustine had recognized it; and it had become a commonplace of medieval thought, percolating down into such manuals of popular preaching as the fifteenth-century *Speculum Sacerdotale.*[25] In each of these periods, Bale demonstrated, the insidious craft of the Enemy (at work in all ages) had sought to draw men from obedience to God. The resistance of English conservatives like "Wharton of Bungay" in Suffolk (one of Bale's favorite enemies)[26] could be understood and therefore lived with, as yet another attack of this kind. But the future held out high hope: God would not permit the perfect law of Christ to be twisted and perverted forever, but would appear in His time to defeat Satan once and for all and restore the three laws to their proper function in the Christian's life.[27]

Bale, of course, offered no prediction in *thre laws* about the timing of the Lord's return, and made no attempt to describe the specific events which would be associated with the *Parousia*. The play did not deal with concrete historical events, nor was it really so much concerned with the future (though that element was there) as with the past. *A Comedy concernynge thre lawes* was important not so much as an expression of apocalyptic longing (a tendency distinctly muted in Bale) but for the rudimentary pattern of history which it offered. The play showed that Bale was turning to the Bible for such a pattern. *Sola Scriptura* now not only meant for him that the Bible supplied the norm by which to test doctrine, morals, and church government. It also confirmed and strengthened in his mind the age-old Christian belief that the God who revealed His will in history also revealed it in His Word: that the Bible held the key to understanding the past, the present, and the future. "Surely the Lord God will do nothing," Amos of Tekoa had said, "but he revealeth his secret unto his servants the prophets."[28] Hence from the very beginning Christians had sought the meaning of history not primarily in the empirical data or in the objective "tracks" of the past, but in revelation, in the inspired messages of those who spoke God's word. So it is with no surprise that one finds Bale turning to the Bible via St. Augustine and the *Speculum Sacerdotale* for his pattern of history in *thre lawes*. The play marks an important stage in his intellectual development, for it shows that by 1538 he was grappling with the problem of periodization. His eventual solution—which was some five years in emerging—would be a seminal contribution to the historical thought of the English Reformation.

For the present, however, the pattern for history which Bale used in *thre lawes* raised a problem. The division of time into the ages of Nature, Law, and Grace was not really relevant to the issues which were dividing the reformers from Rome, and dividing reformers among themselves. The historical territory over which all parties were struggling was, after all, the period since Christ's Ascension. The magisterial reformers (and Bale the Cromwellian playwright was manifestly in that camp) were engaged in a two-front battle. On the one hand they had to show how the Roman Church had deviated over the centuries from the purity of New Testament Christianity. Robert Barnes, as noted just above, had attempted something like this, with Luther's blessing, in *Vitae Pontificum Romanorum*. There had been other Lutherans too who had made similar beginnings, like Joachim von Watt who had published his *Vom Alten und neuen Gott* in 1521. On the other side the magisterial reformers had to fight off the Anabaptists, whose battle cry of *restitutio* represented aims that were unacceptably radical. No Henrician—or Lutheran, or Calvinist, or Zwinglian—was willing to leap back into the New Testament Church feet first. The magisterial reformers balked at the notion of imitating the apostolic Church down to the tiniest detail, and they insisted on certain institutions and practices, such as infant baptism, which Scripture did not in fact support unequivocally. These magisterial reformers had to make some recourse to the example of the post-apostolic Church, then, however much they might protest that the Bible was the only norm.[29]

But how long had this post-apostolic Church remained acceptably "pure" and worthy of emulation? The pontificate of Boniface III in the early seventh century was a terminal point which caught the Lutherans' fancy very early,[30] but the point was that this periodization had no scriptural support. It was purely a human suggestion. So among the magisterial reformers in the 1520s and 1530s there was considerable need for a pattern for post-apostolic Church history, derived from the Word and carrying the Bible's authority. The three-age pattern was no help.

Neither were a couple of alternative schemes which had found favor in Germany. The first big historical work of the Melanchthonian school, Johann Carion's chronicle of 1532, mentioned the three ages of Nature, Law, and Grace briefly, but then settled for a four-monarchy plan drawn from the Book of Daniel.[31] Since the fourth monarchy (Rome) spanned the whole length of Church history and more, this system was of no help in breaking the post-Ascension age into smaller segments. Luther himself tended to lean toward a six-age chronology of world history, which derived (in the Christian tradition) from at least as far back as the Epistle of Barnabas, about 135 A.D. Taking each of the six days of Creation to represent a thousand years, this scheme assumed that Jesus had been born early in the sixth millennium, and that a seventh age (representing God's sabbath rest) should follow His return and the Last Judgment. St. Augustine had also used this chronology with modifications long ago, and in his vigorous struggle against chiliasm, he had argued that the seventh age was not to come, but had represented the peace enjoyed by the faithful in all six eras. Augustine had posited an eighth age, outside of time, to follow the *Parousia*.[32] *Mutatis mutandis*, this scheme had been adopted by any number of medieval historical writers, and had become as much a part of Christendom's common patrimony as the Pauline three-age pattern. In the Renaissance it was known and employed (for example) by the French humanist Charles de Bouelles, whose *Aetatum Mundi Septem supputatio* of 1521 Bale would later use (for specific details, not for the pattern) in the 1540s. So this was the scheme which Luther himself favored during most of his life, and which he would embody in his *Supputatio annorum mundi* in 1541.[33] Taken by itself, however, without further modification and subdivision, this system of periodization offered no more help in thinking about Church history than did the three-age or four-monarchy models. Since the sixth millennium covered the whole period from the Ascension until Christ's return, Protestants found no clues here for dating the precise stages of Rome's *descensus Averno*, or for fixing the duration of the acceptable early Church.

Fortunately for the reformers (and especially for Bale) there was one other alternative, a chronology based upon the Book of Revelation which also carried with it the weight of scriptural authority. As Bale searched for a "vision of history"[34] in the late 1530s, some imaginative way of understanding England's present turbulence as part of a clear and God-ordained pattern for the whole of history, it was in the Apocalypse that he eventually found what he sought. By 1538 his thoughts were already turning in this direction, as the conclusion of his *Comedy concernynge thre lawes* made clear:

> The apostle John, in the Apocalypse, doth say
> He saw a new heaven, and a new earth appearing . . . .
> A new Jerusalem, the said John also see (*sic*)
> As a beautiful bride, prepared to her husband.
> Our true faithful church is that same fair city,
> Whom we have cleansed by the power of our
>   right hand . . .
> Now we have destroyed the kingdom of Babylon,
> And thrown the great whore into the bottomless pit,
> Restoring again the true faith and religion. . . .[35]

At the time that the Book of Revelation had originally been written, it had answered a need similar to the one which Bale felt in the late 1530s (though no doubt more acute). The early Church had stood utterly convinced that with Jesus's resurrection, the midpoint, the critical moment in history had been reached. Jesus had won the battle over death and sin. However the Kingdom might grow and increase thereafter, these achievements would be simply the fruits of a victory already won. In this sense the early Christians radically modified their heritage of Jewish messianic hopes—they felt that the climax of history was not to be awaited at the end of the world, but had already come.[36]

But if Jesus really were the Son of God and therefore Lord of Time, why was it that evil manifestly continued to flourish? The "already—not yet" tension (the tension which Bale too would feel in the 1530s) became especially painful in the reign of the megalomaniac Domitian (81-96 A.D.), and it seems to have been the persecutions which he ordered that produced the apocalyptic book known as the Revelation of St. John. Drawing on the ripe harvest of images in the Jewish eschatological tradition, transforming them by relating them all to the central figure of Jesus, the Book of Revelation reasserted emphatically the lordship of Christ over history. The Lamb alone was worthy to open the seven seals of the book:[37] He was both the unique key to the meaning of time and its Master. The ravening beasts of war, famine, and plague (loosed as the second, third, and fourth seals opened) might go forth, but the mighty warrior of the Gospel astride the white horse (in the first seal) alone "went forth conquering, and to conquer." The later visions in the book represented the ultimate defeat of those embodiments of evil, the imperial house and the imperial priesthood. The visions promised a respite of a thousand years during which Satan would be banished to the bottomless pit. Then after a brief and futile revival of wickedness, the Last Judgment would come with the appearance of a "new heaven and a new earth" and "the holy city, new Jerusalem coming down from God out of heaven."[38] So the Apocalypse of St. John offered the beleaguered Church late in the first century a "vision of history" which allowed Christians to see the sufferings of their present age as the transitory phenomena which Jesus had promised. And it held out hope for a golden age in the future when the fruits of the victory already won might be fully enjoyed.

Despite the power with which the Book of Revelation spoke to the concerns of the early Church, unanimity in interpreting its imagery was short-lived, if indeed ever achieved. Many of the early Fathers continued to believe that the horsemen and beasts, the trumpet-blowings and vial-pourings and so on, referred to concrete and specific historical figures and events. They took the beast rising from the sea in Chapter 12 to represent the Roman imperial power, a ghastly quintessence of Caligula, Nero, and Domitian combined: *regnum caesaris regnum diaboli.* And they took the future victory of the Lord and the eradication of Satan's hosts to be actual historical events, to occur within future time on earth. Fathers of the Church as widely respected as Irenaeus believed literally in the millennial reign of Jesus and His saints (identified with the seventh age of the world, the Sabbath) in this world and before the Last Judgment. Irenaeus, Tertullian, Commodian, and writers as late as Lactantius in the fourth century refused to repudiate the belief that the Book of Revelation offered a key to God's plan for the Church in the world, a way of understanding the Church's conflict with forces (like the emperors) who sought to draw Christians away from worship of God. But other influential writers denied the applicability of the Apocalypse of St. John to concrete historical events. As early as the second century A.D., Origen was rejecting the notion of a millennial kingdom on earth, and asserting that the images in Revelation referred to the spiritual and psychological life of the individual Christian, not to external events in time. This internalizing, allegorizing bent characterized Alexandrine exegesis as a whole. Nor did the Roman church follow the more literalist millenarians like Irenaeus. So at least two of the major centers of Christianity were already predisposed to reject the Book of Revelation as a key to world history, even before the tide turned decisively in that direction during the fourth century.

The triumph of Christianity, the developing institutional Church's bias against boat-rocking, the influence of strongly ahistorical Greek traditions on Christian thought—all these encouraged the Church in the fourth century to quash any hopes for an imminent millennium, or any too-literal identification of beasts and dragons with political figures in the Roman Empire. The Donatist heretic Tyconius (around 380 to 400 A.D.) led the way in bringing the interpretation of the Apocalypse into line with fourth-century needs. Like Origen, he saw in the repeated series of sevens (seal-openings, trumpet blasts, and the like) an allegory of the individual Christian's spiritual pilgrimage, not a pattern for elucidating world history. And he strongly believed that the thousand years of Revelation 20 referred simply to the period since the Ascension, not to any golden age yet in the future.

These and other ideas (notably his image of two "cities" were among the legacy of Tyconius to St. Augustine (354-430), who made the allegorical approach to Revelation the standard one for the next seven hundred years and more. The important events in history, Augustine believed, were not the visible and external phenomena like wars, famines, persecutions, the rise and fall of empires, and so forth, but rather the inward and hidden journeys which each of the Elect made toward God. Naturally, therefore, he saw the Book of Revelation not as a *speculum historiale* but as a mirror of the soul's pilgrimage, the quest of the *viator* who was in this world but ultimately not of it. Nor was the thousand-year reign of Christ a future age to come; rather, this image or prophecy had already been fulfilled in the Church since Christ's Ascension. Augustine of course accepted and transmitted to medieval historical thought the pattern of seven ages in world history. But generally he located the seventh age or Sabbath rest in the hearts of the faithful in all ages. In any case, there was nothing yet to come on earth that had not already been brought in by Christ. Augustine restored the early Church's primary emphasis on the "already" rather than the "not yet." His repudiation of chiliasm was confirmed by the Council of Ephesus in 431, and his allegorical and nonhistorical exegesis of the Apocalypse became the standard interpretation in the early Middle Ages.[39]

The reawakening of interest during the twelfth century in the literal sense of the Bible brought with it, however, a revival of the conviction that the Book of Revelation offered a key to history. Commentators like Anselm of Havelburg (d.1158) began to refer the various sequences of sevens to actual events or stages in the history of the Church, to see in the Apocalypse a pattern giving shape and meaning to the Church's experience through the centuries. Though God's self-revelation through Christ was perfect and unchanging, still one could see development and variation (Anselm thought) in the different forms which Satan's attacks on the Church had taken in the course of time. Thus the seven seals in Revelation 6 to 8 could represent subdivisions within the larger sixth age of the world, from the Ascension to Christ's return. The first such subdivision, the era of the apostolic Church, was followed by the time of persecutions under the emperors up through the age of Diocletian. This period of trial was the second age, indicated by the second seal. The third age was the era of major heresies, after Constantine had bestowed external peace on the Church. Following this came an age of "false Christians" and hypocrites—not a very precise conception, nor did Anselm try to give it specific historical content. His notion of the fifth age was even more opaque, representing as it did the "consolation" enjoyed in all ages by Christians on their earthly pilgrimage. The sixth and seventh seals, finally, stood for the apogee of evil during the reign of the Antichrist, and then the eternity of heavenly bliss, beyond history. Anselm felt that he was still living in the fourth age (presumably with a bit of the fifth added to it). The importance of his exegesis was hardly that he supplied a clear or systematic interpretation of Church history—as he manifestly did not. Rather, what Anselm did do was to reassert the principle that the external history of

Christendom was significant and that the Bible did supply a pattern for it—that this pattern, in fact, was to be sought precisely *in* the Bible and not in any empirical historical data. And Anselm helped open up the way for mentioning specific historical events in the course of commenting on the seven seals, trumpets, and vials. Though he did not do much of this himself, his near-contemporary Rupert of Deutz (d. circa 1130) had been quite acutely aware in his exegesis of Revelation that the early persecutions of the Church had been ended by a concrete historical figure, the Emperor Constantine, and that this outward event had marked a critical turning point in Church history. It was the Abbot Joachim of Flora (d.1202), however, who opened the floodgates for the introduction of specific historical data into commentaries on the Apocalypse. The Vandal and Lombard invasions, the rise of Islam, the Crusades, and so on all figured for Joachim as examples of the stages in the Church's experience. From the beginning of the thirteenth century onward, the validity of Revelation as a mirror for history had been clearly re-established.[40]

Joachim of Flora, of course, was significant for far more than simply for introducing the likes of Saladin and Frederick Barbarossa into his exegesis. For Anselm of Havelburg, Rupert of Deutz, and their contemporaries, the Apocalypse had supplied primarily a pattern for the Church's past. In the fertile thought of Joachim the book also became once more a timetable for the future. Adopting and revising the seven-seal scheme from Revelation, the Calabrian abbot claimed to deduce from patterns in the Bible as a whole that the seventh seal-opening would mark a completely new status in the history of the world. Blending a pattern of threes with the sevens in the Apocalypse, Joachim argued that the Age of the Father (the Old Testament period) and the Age of the Son (beginning with the Incarnation) would be succeeded by an Age of the Spirit—and that this would commence *within history*, at the beginning of the seventh epoch since Jesus's birth. Joachim felt that he was living in the sixth such epoch, the time in which the power of Satan would rage most savagely. But soon (he was not clear as to how soon) a new order of "spiritual men" would usher in the millennium, or seventh age, or third status. Satan would be utterly defeated and bound, and a new spirituality would suffuse the old and tired institutions of the world. Joachim conceded that total perfection was not possible on earth, within history—evil would once more burst forth for a brief moment before Christ's second coming and the Last Judgment. But still Joachim's Age of the Spirit made the future of this present world sound rather promising. Joachim stood foursquare against the age-old Christian pessimism which foresaw only a downward spiral of decay until the *Parousia*. His ideas—not surprisingly—met with stiff reaction from the institutional Church. In particular the adoption of Joachite and pseudo-Joachite ideas by the Spiritual Franciscans led to wholesale condemnations of the tradition during the thirteenth century. The great school-men of the period reaffirmed the Constantinian Church's repudiation of chiliasm. Yet of course the hopes and aspirations persisted underground, fostered by the multiple traumas (plague, Schism, Hundred Years' War, and so on) of the late Middle Ages. So the Joachite radical approach to the Apocalypse as a mirror of history ranged alongside the more conservative tradition stemming from Anselm of Havelburg and formed part of the heritage available to Bale in the 1530s.[41]

The stream of Joachite thought flowed into and reinforced another current of prophecy in the later Middle Ages—a complex of ideas which were partly extra-biblical in origin, but which had a strong impact on the way men read and interpreted the Book of Revelation. This was the current of prophecy represented by the so-called "Sibylline oracles," the oldest of which in the Christian tradition dated back to the fourth century. To the image of the eschatological warrior-Christ in Revelation, these books added the figure of the Emperor of the Last Days, who would crush the forces of evil decisively and reign over a

Christian golden age of peace and plenty just before the final outburst of Satan and the Second Coming. The Sibyllines also added frightening imagery to the demonic being mentioned in the epistles of St. John: the Antichrist. This enemy of mankind had been gradually associated in Christian apocalyptic thought with the "Man of Sin" in St. Paul's second letter to the Thessalonians and with the beast-dragon-Satan of chapters 13 and 20 in Revelation. According to the Sibylline prophecies, the Antichrist—the epitome of all the dark forces in the earth, the stuff of nightmares since the childhood of the human race—would reign for a brief but terrifying period between the death of the Last Emperor and the Second Coming. A widely-read compilation of both Sibylline and biblical apocalyptic lore (the *Libellus de ortu et tempore Antichristi*) was made in the tenth century by Abbot Adso of Burgundy.

It was particularly in the thirteenth century and thereafter, however, that the search for "signs" of Antichrist's approach became a feverish preoccupation—and not merely in times of famine, plague, and war. In the struggle of papacy and empire dating back to the time of Pope Gregory VII, it had become commonplace for each side to perceive in the other the lineaments of Antichrist, and to couch their incessant polemic in those terms. Yet for all this repetition, the figure of the Antichrist lost none of its horrifying fascination. The image of the Antichrist-papacy naturally loomed large in the thought of the Spiritual Franciscans and of their kindred spirits. In England at the end of the fourteenth century, John Wyclif reinforced this identification of Rome with the forces of Satan. The devil had of course been at work in all ages, Wyclif argued, but especially since the growth of papal ambitions from the eleventh century onward, individual popes had been particularly notable members of Antichrist's body. Finally Luther made the association of Rome with Antichrist indelible in the minds of those who opposed the papacy. The whole institution and its doctrine and not merely individual popes represented for Luther the arch-fiend, the beast of Revelation. Luther felt that the transformation of the papacy into the Antichrist had been adumbrated in the claim of Boniface III to universal spiritual authority in the early seventh century, though perhaps the full measure of papal depravity had become clear only after the year 1000. By the 1530s, then, any Protestant who sought a key to Church history in the Apocalypse would naturally view the book in light of this Antichrist tradition. However one might date the seven seal-openings and so on, the thousand-year bondage of Satan would clearly refer to some period (past or future) of restraint on the papacy's power to corrupt men's faith and morals. The images and ideas connected with this late medieval Antichrist lore formed a basic facet of the mind-set with which Bale approached the Book of Revelation, as he searched for some way of viewing the Henrician Reformation within a larger historical pattern.[42]

Several books which Bale knew in the late 1530s reinforced his inclination to study the Apocalypse. One of these was the Latin play *Pammachius*, published by the Lutheran reformer Thomas Kirchmeyer at Wittenberg in 1538. The play most likely appeared too late to have had any influence on Bale's *Kynge Johan*, as used to be thought,[43] but he later translated it, probably in the early 1540s, and referred to it in his *The Image of bothe churches*.[44] *Pammachius* had an apocalyptic structure: the pope conjures up Satan after the thousand-year bondage, uses demonic power to depose the Christian emperor, and substitutes his authority in Christendom for that of Christ and the Bible. Just as he and his minions are celebrating their victory, however, a messenger sounds the alarm that the Gospel has got loose at Wittenberg, and God's forces are counterattacking. *Pammachius* ends with the battle still in doubt, and the Second Coming expected imminently. The play (issued from the fortress of the magisterial Reformation) naturally took a postmillennial stance: the thousand years were in the past, and no golden age was to be looked for within history—only continued strife until the end of the world. Nevertheless the millennium of Revelation 20 was taken to represent a real (if unspecified) historical period, indicating Kirchmeyer's confidence in the Apocalypse as a key to understanding the past.

Another book pointing Bale in the same direction was Joachim von Watt's *Vom Alten und neuen Gott*, published first in 1521 and translated into English in 1534 by Thomas, Lord Wentworth's protegé (and Bale's later friend in exile) William Turner.[45] Bale had read a Latin version of the book in his early Cambridge days and had not liked it a bit.[46] Now he was more receptive. Von Watt's purpose was to trace the growth of idolatry from the time of the early Greeks and Hebrews on up and to show how at last the papacy itself had been exalted above God in Christian worship and was now spewing forth errors, vile ceremonies, and so on, all over the earth. Von Watt thought the papacy was probably the full manifestation of Antichrist. Though the book did not mention Satan's loosing after the thousand years, another typical chronological theme was stressed: the crucial pontificate of Boniface III (607), who persuaded the Byzantine Emperor Phocas to grant the Roman See primacy over all other churches.[47] Despite the absence of specific allusions to historical patterns in Revelation, von Watt's work was full of apocalyptic references[48] and assumed the relevance of prophecy to an understanding of the papacy's development.

Perhaps the most important work leading Bale into a study of Revelation was *Fasciculi Zizaniorum*, the Carmelite collection of documents relating to Wyclif and the early Lollards. Bale probably obtained the Norwich Carmelites' manuscript copy when that house was dissolved in 1538, and he annotated the volume heavily during the next few years.[49] One of the collected tracts which caught his eye was an attack by John Tyssington, O.F.M., on Wyclif's assertion (*inter alia*) that all the doctors of the Church since the year 1000 had erred, and that Satan had inhabited the Church in particular strength since that time. Bale underlined phrases like *post solutionem Sathanae* and

Apocalypsis solutum fuisse Sathanam post annos Domini mille.[50] Wyclif had in fact claimed that Satan had taken over the Roman Church "more fully" since the year 1000.[51] This was certainly sufficient (even had there been no other clues) to point Bale in the direction of the Apocalypse in his search for a periodic structure in history. And the authority of Wyclif behind this periodization was coming to have a good deal of weight for Bale. He seems really to have discovered Wyclif as a kindred spirit, now for the first time. One can almost see Bale's eyebrows raised in surprise, as he noted on one of the volume's fly-leaves that concerning the Eucharist, Wyclif "raises this question. . . . Whether after the consecration the substance of bread remains essentially . . . . He confesses not only that bread remains, with Luther, but bread alone, with Oecolampadius and Zwingli."[52] In point of fact, when Bale had had a chance to think about Wyclif a bit more, and had had time to study Revelation, he would conclude that the appearance of this "morning star" had marked an important stage in God's plan, too. For the time being, in the late thirties and the early forties, his new acquaintance with Wyclif served to confirm his suspicion that the pattern he sought could be found in biblical prophecy.[53]

The final impulse, turning Bale's attention to the Apocalypse, was his flight into exile in 1540. The fall of Cromwell in June of that year left Bale defenseless and exposed, and the burning of his old acquaintance Robert Barnes the following month showed what could happen to conspicuously Protestant ex-friars. Bale's marriage in any case (on top of his association with Cromwell) had made him an obvious target for retaliation by the Norfolk-Gardiner faction. So Bale fled with his "poore wife and children" to the Continent. He probably settled in Antwerp for the next five or six years, perhaps eking out a subsistence by working for the printers in that city.[54] In his penury and exile he came to identify with St. John on the island of Patmos. He came to feel that the Book of Revelation could best be understood by exiles, their vision purified by austerity, and indeed he thought that God laid upon certain exiles the duty of interpreting the Apocalypse to their brethren back at home.[55]

So Bale in exile naturally began to cast about to see how other reformers had understood the book—and in particular to see whether they had derived from it an historical schema in which to place the Reformation. His own plight would be easier to put up with if he could see it as part of a recurring pattern in God's plan for the Church. Judging from the works which Bale cited when he finally published his own commentary, *The Image of bothe churches*,[56] there were four Protestant interpretations of Revelation which he had read (along with a mass of older works, to be sure). Two of these Protestant works were very brief and not of much use to him: Luther's *Ein Kurtze und klare anlaitung* to the Apocalypse (printed in Wittenberg in 1530), and Georgius Aemilius's *Imaginum in Apocalypsi Iohannis Descriptio* (Frankfort, 1540). Luther's work was merely a brief preface of eight leaves, and Aemilius's a collection of woodcuts and Latin verses. Bale's marginal notes to the first book of *The Image of bothe churches* (the only one of the work's three parts which contained such notes) do not indicate that he got much from either of these.[57] A third Protestant commentary was rather more useful to him: a work entitled *In Apocalypsim Ioannis Apostoli . . . Commentarius*, published at Zurich in 1539 by Dr. Sebastian Meyer of Bern. In Part I of *The Image* Bale referred to Meyer's commentary more than twenty times, though only on minor points of interpretation (and indeed he sometimes misrepresented the Bernese reformer's ideas).[58] He did find reconfirmed in Meyer's work the notion that Satan had been loosed about 1000 A.D. after his millennium of bondage. And Meyer did concede that the first four seal-openings in Revelation 6 had been applied by other commentators to specific stages in Church history—though Meyer himself much preferred the belief that they symbolized events in the life of Christ.[59] So here and there Bale found suggestions about a pattern of Church history in the Swiss reformer's commentary, despite the fact that Meyer himself did not pursue that line of exegesis very far. The really crucial influence on Bale's interpretation of the Apocalypse, however, was the commentary published at Marburg in 1528 by Francis Lambert, professor of theology at the new university there.

Francis Lambert had come to embrace the Reformation through many of the same experiences that Bale had shared. Born at Avignon in 1487, Lambert had joined the Observant Franciscans there at the age of fifteen or so. After he had finished his education, his intelligence and speaking ability made him a successful preacher among the laity in and around Avignon, but marked him out for jealous harassment by his fellow friars. Lambert apparently shared something of Bale's prickly temperament. Disillusioned by the lack of love and idealism within his order, he seized the opportunity to escape while on an official trip to Switzerland in 1522. Violently on the rebound from the Franciscans, he was ripe for conversion. He wandered for a bit, preaching where he could, and fetched up in Bern, where (interestingly) he felt the influence of Sebastian Meyer—not regarding the Book of Revelation specifically, but concerning the Church's need for reform in general. It was evidently at Zurich in July of 1522, however, that Lambert was converted once and for all. It was Zwingli himself who convinced Lambert of his errors in a public disputation. From that point on, the ex-friar spent most of his remaining years in Germany. Commissioned by the Landgrave Philip of Hesse in 1526 to plan the reformation of the Church in that territory, Lambert drew up a program which Philip rejected (on Luther's advice) as both too legalistic and too democratic—too much like the later Calvinist polities for Lutheran tastes. Philip nevertheless named Lambert to a chair in theology when he founded his university at Marburg, and Lambert taught there until his death in 1530. His forte as a scholar was evidently exegesis, for commentaries—mostly on Old Testament prophets—

outnumber his other printed works. The lectures which he
gave on the Apocalypse during 1527 at Marburg were
published the following year as *Exegeseos Francisci
Lamberti in sanctam Divi Ioannis Apocalypsim Libri VII.*[60]

Francis Lambert seems to have been the first
Protestant reformer to use the patterns in the Book of
Revelation as a scheme for understanding Church history.
In his comments on the seven seals in Chapters 6 to 8, on
the number 666 at the end of Chapter 13, and on the
thousand-year bondage of Satan in Chapter 20, Lambert
offered his answers to the problem of periodization. The
seven seals, he said, represented (as Anselm of Havelburg,
Joachim of Flora, and their tradition had held) the
successive ages from the early Church to the end of the
world. First came the outpouring of the Spirit at Pentecost,
and the mission of the Apostles throughout the Roman
world. Following this was the second age, when a few
heretics crept into the Church but especially when the
Roman emperors savagely persecuted the faithful. Then
came the third age, after the peace given to the Church by
Constantine; this was the period of heresies *par excellence*.
When the Church had more or less effectively suppressed
these errors, Satan's forces took a new tack by totally
corrupting the papacy itself with worldly ambition, by
spreading the hypocritical monastic life, as well as by
persecuting the Church outwardly through the armies of
Islam. This was the fourth age. The fifth was partly
chronological, partly thematic. It signified the persecution
of the saints in all ages, though their affliction by the
papacy had been especially acute since the seventh or
eighth century. The sixth seal then represented the revival
of the Gospel, which Lambert felt had been going on for
the last hundred years or so. He believed, however, that the
sixth age would conclude with a fearful persecution, the
worst yet, during which the beast from the sea (Revelation
13) would rage for forty-two months. But God would crush
the forces of Satan, tie up the dragon in the bottomless pit
for a thousand years, and usher in the seventh age—the

millennium on earth. Lambert was quite unequivocal on this point. The golden age was still to come, and within history. After that he foresaw the final brief loosing of the devil, and then the Last Judgment.[61]

Lambert's unabashed chiliasm may have drawn its inspiration from the Joachite tradition. He did not refer to Joachim in the commentary, but his exegesis paralleled the latter's in his interpretation of the seven seals (except perhaps the fifth) as clear-cut periods in Church history, and in his eager expectation of the Sabbath Age on earth.[62] If Lambert had not actually read the Calabrian abbot's own works, still there were collections of later Joachite tracts (suggesting various seven-fold patterns) that had been published recently and which Lambert might have seen.[63] In any case it seems strange that Philip of Hesse, fresh from annihilating Thomas Muentzer and the peasant rebels at Frankenhausen in 1525, should have invited the likes of Francis Lambert to come and reform his Church. Indeed, Lambert had already been lecturing on the Apocalypse at the University of Strasbourg in 1525;[64] but perhaps he had not yet clarified his chiliastic ideas, or if he had, perhaps the Landgrave of Hesse had not heard the bad news. The publication of his commentary at Marburg in 1528—in the decent obscurity of the Latin, unlikely to encourage peasant violence, at least—apparently left Lambert unscathed. There was even a second impression of the book at Basel in 1539. This may have been the edition which Bale picked up when, exiled to the Low Countries, he began to study the Apocalypse in earnest.

The pattern of history which Bale offered in *The Image of bothe churches*, which he published at Antwerp in 1545 or 1546,[65] was essentially Francis Lambert's minus the chiliasm.[66] Bale agreed with Lambert (and with the long tradition of commentators going back to Anselm of Havelburg) that the Book of Revelation was a mirror of Church history. The opening of the seven seals, he said, not only represented the manifestation of God's truth in each of the seven ages of the world,[67] but especially betokened the periods in the history of the Church since the Ascension.[68] Bale fully concurred in the traditional belief that the meaning of history was to be sought not in experience, or in chronicles and histories themselves, but in the Bible. Chronicles supplied examples of what the prophecies in the Bible foretold, "yet is the text a light to the cronicles, & not the cronicles to the texte."[69] Armed with Lambert's reading of the Apocalypse, therefore, Bale set out to show how the purity of the early Church had gradually grown rotten, and yet how God had always kept His truth alive in a faithful few.

In Bale's interpretation of the first five seal-openings in Revelation 6, he followed Lambert very closely indeed, sometimes simply translating what the French reformer had written in Latin.[70] The first seal represented the out-pouring of the Holy Spirit at Pentecost and the Apostles' preaching of the Gospel over the whole world. The second seal-opening, Bale and Lambert agreed, marked the attacks on the early Christians' faith and belief by the pseudo-apostles, and on their bodies by the Roman emperors. Bale paraphrased much of what the Marburg professor had said here, but added quantities of specific examples—of early heretics, persecuting emperors, and so on—which Lambert had lacked.[71] (This difference between the two com-mentaries was to be typical of the parts in which Bale followed Lambert closely; the Englishman brought with him no originality as an exegete, but an enormous knowl-edge of historical detail.) The third age had seen the loss of spiritual vigor in the Church after Constantine, Bale and Lambert felt. Bale went on at some length about the laziness and worldly ambition of the popes in this age (roughly the fourth through the sixth centuries), and about the heresies and intramural disputes which these negligent pastors had permitted and provoked. Though he did not emphasize the point here, Bale evidently felt that the age of Constantine had indeed marked a crucial turning point for the papacy at least—up through the reign of Diocletian all the popes had died for the faith, but after Sylvester I an altogether different breed of churchmen had aspired to the See of Peter.[72] Yet Bale did not adopt the harsh view of the Lollards or of the radical reformers of the sixteenth century that the venom of worldly ambition poured into the Church in Constantine's reign meant that it had been irremediably corrupt from that early date onward.[73]

Bale put more stress on the collapse of the Church's integrity in the next period, symbolized by the fourth seal-opening. He dated this (following Lambert) roughly from the beginning of the seventh century. This was the period which earlier Lutheran writers like Joachim von Watt had emphasized, when Pope Boniface III had wheedled the title of "universal bishop" out of the upstart Byzantine Emperor Phocas.[74] The near-coincidence of Boniface's pontificate with the explosion of Islam in the mid-seventh century impressed both Lambert and Bale, as it had previous reformers, too. Later on in their commentaries, apropos Revelation 20:8, they would both associate the seventh-century papacy and Mohammed with Gog and Magog, twin leaders of the forces that would oppress the faithful at the final loosing of Satan. Bale and Lambert both stressed the hypocrisy of the Church's prelates in this fourth age, their ostentatious fasting marking them out as the pale horse in the prophecy.[75] Bale typically added quantities of detail, however, which Lambert had lacked: examples of super-stition with which the papacy had begun to corrupt the Church in this age (bell-ringing, censing, holy water, processions, and so on—the whole weight of cultural baggage from Bale's past which he now was rejecting so emphatically). So in the fourth seal-opening, the papal monarchy was approaching full growth and its odious human traditions were corrupting the faith throughout Europe, Bale and Lambert thought.

In the fifth age (again, Bale followed Lambert), the full-grown papal tyranny had persecuted all its oppo-nents with starvation, burning, hanging, and beheading. Both authors conceded that this seal-opening was part-ly thematic rather than chronological, that it indicated the persecution of the faithful during each age since the Ascension.[76] But Bale's specific interest in periodization—the fact that he was an historian and antiquary first, and an exegete only secondarily—led him to be a bit more specific than Lambert about the beginning of the period. He thought that the papal tyranny had waxed especially hot after the eleventh century, with the Church's attacks on the Waldensians and the Albigensians (Bale, as will be seen, accepted some strange bedfellows as allies against the pope). The fifth age, in any case, was still going on in the sixteenth century, in the sense that the burning, hanging, "heading," and so forth by the Roman Church and its cohorts were still in progress. Thus far Bale had drawn heavily on Lambert for the historical pattern he derived from Revelation 6, sometimes following the Frenchman almost word for word.

With the sixth age, however, the two parted company. Bale did agree with the French reformer that the opening of the sixth seal represented the revival of the Gospel. Lambert, however, had said merely that he thought this had been going on for over a hundred years; Bale (with his growing feeling for the significance of Lollardy) linked the dawn of the sixth age directly with Wyclif.[77] There were some passages in this section in which Bale translated Lambert's comments directly, as well.[78] But when one compares the interpretations which the two men later on in their commentaries placed on the "number of the beast," 666 (Revelation 13:18), it is clear that they saw the sixth age through radically different eyes, and had quite dissimilar expectations about the future. For Lambert, the sixth age (his own) had seen a reawakening of true preaching, it was true. But he foresaw at the end of the period a horrible persecution, the forty-two months in which the dragon would make war on the saints and overcome them (Revelation 13:5-7). After this would come the exile of Satan to the bottomless pit, and the millennium on earth (the seventh age).[79] By comparison with this future Sabbath age of peace and joy, the historical importance of the Reformation therefore paled considerably. Bale, on the other hand, saw his own age in a very different light. In the first place, he did not share Lambert's ominous feeling that the most frightening manifestation of Antichrist was yet to come—and coming soon.[80] Rather, Bale took the long view: any future appearance of Antichrist would be no more than a "member" of that "one general Antichrist for all, which hath regned in the church in a maner sense that Ascencyon of Christ."[81] To allow that there was one *major* Antichrist in the offing would concede a point to the chiliastic hopes and fears which, since Lambert had written his commentary, had encouraged the Kingdom of the Saints at Muenster. To play down the magnitude of the Antichrist at the gates (as compared with the beast already abroad) was, by the same token, to bank down dangerous enthusiasm. And like the English reformers in general, Bale needed to make his scorn for Anabaptists (particularly of the chiliastic variety) very explicit. Likewise, just as Bale rejected Lambert's belief that the sixth age would see the apotheosis of Antichrist, he also put a much higher value on the Reformation which that period was now experiencing. The sixth seal-opening, which he believed had begun with John Wyclif's first preaching back in the 1370s, had already seen the "second Sabbath"—the golden age was already abroad, there was nothing more to await. "The second sabbath here, or lyberte of God's truthe, hath had his shewe in Englande alredy, yf ye marke it wel."[82] So again, Bale's stress was on the "already" rather than Lambert's "not yet."

The differences in their interpretations of the sixth seal-opening were naturally linked to their disagreements over the seventh. Bale, to be sure, seemed to follow Lambert's belief in a millennial kingdom on earth when he commented on the seventh seal (and also, later, on the seventh trumpet-blowing and vial-pouring). He wrote consistently in the future tense: "This sygnfyeth that there shal be in that age, that peace in the Christen churche, which Christ brought with him from heaven and left here with his disciples."[83] And he even seemed to acknowledge the possibility of a *future* thousand-years' peace: "This sylence shall endure but halfe and (*sic*) houre space, whiche maye be the thousande yeares that are spoken of here afore, consyderynge that all the age after Chryste is but the laste houre. . . ."[84] But whatever he may have been thinking of when he wrote this—and considering the quantity of material he borrowed from Lambert, it could be that he simply did not bother to write his own exegesis of these verses—when Bale came to comment on the thousand years of Revelation 20, he rejected Lambert's apocalyptic longings explicitly. The millennium, he said—following out the suggestions he had picked up in Kirchmeyer's *Pammachius*, in the various Wycliffite tracts and elsewhere—represented the thousand years from the Ascension to the days of Pope Sylvester II, who had released Satan from the pit by necromancy. Roughly at the beginning of the fifth age, therefore, the devil had begun to walk abroad in force (though Bale did not here superimpose the thousand-year scheme on the seven ages explicitly).[85] Although the power of Antichrist had been abroad in the world literally since Cain slew Abel, and more especially since the Ascension,[86] nevertheless for the thousand years before Sylvester II Satan had had no power over the souls of the faithful. He had never been able to sit in their consciences as God, or to corrupt their faith with legalism. Vis-à-vis the damned, of course, the dragon had never been bound at all.[87] The machinations of Boniface III and Phocas and the expansion of Islam had shown him hard at work in the seventh century, for example.

At any rate, the millennium, such as it had been—an inward peace for the elect, not an outward and visible golden age—was past. This made the sixth age decidedly eschatological. If there were nothing more to expect save a worsening conflict between Antichrist unchained and the Gospel, and if Satan had already been loosed these five hundred years and more, then surely the end must be approaching. Bale shared the generally low-key pessimism of sixteenth-century Europeans, the sense of senescence and decay, of living at the "latter ende of the worlde," as Bale put it[88]—not that this probably made any more emotional impact in his daily life than his elegiac awareness of death had done, back when he had been a friar. The point is that insofar as he looked for release (and as an exile the thought can scarcely have failed to cross his mind now and then) he put his hopes in the Second Coming, not in any renewal of this present world. This frame of mind, linking Bale with the Lutherans and separating him sharply from chiliasts like Lambert, was to have important consequences for the way Bale thought about the future of the Church, and especially that of the English Church.[89]

But of course Bale's primary interests as an historian and antiquary lay with the past, not with the future, and this orientation also influenced his repudiation of Lambert's chiliasm. As has been often remarked, Revelation offered Bale not so much a timetable for the Latter Days as a key to the past—and in particular, a key to understanding the decline of the Roman Church. How long had its life and doctrine been pure? At what point had it ceased to be a true Church? In the magisterial reformers' search for tentative, post-scriptural norms, these questions had naturally arisen immediately, and in *The Image of bothe churches* Bale was able to suggest at least a rudimentary periodization. He asserted, first of all, that all the popes down to the reign of Constantine (that is, through the second age or seal-opening) had been faithful preachers of the Word and had sealed their testimony with their blood.[90] Like the popes, the doctors of the Church in this age (Ignatius, Irenaeus, Justin Martyr, Polycarp, and others) had generally preached God's truth as well, Bale felt.[91] So the institutional Church during this period of persecution had enjoyed a certain legitimacy. From the reign of Constantine onward, however, the light of the Gospel in the Roman Church had gradually faded. The true Church had come more and more to consist of "a fewe poore soules in corners."[92] With the advent of the seventh century, the hierarchy of the Church had gone over almost entirely into the enemy camp; and at the end of the millennium Satan had captured the institutional Church so completely that the truth could persist only among the hidden, persecuted remnant. In other words, the true Church had now come to consist of the Waldensians, the Lollards, and other beleaguered minorities who were enemies of the papacy. Bale followed the well-worn path of earlier Protestants in emphasizing these precursors of the Reformation, whose example served to show that the sixteenth-century reformers were doing more than indulging the singularity of their own wits, and that the Gospel had been known and taught at least *semper*, if not *ubique* or *ab omnibus*.[93] All of this was a bit vague, as far as specific chronology went; in *The Image* Bale was not as precise as he would be later in his histories, in which he would flesh out his interpretation with copious detail. But the outline of post-Ascension history which he offered (thanks largely to Lambert) went a long way toward fulfilling the magisterial reformers' need for some means of assessing the validity of the early Church and of understanding the stages in its later decline.

In *The Image of bothe churches*, Bale hardly attempted any systematic definition of the true Church down through the centuries, or any discussion of such questions as the relationship between the universal community of the elect and the particular, national, institutional churches. On the latter topic, 1545 was a bit too early to expect mature reflection. The separate Church of England under its supreme head was only a dozen years old, the theological differences which would distinguish the Anglican from the Roman Church had not yet emerged clearly—and Bale was simply not the man of ordered brilliance who might have sorted out this complex problem. The issue would still cause much confusion among the Elizabethan divines.[94] Regarding the definition of the universal Church or the "true" Church itself (the first point), Bale had rather more to say—not in any single passage or systematic fashion, which his exegetical format would not permit, but here and there in his commentary. And his understanding of the true Church did of course influence his vision of Church history, for it underlay the severe judgment which he passed upon Rome, the visible embodiment of the false Church from at least the seventh century onwards. As Bale used the word *church* in the title of his commentary, that is, in its broadest sense, he understood it (after Augustine) as a society or fellowship obeying either God or the devil. And both groups had existed since the days of Abel and Cain; from the time of the first family onwards, God had called those who would worship him truly. This was traditional late-medieval teaching, which the English reformers in general had also shared.[95]

Bale saw the activity of God as the same in every age—the patriarchs and prophets of the Old Testament had not merely possessed the Word in the form of God's promise, but had known God's truth fully and had enjoyed the fruits of Christ's sacrifice.[96] (This belief was consistent of course with Bale's former mind-set as a Carmelite hagiographer, when he had assumed that the saints represented static and ideal types in the mind of God.) So the true Church, the city of God, was first of all perennial. Secondly, Bale tended to emphasize its invisible or hidden nature. As usual, he attempted no systematic exposition of this point. But he stressed repeatedly that God dwells not in churches made with mortar and stone but in men's hearts—still repeating what had evidently been one of his principal themes as a preacher in Yorkshire during the mid-1530s.[97] Likewise, Bale emphasized that the true Church usually consisted of a persecuted remnant,[98] and was not typically an institution wielding power in human society. Thirdly and finally, Bale felt that the Gospel, internalized and understood in Protestant terms, was the crucial mark of the true Church. Dependence on God's grace rather than on man's works, the Christian liberty which followed therefrom, humility (including obedience to divinely-ordained rulers), worship in spirit rather than in outward pomp—these were the marks of the true Church

which Bale stressed. His emphasis on inwardness, on Christocentricity, on grace alone, on the Lutheran understanding
of St. Paul—these are most clear perhaps in his understanding of the millennium during which Satan had been
bound. This had been the period in which the forces of evil
had not been able to coerce or entice the faithful into
legalism, the age in which complete dependence on Christ,
the one indispensable feature of the true Church, had
survived intact.[99] In contrast to this preoccupation with
the Word in his comments on the nature of the true
Church, Bale had rather little to say about the sacraments.
His few comments on the Eucharist express the importance
of spiritual communion, and on feeding on the Word
through faith. Clearly the Word outweighed the sacraments
in Bale's post-conversion piety.[100]

The false Church, the community of Satan, was
naturally the opposite of the true Church and represented
everything which the latter repudiated theologically and
morally. Like its counterpart, the false Church had existed
since the time of Cain;[101] its distinguishing marks had
been idolatry, putting man and his laws in the place of
God, disobedience to God's revealed Word, and animosity
toward the true Church. Likewise, as one might expect, the
"old superstitious Babylon" or synagogue of Satan had
typically assumed visible and institutional form in the
world far more often than the community of the elect had.
Despite the tentative legitimacy of the early Church, for
example, Bale felt that the Antichrist had reigned in that
outward institution even "in a maner sens the Ascensyon of
Christ."[102] Of course, the emperors in the later Roman
Empire had been visible representatives of the false Church,
too. But the Antichrist-papacy, fully manifest since the
seventh century and wielding universal power since the end
of the millennium, naturally had been the clearest
embodiment of the old Babylon. "The proude degree or
abhominacion of the papacye"[103] had been the Antichrist.
Bale fully supported the Lutheran onslaught against the
whole institution, rather than (for example) the Wycliffite

identification of various individual popes as limbs of the Antichrist. For Bale agreed wholeheartedly with Luther that the essence of the papacy's depravity (and the depravity of the whole false Church) was theological, not moral. By claiming unique and supreme authority in Christendom, the papacy had usurped the rightful place of Christ and of the Bible. And by imposing on Christians all sorts of legalistic obligations, together with a Pelagian doctrine of salvation, the papacy had driven countless men into desperate anxiety.[104] Bale of course stressed other facets of the Roman Church's depravity, too, such as its various (and all too successful) campaigns during the last six hundred years to make puppets of the kings and princes of Christendom—the old theme, in other words, of Tyndale's *The practyse of Prelates* and Fish's *A supplicacion for the beggers*, and the central topic of Bale's *Kynge Johan.*[105] And Bale emphasized, too, how the synagogue of Satan had always been given to that luxuriant proliferation of rites and ceremonies which he himself now (in a kind of proto-puritan frame of mind)[106] was repudiating in his own Carmelite past. "Workes of bondage" and "ydell observacions, having no expresse commaundmentes of the woorde of God"[107] had above all characterized the Roman Church since the loosing of Satan by Pope Sylvester II.

So *The Image of bothe churches* offered to Englishmen, in English, a rough periodization for the history of these two societies, the city of God and its antitype, during the period since the Ascension. Bale's use of the Apocalypse as a *speculum historiale* was in no way original, nor was most of his exegesis. What he did do was to mediate the established tradition into English, and to flesh it out with specific historical references. It was this latter activity that he continued in the twenty-five-odd histories, pamphlets, and plays which he published in the years following his composition of *The Image of bothe churches.*

IV / The English Past

Bale's chief originality as an historical thinker lay in the way he adapted the pattern of history which he had found in the Book of Revelation and enlisted it to help explain (in the light of the Reformation) England's place in European history. His belief in the Bible as a key to history may have been centuries old and in its deeper assumptions basic to the Judaeo-Christian heritage, and his specific exegesis may have owed almost everything to the tradition leading back through Francis Lambert to Anselm of Havelburg and beyond. But it was Bale who mediated these ideas to the English reading public. He purged Lambert's Apocalypse exegesis and disassociated it from the chiliasm which had been stirring the lower orders of European society (and frightening the upper) since the time of Tanchelm and Eudes de l'Etoile in the twelfth century. By firmly quashing the notion of a millennium to come, by rejecting Lambert's exegesis on this crucial point, Bale reassured his English readers that they might take Revelation seriously as a guide to history without falling prey to Anabaptist enthusiasm. The immediate popularity of *The Image of bothe churches*—four editions between 1545 and 1550[1] —shows that some Englishmen were already eager to find in the Apocalypse a means of relating the present to the past. But Bale did more than merely help establish that general interest in biblical prophecy which, coupled with belief in the more or less imminent end of the world, would characterize the thinking of the soberest of Englishmen for the next century and more.[2] Though *The Image of bothe churches* was influential in this respect, the chief importance of the book was that it suggested how the Apocalypse could enlighten the specifically English past, could provide an organizing principle for the nation's whole history. Bale would remark in one of his later works that he had "alwaies bene of thys opinion, that S. Jhons Apocalips hath as well his fulfilling in the particular nacions, as in the universal church."[3] In his propaganda tracts, histories, and literary catalogues he proceeded to demonstrate just how that fulfillment had come to pass.

Bale's new pattern for English history answered a need not only because the Henrician Reformation had made a rewriting of the national past imperative, but also because the late medieval traditions of historical writing had bequeathed a good deal of organizational confusion in any case. All the English chronicles—including Ranulph Higden's *Polychronicon* and the chronicle of the *Brut*, the two most popular ones—had assumed the sovereign hand of God in history, and the relevance of Scripture for understanding the same. But the problem was that none of the accepted and biblically-based methods for periodizing history were of much use for the kind of insular, national (to say nothing of civic) chronicle which English audiences had come to expect. Writers of chronicles knew all about the seven-age, three-law and four-monarchy patterns, but these schemes were as little help in making sense of the British past as they were in supplying a structure for post-Ascension Church history. So the late medieval English chronicle exhibited considerable shapelessness.[4] To be sure, the new sense of history adumbrated by humanists like Polydore Vergil and Sir Thomas More was slowly catching on—that approach which involved, among other things, the search for principles of periodization more in human affairs (the reigns of kings in Polydore's work, for example) than in

Scripture. Eventually this humanist frame of mind would alter radically the European historical tradition, and not least its English branch. But for Bale's generation, the humanist sense of history was hard to grasp, though in a way it was akin to the manner in which the Reformers viewed the past, in terms of a progression from purity to degeneration to revival.[5] Amid the confessional strife of the mid-sixteenth century, in any case, interpretations of history which claimed the authority of God would generally outbid in popularity the more this-worldly explanations of the humanists, however technically competent the latter might be. Bale's demonstration that the Apocalypse had its "fulfilling" in English history therefore met a real need as his contemporaries sought to reinterpret their national past in light of the Reformation. Bale's vision of history was at once scripturally-based, coherent, and gratifyingly Anglocentric.

Bale's most productive years as an historian and partisan pamphleteer, during which he vigorously communicated this vision to his countrymen, spanned the period from Cromwell's fall to Elizabeth's accession. Bale spent the better part of it in exile on the Continent. It was to Antwerp that he had most likely fled, as noted above, in the summer of 1540. Probably he made contact with the community of Protestant printers there fairly quickly, for by 1542 he had won a place on Henry VIII's list of forbidden authors.[6] In the next three years Bale got off a series of five hard-hitting tracts for distribution back home, besides the first edition of *The Image of bothe churches*. All but the first (an attack on oaths which may have been influenced by Bale's rediscovery of Wyclif and the Lollards)[7] stressed heavily the apocalyptic themes which Bale was working out in his commentary. He seems to have been in close touch with Lord Wentworth's former protegé William Turner in 1543 and 1544, as two of the pamphlets show signs of cooperation and collaboration between them. *A dysclosynge or openynge of the Manne of synne*, a broadside against Bishop Bonner of London which Bale shot off in 1543, claimed on its title page to be "Yet a course at the Romyshe foxe"—referring to Turner's *The Huntyng & fyndying out of the Romishe Foxe* printed at Bonn the same year. And *The epistle exhortatorye of an Englyshe Christyane* (1544) contained a section at the end in which Turner fired another round in his running battle with Bishop Stephen Gardiner.[8] Turner's marked anti-ceremonial bent[9] gave Bale added encouragement in attacking this face of Antichrist in the English Church.

Another pamphlet of 1544 showed Bale taking a different tack: identifying the fifteenth-century Lollard rebel Sir John Oldcastle not only as a worthy precursor of the Reformation, but as one of the few valid saints in England since the mission of St. Augustine in 597.[10] This early shaping of a Protestant martyrology was to be one of Bale's major accomplishments, a job for which his Carmelite labors eminently fitted him.[11] The final tract in these years when Bale was preparing *The Image*, a little piece called *A mysterye of inyquyte*, treated (among other things) the same themes of gradual decay in Rome and eventual revival of the truth, which were so much on his mind.[12] After publishing this tract, however, Bale tended to concentrate the exposition of his scheme of history in works that were specifically historical (rather than merely polemical) in nature. His *The Actes of Englysh votaryes*, attacking the clerical caste in medieval England, appeared at Antwerp (or perhaps secretly in London) in 1546,[13] and represented Bale's first systematic application of his vision of history to the English past. About this time Bale left Antwerp, moving east to the city of Wesel, in the duchy of Cleves near the meeting of the Rhine and the Lippe.[14] Here Bale worked closely with the Protestant printer Dirik van der Straten, who published no fewer than ten of Bale's works in the next two years.[15] These included a second contribution to Protestant hagiography (the papers of Mistress Anne Askew, who was burned for her sacramentarian beliefs at Smithfield in July of 1546); four of Bale's plays including *A Comedy concernynge thre lawes*;

and the first edition of his history of English writers, the *Summarium*.[16]

It was probably sometime in 1548 that Bale and his family came back to England. Protector Somerset's toleration of free discussion and his policy of liturgical (if not yet doctrinal) reform would have been manifest by the end of the previous year,[17] persuading Bale that he might safely return. He found a patron in Mary Fitzroy, the Protestant Duchess of Richmond, and met the young John Foxe in her household—beginning a friendship that would be enormously fruitful over the next fifteen years. Probably with the Duchess' support, Bale was able to travel around to libraries in southeastern England and collect information for an expansion of his *Summarium*. He had originally intended that work to be merely a stop-gap measure until John Leland's notes on early English authors could be published, but Leland's insanity threw the burden back on Bale's shoulders. In *The laboryouse Journey & serche of Iohan Leylande* (1549), Bale appealed for support in getting England's old chronicles into print, and in rescuing the country's literary heritage from the ruin of the monasteries. There is no record that the noblemen and London merchants to whom Bale specifically directed his plea diverted great quantities of money from their "belly banketts and table tryumphes" to support Bale's program, though by 1553 he had managed to buy up more than a hundred and fifty volumes for his own library.[18]

Some dependable financial support eventually came from John Ponet, the newly appointed bishop of Winchester, in 1551. Bale served Ponet as chaplain in the spring of that year, and in June the bishop presented him to the rectory of Bishopstoke, five miles south of Winchester.[19] Bale was at Bishopstoke for only a little more than a year—a very unquiet year, apparently, as Bale's pastoral experience at Thorndon in Suffolk fifteen years before had taught him nothing about soothing a divided and inflammable parish.[20] But these tribulations paled into insignificance by comparison with the stormy year to come. Bale's appointment by Edward VI to the wild and unappealing see of Ossory in Ireland, his turbulent seven months there in 1553, and his escape to the Low Countries after Queen Mary's accession, all are vividly described in Bale's little autobiographical tract, *The vocacyon of Johan Bale to the bishoprick of Ossorie.*[21] After this melodramatic year, the hardships of a second exile on the Continent may have come as something of a relief.

Bale seems to have returned first to Wesel, where at the end of 1553 he published his *vocacyon* and an edition of Bishop Gardiner's erastian pamphlet from the 1530s, *De Vera Obediencia* (embarrassing Queen Mary's new lord chancellor with this reminder of his anti-papal past).[22] By September of 1554 he had joined the community of exiles at Frankfort. Bale was one of those who signed the letter of September 24 calling John Knox to the pastorate there,[23] though he later took the Coxian side in the "troubles" which arose. Along with Cox, Jewel, Parry, and others, Bale accused Knox of treason before the Frankfort magistrates. All this fratricidal strife began to weigh heavy on him, however, and he may have felt increasingly uncomfortable at Frankfort. He was still there in November of 1555,[24] but by the following May 10 he had joined his friend John Foxe in Basel.[25] Foxe was earning a living by reading proof for the printer Oporinus, and Bale may have done likewise. The two friends probably lived together in the Clarakloster.[26] Oporinus proved extremely sympathetic and cooperative with Bale's scholarly labors, publishing his much-expanded history of English authors, the *Catalogus* (in two parts, 1557 and 1559), and a history of the papacy entitled *Acta Romanorum Pontificum.*

Bale's congenial and productive relationship with Oporinus and Foxe might have made the years in Basel generally happy ones, had it not been for a revival among the English community of the same strife between nascent Anglican and Puritan factions that had wracked the Frankfort congregation. Writing to his friend Thomas Ashley sometime in 1556, Bale bewailed the new "Church of the Purytie," a group of zealots who were trying to establish "a seditious secte in contempte of the Englishe order for their owne pharisaycall advancement. . . ."[27] Bale was certainly not used to being outflanked on the left by other English reformers. But his loyalty to Edward VI had led him to support the 1552 Prayer Book, and it grieved him to see erstwhile allies falling into a new kind of work-righteousness. In any case, Elizabeth's accession in 1558 transferred the problem onto a larger stage. Bale did not return to England at once, since the second part of his *Catalogus* was still in press. He was still at Basel on March 4, 1559, when he wrote to Josias Simler at Zurich.[28] Soon after that he made his way home. A letter to Bale from Robert Roll in November mentions that the old reformer had been in London earlier in the year.[29] Either Bale declined to return to the firing line in Ireland, or Elizabeth chose not to send him; in any case, he was admitted to a stall in Canterbury Cathedral in February of 1560 and had to be content with that as a reward.[30]

The last three and a half years of his life, one regrets to say, were no more peaceful than the ones which had gone before.[31] But the labor of publishing, at least, was largely behind him. He got off one belated Parthian shot at Bishop Bonner in 1561,[32] and several of his works came out in further editions, but the primary focus of his polemical activity had shifted from the printed page to the town of Canterbury. By this time, however, his books and pamphlets had forcefully impressed his sense of the English past on the Protestant reading public in the land.[33]

When Bale said he thought that the Apocalypse had had its "fulfilling" in individual nations as well as in the universal Church,[34] he did not mean that the prophecies necessarily had been or would be fulfilled exactly the same way in each case. Just as a skeleton key might unlock several different doors, so Revelation supplied a pattern which one might use to understand a number of different national traditions of folklore and history. Now Bale did not feel any burden to prove to his readers the relevance of prophecy as a pathway into the understanding of history. Since he could take this for granted, he likewise felt no pressure to demonstrate (for example) that the patterns in Revelation had been fulfilled exactly the same way in the Roman Church, in England, in Germany and so on. Bale enjoyed a certain flexibility in relating the apocalyptic scheme of history to England's national past. In practice this meant in particular that Bale did not feel obligated in each and every one of his works to rehearse the six-age scheme, or supply exact dates for the beginning and ending of each period in England. But he always stressed certain other themes from the Book of Revelation. The fundamental pattern of purity, decline, and renewal always came through clearly in his works; the crucial apocalyptic "moments" (especially the years 666 and 1000) were always emphasized; and often the six-age pattern did in fact come to the surface in explicit detail.

It was naturally in Bale's generally *ad hominem* polemical tracts of the 1540s that he was least concerned to elaborate a systematic apocalyptic interpretation of English history. Nevertheless the basic assumptions undergirded all these pamphlets. There was for example the age-old belief in a golden age (writ Protestant now), followed by decay and then revival: "In the prymatyve churche was the gospell gredylye recyved of the unyversall worlde, In the myddes thereof whan Sathan was at lyberte, was yt in a maner contempned of all menne, and hypocresye taken up in the stede thereof. Now in the latter ende are menne agayne verye desyerouse of yt. . . ."[35] Of course there were multitudes of Englishmen in the 1540s who were anything but "desyerouse" of the Gospel as Bale understood it. So in his diatribes against the persistent features of late medieval piety in England, Bale naturally sought to tar these practices with the brush of papistry—to link them not only with Rome in general, as William Turner was doing in his "Romyshe foxe" books, but also with the domineering papacy which was condemned explicitly out of the Apocalypse: "Thys gloriouse lordshypp came in when phocas the false emproure made Rome the head churche of the worlde for moneye. And yt was spred abroade after a thousande years from Christes natyvyte, whan Sathan was losed out of hys preson, and permytted to go at large to decyve the ungodlye multytude for ther unbeleves sake."[36]

Along with the spiritual deceit practiced by the Roman Church, Bale (as might be expected) thumped the political subversion England had suffered—the theme he had inherited from Tyndale, Barnes, and their colleagues: "By these your fylthye forefathers and soche other / hath this realme bene alwayes in most myserable captivite eyther of the Romanes or Danes / Saxons or Normannes / and now last of all undre the most blasphemouse Behemoth your Romishe Pope...."[37] But the revival of the Gospel had begun to turn the tide, and Bale sketched out in his briefer tracts the mythology of John Wyclif (now the proverbial morning star of the Reformation) and the Lollards, which he would expand in his histories. He announced his hopes of doing a large work on Wyclif,[38] and in one tract published a preliminary list of Lollards (and some early Lutherans) who had testified and suffered for their faith.[39] So both the English authorities and Bale's readers in the early 1540s had fair warning of what the irate exile had in store for them.

The Actes of Englysh votaryes (in two parts published in 1546 and 1551) represented Bale's first elaborate revision of English history. Though he allowed at the beginning that he intended to uncover only one face of Antichrist in England, the evil consequences of clerical celibacy, the book's implications were in fact a good deal wider than that. What Bale did in *The Actes of English votaryes* was to shape the myth of the "beleaguered isle," that epic view of the nation's past in which England had striven heroically (if in vain) down through the centuries to keep out Romish spiritual corruption and political subversion.[41] He evidently foresaw some unseemly levity on his readers' part when on the title page he urged them to "read, but laugh not," but the scurrilous clerical horror-stories notwithstanding, Bale was in no light humor. He had originally planned a four-part treatise, dividing the clergy's "actes" into four periods—"rising, building, holdynge, and falling"[42]—but he only got as far as the first two. This was nevertheless quite enough to make his point.

England had accepted Christianity, Bale said, when Joseph of Arimathea (from Jerusalem, not Rome) visited the island in 63 A.D. "The Brytains toke the christen faithe at ye very spring or fyrst going forth of the Gospel, whan the church was moste perfit, and had moste strengthe of the holy ghost."[43] Purity of worship had lasted unblemished up to the time of the emperor Diocletian, when Britain was divided into dioceses (the first sign of institutional rigidity). But despite the insidious infiltration of monks into England during the next three hundred years, bringing with them Pelagian notions of work-righteousness, the English Church's original vigor had enabled it to withstand most corruptive influences until the fateful mission of St. Augustine in 597. This minion of Antichrist had introduced "candel-styckes, vestymentes, surplices, alter clothes, syngyng bookes, rellyckes"[44] and ever since 600 (a significant number) especially, the monks had labored "to prepare Antechrist a seate here in England, agaynst the full tyme of his perfight age, of .666."[45] The latter date marked (Bale said) the arrival of Theodore of Tarsus, sent to finish what Augustine had begun.[46] So the seventh century crisis in the Roman Church had its noxious impact on England too. Bale emphasized that both Augustine and Theodore had supported the Saxon conquerors against the native Britons, copying the subversive tactics of their papal superiors. As the year 1000 approached, matters got even worse. Dunstan's enforcement of clerical celibacy was a sure sign that Satan was about to emerge from the pit, and the Danish invasions (abetted by treasonous monks) supplied the final portent.[47] This was where Bale ended the first part of his treatise, the "rising" of the clergy—using the millennium of Revelation 20 (if not the six-age pattern) as the key feature of his periodization.

The second part (the clergy "building") covered simply the eleventh and twelfth centuries, emphasizing the same themes of idolatry and worldly ambition in the Church. Things predictably got worse after the loosing of Satan. Finding the Saxon rulers recalcitrant puppets, the clergy engineered the Norman Conquest. Then Anselm proceeded to undermine the new dynasty in turn, as well as to legislate clerical celibacy once and for all. And the pernicious activity of Thomas Becket of course gave Bale ample scope for invective.[48] Bale closed Part 2 with stories of how the Church had wickedly manipulated Richard the Lion-Hearted.[49] The third and fourth parts would have traced England's recovery, through Wyclif and Henry VIII, but what Bale did publish was enough to make clear the picture of England holding out against Rome longer than the rest of Christendom, albeit (until the fourteenth century) unsuccessfully.

If Bale chose not to refer specifically to the six-age scheme from Revelation in *The Actes of Englysh votaryes*, it was probably because of England's unique experience within the universal Church. Happily the island had avoided the second age (false Christians and Roman persecutions) almost entirely. The third age (heresies) had effectively been delayed in England until the onset of the fourth, the period of the papal monarchy which (Bale thought) had reared its head early in the seventh century. So England's peculiar destiny—last corrupted, first revived—meant that the nation and the Roman Church had been out of step at times. Bale felt no compulsion to apply in *The Actes* his exegesis of the seven seals and so on, if this particular part of Revelation were not the key to the national past. But his stress on the years 666 and 1000 showed where his vision of English history in this book drew its inspiration.[50]

In Bale's next important historical work, the *Summarium* (published at Wesel in 1548), he decided that his interpretation of the seven seals was relevant to English history after all, at least in its general outline. At the end of the volume, Bale described the six ages of the Church's history just as he had done in *The Image of bothe churches*, and went on to say that he had done so in order that his readers might realize that the prophecies in Revelation had in fact been fulfilled in national churches as well as in Christendom at large.[51] All the information which Bale had supplied about medieval English writers in the *Summarium* was to be viewed through the lens of these prophecies, and to be considered an illustration of the way these prophecies had come true. Therefore it would be a trifle misleading to assert that the *Summarium* began "as a nonpolemical biobibliographical work" which Bale "forced into the mold" of his apocalyptic sense of history.[52]

It is not at all clear that the antiquarian motive preceded the polemical one. It would of course be idle to deny that Bale shared that exhilaration in discovering the tracks of the English past which his friend John Leland fervently expressed. But since Bale now took the Bible as his touchstone for interpreting history, he simply assumed that the fruit of his antiquarian labors would naturally confirm and illustrate what the Book of Revelation had predicted. Patriotism, anti-Roman polemics, and antiquarian enthusiasm were all perfectly compatible for Bale. To argue that the antiquarian motive was primary (either in time or in importance) would be to impose our modern preferences upon him. In fact, just as in the 1520s Bale had collected Carmelite information with an explicit axe to grind, so now he was publishing his data on English authors not only to inform his countrymen, but also to teach them the truth about Rome and the English past. One facet of Bale was the antiquarian, it is true. But at the very core of his being he was a preaching friar turned reformer, who used his antiquarian skills to supply himself with ammunition.[53] So Bale communicated his vision of the nation's history as vigorously through his scholarly works like the *Summarium* as he did through his popular works like *The Actes of Englysh votaryes*.

Bale took some pains to use the division of the

Summarium into "centuries" (groups of a hundred authors)
to point up his view of British history, and to use his brief
biographical sketches of each writer for the same purpose.
(Bale used here the same format as in *Anglorum Heliades*,
the organization which he had perhaps borrowed from
Trithemius' catalog, one of his major sources: a short summary of the author's life, followed by a list of works with
their incipits.[54]) Bale tried to give each century an
explicit theme, consistent with the chronological period it
represented. With the second, third, and fourth "centuries"
he had the most success. The first hundred writers formed
an amorphous and variegated group, stretching all the way
from the legendary pre-Christian heroes whom Bale had
borrowed from Annius of Viterbo and Geoffrey of
Monmouth down through Rabanus Maurus in the tenth
century.[55] In his biographies, Bale stressed the pure
monotheism of the pre-Roman Britons, the pristine
Christianity which Joseph of Arimathea had planted, the
fiendish machinations of Augustine and Theodore of
Tarsus, and the "faithful in each age" like Bede, but there
was no single, dominant motif in this century. The second
century (from the late 900s to the early 1200s) proved
much easier to organize around a single topic. Bale began
the section with the legendary English Pope "Joan," whose
harlotry typified the age in which the Church began to
enforce clerical celibacy. So the evils produced by a
sacerdotal caste (including tyranny over men's consciences
and political ambitions) were the theme of Century II.

In the next group of a hundred authors, Bale singled out
the complexities of scholastic theology as his leitmotif. Beginning the section with Archbishop Robert Kilwardby,
O.P., Bale fulminated against the mendicant friars and the
doctrinal pollution which they had spread throughout the
English Church.[56] But the fourth century, commencing
with John Wyclif (who set the tone for the whole section),
showed the tide beginning to run in the other direction.
This fourth section represented not the victory of the
Gospel by any means (for Bale listed any number of

unreconstructed scholastic theologians from this period, roughly 1360-1430) but rather the conflict of good and evil which the sixth seal-opening in Revelation symbolized. The final century, like the first, lacked its own peculiar theme— the writers whom Bale recorded (late scholastic doctors, Lollards, and then early Lutherans) simply carried on the struggles of the sixth age. But the structure of the middle three centuries in the *Summarium* had pointed up very clearly the essential characteristics of the fourth, fifth, and sixth seal-openings in Bale's apocalyptic scheme. And passing shots amid his biographical sketches ensured that his readers would not forget the crucial years 666 and 1000 either.[57]

When Bale came to publish his much-expanded version of the *Summarium* (his *Catalogus*) at Basel in 1557, he made even clearer the relationship between the authors he listed and the six-age chronology of Church history. He took extra pains to make the *Catalogus* what the *Summarium* had aimed to be, a history of the English Church and people in biobibliographical form.[58] At frequent intervals Bale inserted historical appendices, drawing on his immense knowledge of the medieval English and Continental chronicles; he dealt in these sections not merely with the political history of the island kingdom, but especially with the development of the papacy and the maleficent activities of papal agents within England. English history could not be understood apart from that of the Roman Church, since the two were the major champions in the struggle of Good and Evil since the time of Christ.[59] So Bale again took ample occasion to blacken the names of the usual people, antitypes of the virtuous Englishmen who had held out against corruption the longest.[60] The centuriate structure of the *Catalogus* (as in the earlier volume) served to emphasize the stages of the conflict too. Century V began with John Baconthorpe, embodying scholastic theology; this was set off against Century VI headed by Wyclif. And so on. No more than the *Summarium* was the *Catalogus* simply the product of disinterested antiquarian research. Basic to its conception was Bale's desire to communicate, through the scholarly weight of the evidence he had collected, the sense of history he had evolved.

In 1558 Bale abstracted the material describing the papacy from the *Catalogus* and published it in a separate little volume entitled *Acta Romanorum Pontificum*.[61] The scheme of periodization for papal history in both these books was significantly different from the one Bale had adopted from Francis Lambert in *The Image of bothe churches*,[62] and the reasons why Bale here changed his mind towards the end of his life are worth considering. What he did in the *Acta* was to divide the history of the papacy into three periods, over which he superimposed the first four seals of Revelation 6. The first period extended to the death of Sylvester I in 324 (instead of merely to the close of the apostolic age, as in *The Image*) and was represented by the first seal and the white horse. During the second period, from Sylvester's successor Marcus through the pontificate of Sabinianus who died in 606, the papacy experienced the second seal-opening and embodied the red horse. The third period of the institutional Church was the longest, stretching from the traditional villain Boniface III up to the beginning of Julius II's reign in 1503, at which point Bale thought the papacy had begun to crumble. This lengthy age had four subdivisions. The first two (from Boniface III through Gregory V, just before 1000 A.D.) stood for the third seal-opening and the black horse, and the latter two (Sylvester II and the loosing of Satan through Pius III in 1503) for the fourth seal and the pale horse named Death.[63] What Bale was doing in this new pattern was essentially stretching the first age to cover the whole pre-Constantinian Church, rather than merely the apostolic age, and therefore pushing the succeeding seal-openings farther down in time. The reason for this alteration had to to with the problem which bothered the magisterial reformers so acutely—the search for a normative period in the Church's past, a standard beyond the Bible against which to measure doctrine and ceremony in the Church.

The *sola scriptura* criterion was generally sufficient when reformers of Bale's generation were attacking the remnants of late medieval piety in English life—when it was a matter of hunting out the "Romyshe foxe" in the English Church. It was on the Bible alone that Bale had stood (as explicitly as he dared) at Thorndon in 1536; and it was to the Biblical norm that he and Turner continued to appeal in the 1540s when they harried the conservative English prelates with pamphlets from the Continent.[64] But when it came to fending off enemies from the opposite direction— zealots who carried the *sola scriptura* principle to the extreme and repudiated bishops, infant baptism, and the like—the Biblical norm would hardly do. A later period was needed, one in which the institutions defended by the magisterial reformers had flourished, and yet in which the Church had remained tolerably pure. This was of course where the periodization of ecclesiastical history drawn from Revelation was indispensable.[65] It is doubtful whether Francis Lambert had had this problem in mind when he worked out his exegesis of the Apocalypse in the 1520s—his chiliastic longings make one doubt his empathy *au fond* with Luther and with the magisterial reformation. Nor is it clear from *The Image of bothe churches* that in the 1540s Bale recognized the usefulness of his scheme of history for coping with the radical reformers on the left. He was still more concerned with tracing the decline of the Roman Church than with determining exactly how long purity had lasted. The same is largely true of *The Actes of Englysh votaryes*. Bale did establish the myth of the pristine pre-Augustinian English Church, the golden age before 597, which was to be influential in Elizabethan thought and a useful weapon against Puritan iconoclasm.[66] But Bale's target in *The Actes* was still the Roman Church. His purpose was not to show that in this golden age surplices had existed, but rather that clerical celibacy had not. The hint of a different attitude appears in the

Summarium, however. In the dedicatory epistle to Edward VI, explaining the purpose of the work, Bale said he thought his readers would be greatly edified to see how at least a few "faithful in each age" had believed the Bible rightly. But he went on to say that as far as concerned the settling of disputes over dogma (such as were raging at present), no doctrine was to be accepted as valid unless witness to it could be found "among the doctors of the early Church."[67] This was a significant departure from his earlier rigid Biblicism. In the *Summarium* he neither explained why he was stretching his normative period to include the first few centuries, nor took the time to define precisely which "doctors of the early Church" he meant to include. Bale's statement may even have been a slip of the pen; 1548 was extremely early for the need to fend off proto-puritan enthusiasts to have become clear in the minds of moderate English reformers, and bilious Bale was the last person one would expect to have sensed that need so soon.

In any case, during the next eight years Bale's stormy experiences did force him to accept the need for a post-scriptural normative period. In his diocese of Ossory in Ireland he fought strenuously to impose the 1552 Prayer Book, authorized by the "new Josiah" Edward VI, and he nearly lost his life in the process. When he reached Frankfort in 1554 he did feel willing to accept certain minor deviations from the prayer book, which the congregation felt necessary in their current state of exile.[68] But he was appalled when the Knoxian faction pressed for more radical changes. And two years later he was writing from Basel to his friend Thomas Ashley, wringing his hands over the "new catharytes" who claimed that the communion service in the 1552 Prayer Book had a "popishe face."

> I fynd the admonishment of St. Pawle to Timothy and of St. Peter to the Dispersed brethren most true and in full force in this miserable age. They sayde that in the Latter tymes should come mockers, Lyers, blasphemers and fearse despiters, we have them wee have them Mr. Ashley, we have them even from amonge our selves. . . . they blaspheme our Communion calling

it a popishe masse, and saye, that it hath a popishe face, with
other fearce Despisinges and cursed speaking. . . .[69]

If this was Bale's frame of mind as he worked on the *Catalogus* and *Acta Romanorum Pontificum*, it comes as no surprise that he should have sought a valid post-scriptural period,
whose example would support the liturgy of the second
prayer book.

So this seems to have been what Bale was doing, as he
wrote the appendices to the *Catalogus* which he published
separately in 1558 as *Acta Romanorum Pontificum*. He
argued now that the whole span of Church history through
324 (the death of Pope Sylvester I) represented the white
horse, the first seal, or the age of true Gospel-preaching.
Here was a precise period to which one could refer in
defending the "laudable ceremonies" of the second prayer
book. To be sure, Bale never did state explicitly why he
had thus changed his mind on the dating of the first
age—indeed, he never conceded that he had in fact altered
his views. But his agonized reaction to the "new
catharytes" in 1556 shows that he was acutely aware that
the 1552 Prayer Book needed an historical defense. How
Bale went about establishing a normative period for the
Church (and especially the Edwardian Church in England)
may be clearer if one compares *Acta Romanorum
Pontificum* with the earlier work which Robert Barnes had
published at Wittenberg in 1536, entitled *Vitae Pontificum Romanorum.* Both Barnes and Bale drew heavily
on the history of the popes written by the fifteenth-
century papal librarian Bartolomeo Platina, as well as on
other medieval chroniclers of the Church. But Barnes
and Bale differed radically in their attitude toward what
these writers had said about the pre-Constantinian Church.
Barnes' intention had simply been to demonstrate the post-
scriptural origin of the Mass, the veneration of images, and
the various other ceremonies and traditions which the
Protestants now were rejecting. Since the Bible was his only
norm, he quite happily copied all the material he could find
in Platina and the others which showed the early popes

inventing rites and pious observances. He recorded without question, for instance, Platina's statement that the third-century Pope Felix I had ordered yearly *officia* to be celebrated in honor of certain martyrs.[70] Bale, on the other hand, had to show that the pre-Constantinian Church had not been marred by the kind of superstition which he and the English Church had rejected—otherwise, the period would simply not do as a standard by which to defend the ceremonies the English Church had retained. And so when Bale found in Platina the story of Pope Felix's innovations, he copied it but with the exclamation, "This is manifest blasphemy!"[71] In another place Bale and Barnes diverged in their treatment of Pope Calixtus I, Bale remarking, "I think it is a fable, that he turned the people of God into judaizers, by (instituting) four periods of fasting."[72] Finally Bale's irritation with Platina and his ilk exploded, and he exclaimed, "Carsulanus, Platina, Stella and others who flatter the popes have falsely attributed whole wagon-loads of decrees and lies to these martyrs of Christ—to buttress the diabolical institution of their ceremonies (or should I say blasphemies) with the authority of these men."[73] It is true that Bale did hedge his bet at the end of this section, conceding that various "trivial, worthless and unscriptural" decrees just might possibly have originated with the early popes, but this was not the impression he conveyed in everything else that he said about the period.[74] Though this brief section on the pre-Constantinian Church did not explicitly establish it as a pattern for emulation by the English Church (or by the Marian exiles), Bale did lay the groundwork here for future argument.

When Bale came to describe the second age of the Church, after Sylvester I, his tone altered abruptly. Using the same sources as for the earlier period, he now accepted without a question whatever ill they had to say (from the Protestant point of view) about the popes, their ceremonial innovations, and their doctrinal novelties.[75] So Bale's disagreement with Barnes about the first era of the Church's history, one should emphasize, did not arise from any greater critical sense on Bale's part, or from any more highly-developed sense of anachronism. He did not immerse himself in the records of the primitive Church and then conclude that Platina, Stella, Carsulanus, and Barnes had got it all wrong. Bale continued to work deductively, just as he had done since his first forays into Carmelite history. Beginning with the intuition (or the need to prove) that the pre-Constantinian Church had been pure in life and doctrine, and finding this notion supported by his revised chronological scheme based on Revelation, Bale concluded that any evidence to the contrary must have been a papist forgery.[76] Where Bale did rise above his predecessor Barnes was, of course, in his vision of a pattern in Church history. But this very pattern (derived from the Bible rather than from the historical data) reinforced his inclination to interpret his evidence in light of the revealed Truth. Bale's assumptions about the historian's function had not altered significantly since his Carmelite youth; it was simply that the Bible had become the lens through which he read the past. The text was (as he said) a light to the chronicles, and not vice-versa.

The scheme of history which Bale had thus evolved by the late 1550s—whatever its shortcomings from a modern critical standpoint—had of course a major influence upon England's attempt to reconsider its national history in the light of events since 1529. Back in 1544, Bale had mapped the territory that needed to be explored, when he had called for a thorough rewriting of the chronicles to purge them of clerical lies and "Italyshe beggary."[77] If the fruition of the project had to wait until Foxe's *Actes and Monuments*, the artistic synthesis of Bale's more fragmentary suggestions, nevertheless by the 1550s the broad outlines of Bale's new vision of history were clear. For one thing, England's past and the history of the Roman Church were indissolubly linked. Though both England and Rome had begun on a more or less equal level of purity, after the age of Constantine they had increasingly become type and antitype in the cosmic struggle of good and evil. As the institutional Roman Church had ceased to be a part of the true Church, and after the seventh century became the actual seat of Antichrist, England increasingly had become the primary refuge of the remnant who continued to respond to God's call in each generation. England had withstood subversion the longest, and thrown it off the soonest—doctrinally by the "morning star" of Protestant theology, John Wyclif, and jurisdictionally by Henry VIII. But naturally the struggle went on, and would do until the *Parousia*. Bale's reworking of the national myth, making opposition to Rome the central theme of English history, found a responsive audience even before the reign of Queen Mary burned it indelibly into the nation's self-consciousness. Three separate editions of *The Actes of Englysh votaryes*, part I, were called for between 1546 and 1551,[78] and Bale's dramatic account was being picked up and broadcast by other popular pamphlets as early as 1549.[79] Though the Marian experience and events of the Elizabethan and early Jacobean period (the Bull of 1570, the miraculous deliverance in 1588, and the Gunpowder Plot of 1604 being the most obvious) combined to heighten and reinforce English anti-Catholicism, its historical justification stemmed from Bale's earliest works in the 1540s. Along with John Foxe, Bale must shoulder the responsibility for whatever bitter fruit this tree has produced.[80]

The unabashed Anglocentricity of Bale's sense of the past raises a question concerning his relationship to the growing national self-awareness of the English people as a whole in the sixteenth century. William Haller's provocative study, *Foxe's Book of Martyrs and the Elect Nation*, offered one interpretation which until recently has gone practically unchallenged.[81] In the course of explaining the origin of Foxe's ideas, Haller noted that Bale vigorously repudiated the brand of millenarianism which the Muensterite radicals had represented. Bale put no stock in the notion of a future golden age, a Joachite third *status* or whatever, brought in by supernatural power. Rather, in

Haller's pithy formulation, Bale's "apocalyptic urgings took a different turn. They led not to the pursuit of a millennium but to the aspiration after nationality, not to the expectation of a messiah out of the blue but to the idea of an hereditary monarch called by the grace of God to rule the realm and defend the faith, not to the desire to cast down the mighty but to the resolution to cast out the interloper."[82] A reading of Revelation had convinced Bale and the other Marian exiles that the New Jerusalem represented not some future reign of Christ and His saints, but the true Church of the predestinate in all ages, Haller said. As the exiles returned, however, Haller believed they were determined "to associate the idea of the communion of true believers with the Church of England, the Church with the nation, and the nation with the indispensable though enigmatic young woman now coming to the throne."[83] It was the genius of Foxe, Haller felt, to articulate all of this powerfully and lucidly, convincing the Elizabethans that they were a "new Israel," an elect people, and that God's will for them lay in national unification under a godly queen, a new Constantine, so that they might serve the Lord of Hosts effectively against the Romish foe.

One can indeed find passages in Bale's works which support Haller's argument that he longed most of all for a purified national Church under a godly ruler, and that he aspired to build a this-worldly "Jerusalem in England's green and pleasant land." There is that heartfelt expression of Tudor patriotism in *The laboryouse Journey & serche of Johan Leylande*, in which Bale (perhaps celebrating his return from exile in 1548) wrote,

> The byrdes that flye abroade, do love their owne nestes. The
> beastes that ronne astraye, seketh their accustomed cowches.
> And the fyshes within the water, resorteth to their hollow
> dennes. Ryght notably was it alleged of Plato that we are not
> borne onlye to our owne commodities. But we ought to have
> respect both to our countrey and kyndred. Of our natural
> countrey we have our fode, our nourishment, frendship, frindes,
> acquayntaunce, howse, wyfe, chyldren, with such lyke. . . .[84]

In explaining the motives which had led him to collect and publish his records of ancient and medieval English authors in the *Summarium*, Bale also referred to his "natural and dutiful love towards my native land."[85] And in his account of that stormy year in Ireland, *The vocacyon of Johan Bale to the bishoprick of Ossorie*, Bale went so far as to say of England that "God chose the (*sic*) for hys elect vyneyarde,"[86] all of which would seem to bear out Haller's reading of Bale fairly convincingly. Then there are the passages in which Bale appeared to expect great things of Henry VIII and Edward VI as champions of the Gospel in the sixth age—godly rulers of a purified Church and nation.

Writing in exile in 1543, Bale could still feel positively about the role of the English monarch in God's plan and consider him a true fulfillment of the type established by the virtuous kings of the Old Testament: "Prayse be unto the eternall lorde, for that he hath wrought alreadye by your most victoriouse Iosaphat. I doubt not but here after he will sende soche a Iehu as schal take away all the Idolaters. Soche a full Iosias schall ye have yf ye be thankfull, as will perfyghtlye restore the lawes as yet corrupted, and breake down the buggerye places that are yet in the howse of the lorde."[87] Bale wrote in a similarly laudatory vein about Edward VI in 1552, comparing him with the emperor Constantine who had also destroyed idols and brought peace to the preachers of the Gospel.[88] (Bale's attitude toward Constantine the man was throughout his life one of moderate to enthusiastic approval, a feeling which separated Bale from the earlier Lollards and the radical reformers for whom Constantine's Caesaropapism was anathema.) Finally there was the new conclusion to *Kynge Johan* which Bale wrote sometime after mid-1560 or so, in which he seemed most clearly to aspire after nationality, as Haller argued, and to pin his hopes for the future on "an hereditary monarch called by the grace of God to rule the realm and defend the faith."

Nobility.
Englande hath a quene—Thankes to the lorde aboue—

Whych maye be a lyghte to other princes all
For the godly wayes whome she doth dayly moue
To hir liege people, through Gods wurde specyall.
She is that Angell, as saynt Iohan doth hym call,
That with the lordes seale doth marke out hys true seruantes,
Pryntynge in their hartes hys holy wourdes and Couenauntes. . . .

Civil Order.
Praye vnto the lorde that hir grace maye contynewe
The dayes of Nestor to our sowles consolacyon;
And that hir ofsprynge maye lyue also to subdewe
The great Antichriste, with hys whole generacyon,
In Helias sprete to the confort of thys nacyon. . . .[89]

It sounds as though Elizabeth were not only to bear the sceptre of Constantine over the nation and its Church,[90] but to wear the prophetic mantle of Elijah as well (incidentally assimilating all that was best in the Carmelite heritage). One could scarcely wish for more confirmation of the view that Bale expected England "to lead the world to its redemption in the final reformation of the Church, and Elizabeth . . . to be the ruler and representative of England in that work."[91]

Nevertheless when one reads these words in the context of everything else that Bale wrote, it becomes clear that Haller has grasped only one facet of Bale's thought, and not the dominant one at that. It is of course true that Bale shared the sturdy patriotism which his acquaintance John Leland epitomized, that growing interest in every feature of the country's landscape and history which led to what A. L. Rowse has called "the Elizabethan discovery of England."[92] Nor can one doubt that along with the magisterial reformers in general, Bale had a high view of the responsibility which the ruler bore, to lead his or her people into the paths of righteousness. But national unification under a godly prince was not Bale's ultimate aspiration. However prominent England's historical role might have been and might be in the future, Bale saw it as merely one part of the cosmic drama which the Book of Revelation described. Likewise, England's mission as a "new

Israel" was purely temporary and provisional, destined to last for those few years until the Son of Man should come again. Compared with the imminent Second Coming, England's role in world history paled considerably in significance. Any reading of Bale which misses his eschatological expectation must necessarily go astray.

The importance of the perspective *sub specie aeternitatis* in Bale's thought is clear in many ways. Bale's patriotism, for one thing, was most often coupled with a concern for his countrymen's spiritual welfare and their status vis-à-vis the imminent judgment. In *The laboryouse Journey & serche of Johan Leylande*, Bale followed his paean on the glories of England, as revealed in her ancient chronicles, with a plea to read those chronicles with the Apocalypse in mind: "By the hystoryes of Antiquyte, are the natures of all ages of the worlde manyfested from tyme to tyme, & also both the prophecyes of Daniel and S. Johans revelacyon more easely of their readers understanded. For he that marketh not by the serche of ernest chronycles, the dysposycyon of tymes, shall never beholde those godly prophecyes fulfylled in effect."[93] Reading the Apocalypse and the chronicles together would of course convince Englishmen of the Protestant theology of history, Bale thought, which was the main reason why "vyrulent papystes" sought to keep both out of the hands of the reading public. Rescuing and publishing the old histories, Bale felt, would increase both England's fame and her spiritual health. Here love of country and concern about its status *coram Deo* were intimately entwined. Likewise in the *Summarium*, while Bale asserted that patriotism and love of literature had moved him to publish the work, he also emphasized in his dedication of the work to Edward VI that he hoped specifically that the *Summarium* would help the king understand the age-old struggle between God and Satan and lead England into the ways of truth. The summary of Bale's apocalyptic pattern of history at the end of the volume drove the point home.[94] Finally, Bale's reference to England as God's "elect vyneyarde" in *The vocacyon of*

Johan Bale[95] was followed not by an exhortation to rally round the monarch, God's anointed ruler of the new Israel, but by a call to repentance and obedience to God. So Bale's love for England was in no way a purely secular sentiment, substituting the fatherland for the Heavenly Father as an object of devotion, nor can Bale's patriotism be discussed outside the context of his preoccupation with England's spiritual reformation.

If Bale's love for the heavenly Jerusalem transcended and exceeded his nevertheless very real loyalty to his earthly *patria*, so also he placed more hope in the King of Kings than he did in the Tudor dynasty. Obviously earthly monarchs were extremely important in God's plan. Clearly a godly prince could bring great blessings upon his people by casting down the altars of Baal (where men now worshipped bread in place of Christ) and by encouraging the true preachers who spread the Gospel. But there were limits to what Bale expected from earthly rulers. In the first place one should stress that Bale's works show no sign whatsoever that he was influenced or impressed by the old Sibylline prophecies of a Last World Emperor.[96] Still less is there any indication that Bale saw in Henry VIII, Edward VI, or Elizabeth, specifically, that gargantuan figure of the ruler who would crush Satan and preside over an era of peace and prosperity before the final loosing of the dragon and the Last Judgment. The Tudor monarchs—strong warriors of God though they were—brought in no new era. They merely carried on the struggles against Rome in the sixth age which John Wyclif had touched off. So one catches no echo of the Sibylline tradition in Bale.[97]

Nor did Bale overemphasize what the godly prince could be expected to accomplish. Constantine, after all—the post-Ascension type *par excellence* of the holy monarch—had not been able to prevent the steep descent of the Church into worldliness and superstition from his reign onwards.[98] What Bale implied (though he did not spell it out explicitly) by combining praise for Constantine with condemnation for the post-Constantinian Church[99] was that although a Christian ruler might earnestly seek to do God's will, the cosmic struggle in progress was so grave that the Church he governed might nevertheless become the fortress of the devil.[100] In which case—if the power of earthly monarchs were ultimately so limited—it would indeed be better to take refuge in the Lord than to put confidence in princes. And this was of course what Bale stressed throughout his works.

In speaking of the forces of evil, in *The Image of bothe churches*, he argued that "Moste vaynely are we occupyed, if we assertayne our selves to have the victory over them by any other waye than the Lorde hath apoynted. . . . Onely hath he promysed to destroye them all with the breath of his mouth and with no bodely armour not strengthe of men. . . ."[101] And in the same pamphlet in which he praised Henry VIII as a new Jehoshaphat and looked forward to a full purification of English religious life under his descendents, he distinguished clearly between penultimate victories (within the power of godly monarchs) and the final end of the war:

> I denye yt not, but those godlye gouvernours of the earthe whych schal in these dayes brynge their glorye and honour ryghtlye to the newe cyte of God (as some hath done all redie) shall shewe themselves faythfull mynysters, and seke hys glorie in that behalfe. But they schall not performe thys. For yt maye be non acte of manne by his promes. Onlye ys that wonderful conquest over the enemyes of God reserved to hys worde. . . .[102]

And the "wonderful conquest" would occur only at the Second Coming of Christ. But the Lord's return was not some hypothetical possibility, or some future event too distant to be taken seriously. In the "latter ende of the worlde"[103] it could happen at any moment. So if the sixth age had now lasted nearly two hundred years, and if "the second sabbath here, or lyberte of God's truthe"[104] had already appeared, there was nothing which Bale could look forward to within history save a continued struggle with the Antichrist of Rome until the end.

In the short run, a strong and Protestant ruler of England could make a difference, but not in the long run (which might not be all that long), since that meant the end of history and the Last Judgment. This vindication of the elect, and not the national unification of England, was the consummation which Bale devoutly wished. One is hard put to find in Bale anything of the Calvinist assumption that the world's end might be indefinitely postponed, and that in the meantime the people of God had best busy themselves building godly Genevas on earth. Bale had far more in common with the Lutheran mentality for whom the world seemed old and tired, and its ultimate collapse not far off.[105] More than anything else, therefore, it was Bale's expectation of the imminent *Parousia* which made him consider any unified and Protestant English nation merely provisional. To use Haller's words, it was precisely a "messiah out of the blue" whom Bale eagerly expected. In a later generation, to be sure, when in people's minds the Second Coming had begun to recede into the hazy future, Bale's identification of England as the new Israel may (through Foxe) have supplied the ideology for secular national unification. But that is another story. In the 1540s, Bale's vision of the English past offered to him and his Protestant countrymen (in a way that neither the late-medieval chronicle nor humanist histories could) a way of understanding and coping with the turbulence of the Reformation, at home and abroad, in the interim before the Lord should return and scatter the papists with the breath of His word.

Before leaving the subject of Bale's reinterpretation of English history, one should perhaps consider for a moment the question of his accuracy and trustworthiness. One aberration into which his deductive method led him needs no extensive comment here: his wholesale acceptance of Geoffrey of Monmouth's *Historia Regum Britanniae*, and his invention of British kings and heroes to fill the gap between the Flood and the arrival of Geoffrey's Trojans. Bale (like nature) abhorred a vacuum, particularly in his native country's records, and he was fooled thoroughly by what Annius of Viterbo had written about Britian's primeval history. T. D. Kendrick has explored this topic extensively,[106] and his treatment requires no repetition here.

When Bale left behind the mythical British past and came to deal with the Christian era and England's struggle against Roman subversion, one would expect his use of the records to be equally tendentious. It is interesting to see how far that was so. In his propaganda tracts and in *The Actes of Englysh votaryes*, one finds him (not surprisingly) fitting the data to his preconceived pattern rather frequently. In *The Actes* Bale of course quoted faithfully from his sources upon occasion, when the latter supplied him with useful ammunition. He referred to Polydore Vergil correctly, for example, when citing the *Historiae Anglicae* on the holiness of certain married priests driven from their stalls in Winchester Cathedral in 969; and he quoted Ranulf Higden's *Polychronicon* accurately to the effect that King Canute had bestowed his crown on the Rood at Winchester also.[107] But sometimes Bale would embellish his sources a bit, finding that they did not reveal the true depths of clerical depravity clearly enough. He referred to John Capgrave's *Nova Legenda Angliae*, for instance, for the story that Theodore of Tarsus had established a school at Canterbury teaching not only rhetoric, logic, and philosophy, but also "Magyck, Sortilege, Phisnomy, Palmestry, Alcumy, Necromancy, Chyromancy, Geomancy & witchery" which was a little more than Capgrave had vouchsafed.[108] And sometimes Bale twisted the material in his sources completely. He referred to Capgrave in claiming that Theodore of Tarsus had been consecrated in that fateful year 666 A.D., but Capgrave had said nothing of the kind.[109]

All this is scarcely surprising in light of the assumptions Bale had grown up with and which his conversion had only served to reinforce: that the revealed truth (Carmelite traditions, or now the "plain sense" of the Bible) outweighed any conflicting evidence, and that the purpose of history was to illustrate this truth. But what about Bale's scholarly histories of English life and thought, the *Summarium* and the *Catalogus*? These represent a slightly different intention on Bale's part. For in these massive volumes, he was concerned with transmitting information about his country's authors and their works, while at the same time he communicated his vision of the English past. As far as bibliographical information went, Bale seems to have had no motive for falsification, since a full and complete list for each writer would show either what a prolific agent of Satan or what a mighty warrior of the Gospel he had been. So although the capsule biographies in the *Summarium* and the *Catalogus* (as well as the historical addenda in the latter) contain numerous wilful inaccuracies,[110] the bibliographical data appear not to have been affected by Bale's tendency elsewhere to rewrite history from his Protestant point of view.

One may appreciate the way Bale's bibliographical scholarship remained more or less unscathed when one looks at three manuscripts on which he worked during the years 1548 to 1559, roughly the time between the publication of the *Summarium* and its much amplified successor, the *Catalogus*. One of these was an alphabetical bibliography of English authors, which was published in 1902 as *Index Britanniae Scriptorum*.[111] Bale had not intended the work for publication; it was simply a private collection of notes. Because the *Index* was not intended to persuade anyone of anything, and because of the neutral character of the data he was recording, Bale had no reason not to be methodical and accurate. He acquired the notebook about 1548 and divided it into alphabetical sections.[112] Then in the appropriate sections he listed his authors according to their Christian names, and added the titles and incipits of their works as he came across them. Bale took pains to record the location of every book he saw (offering thus an invaluable guide to sixteenth-century English libraries) or the source from which he had obtained the title. The *Index* forms a kind of corollary to *The laboryouse Journey &*

serche of Johan Leylande, showing Bale at work scouring the London printing shops and the libraries at Oxford, Cambridge, and Norwich, as well as various private book collections. The *Index* was as inclusive as possible; Bale's biased and selective approach to the medieval chronicles seems not to have operated when he was collecting bibliographical data. The mere titles and incipits by themselves revealed either scholastic perversity or proto-Protestant virtue, and no revision was necessary. Apart from one or two acerbic comments,[113] this private notebook was free from the polemical ire of Bale's public personality.

A second manuscript from this period included a good deal more vituperative commentary than the *Index* had—a codex containing Bale's excerpts from John Leland's *De Viris Illustribus*.[114] Bale evidently compiled this manuscript sometime after 1552 with the intention of having it published. On the title page he wrote "The work of John Leland, 'On the Famous Men of the English Nation,' epitomized and in many places corrected and amplified by the Englishman John Bale, Bishop of Ossory in Ireland."[115] In *The laboryouse Journey & serche of Johan Leylande*, Bale had said that he wanted to publish the fruit of his former mentor's research, and *De Viris Illustribus* was apparently to be the first installment. Later Bale changed his mind about this manuscript, however, either because he found himself putting too much of Leland's data into the *Catalogus*, or because he finally decided that Leland's conservative theology was too dangerous to his readers' spiritual health. So the epitome stayed in manuscript.

But even at the time when Bale first began working on *De Viris Illustribus*, he was clearly worried about Leland's beliefs: "One thing will perhaps leave the reader discontented, and meanwhile displeases me: the fact that many matters are treated here with no discrimination between doctrines or testing of spirits, and the fact that evil things are taken as holy."[116] Therefore the "amplifications" of which Bale spoke in his title served two purposes. The first was to fit Leland's data into Bale's pattern of history, emphasizing especially the important turning points like the year 1000. "Wolfstan flourished in the year of our Lord 1000. The monks prepared a seat for Satan as he emerged from the abyss. . . . Oswald flourished in the year of the Incarnate Word 1010. The sun in these days was obscured, for the Scriptures were neglected."[117] The second purpose was to rebuke Leland for the popish drift of his theology, especially in his comments about Wyclif and the Lollards: "Weigh carefully the preposterous judgment of Leland here. He says that the most barbarous sophist is a famous theologian. Pious doctors he calls hydras. And he says that the most frigid—actually the most iniquitous—glosses of the papists are the sword of the Gospel."[118] So this manuscript forms a useful contrast with the *Index*. Where Bale was simply recording bibliographical notes for his own use, he was generally content simply to copy the data as he found it, without any commentary. But when he was preparing a history of English literature for the public at large, he took care to ensure that the information (though accurately transcribed) illustrated his vision of the national past, and none other.

So Bale respected and reproduced faithfully the information Leland had collected, though he felt constrained to denounce the construction the antiquary had placed upon it. When Bale left the restricted sphere of bibliography and literary history, however, and searched the medieval chronicles for what they had to say about past events, he was not going to transcribe his findings so passively. The third manuscript from the years 1548 to 1559 shows Bale gathering the kind of ammunition he was going to fire off in *Acta Romanorum Pontificum*, and indicates the selective frame of mind in which he approached the record of past events. This little manuscript book contains notes and jottings which Bale took down over a longish period from the late 1540s through 1559.[119] The first part of the book represents mostly information from two books relating to the Carmelite order.[120] Bale was evidently justifying to himself his break with the past. Towards the middle of the manuscript, Bale began to take notes on various chronicles, and it is interesting to notice the kind of data which caught his eye. From the *Chronica* of Roger Hoveden, for instance, Bale copied the decrees of Pope Gregory VII aganst clerical marriage, a story of how monks replaced priests in Durham Cathedral in 1083, and a decree of Pope Urban II in 1099 against lay investiture. On this last item, Bale felt moved to comment, "Note the great Antichrist."[121] In a similar vein, Bale continued with notes from the chronicle of Gilbert of Hemmingford and then from various of the more historical works of continental reformers like Luther and Gilbert Cousin. There is nothing surprising in this little commonplace book, nothing out of harmony with Bale's assumptions or his methodology elsewhere; it is merely interesting to watch him at work, behind the published *Catalogus.*

In contrast with the scrupulous accuracy of his bibliographical labor (which was widely acknowledged by continental historians like Matthias Flacius Illyricus),[122] Bale treated the record of events in medieval chronicles very selectively. If their authors had been monks or priests, as was naturally true of most of them, Bale naturally assumed that they had lied about most events, but at the same time felt free to spoil these histories of whatever salacious clerical gossip he could use.[123] If, as in the case of the more recent chronicles, the bias was sympathetic to his cause, Bale still took only what he needed.

Bale was obviously no precursor of the modern, critical historical mind; he felt no kinship with that spirit, evolving already in the sixteenth century among continental humanists, which would focus its attention not so much upon the world of nature (or upon the realm of super-nature) as upon "the world of man's making; which seeks out not the typical but the unique; which emphasizes the variety rather than the uniformity of human nature; which is interested less in similarities than in differences;

and which is impressed not with permanence but with change."[124] None of that would have appealed to Bale, steeped as he was in apocalyptic prophecy, and assuming as he did that the latter enunciated God's immutable plan for history. Bale represented that counter-current to humanist historical thought in the sixteenth century, the last great flourish of the Judaeo-Christian belief in history as "the grand design of God."[125] At the same time, he represented and responded to England's search for a usable past, a past which—whether historically accurate or not—helped men grapple with the problems of the present. Bale recognized the need which Englishmen felt, in the age of the Reformation, to re-establish ties of continuity with the past after they had thrown off their jurisdictional connection with Christendom and so much of late medieval piety besides. What Bale was able to show was that events since 1529 had begun to restore the nation's most ancient and venerable past, the "first six hundred years" of pure English Christianity. And for good measure he made clear that the reformed Church in England was patterned (as near as made no difference) after the pristine first three hundred years of the Roman Church as well. By means of the prophecies in Revelation, finally, Bale was able to explain why reform had tarried these many centuries, why one had to reach back so far in time to find a true Church that had not been a persecuted remnant, why the authority of Rome had gone unquestioned so long. The Book of Revelation, in other words, enabled one to rebut the taunt, "Where was your church before Luther?" By re-establishing continuity with the past, a particularly English ecclesiastical past, Bale gave his Protestant countrymen a sense of where they were going in the future, and a list of the tasks left to be done in order to restore that "good old past."

Bale's role in the English Reformation was to be a myth-maker (and through his pupil John Foxe, *the* mythmaker) for his disoriented age, craftsman of a past which could give Englishmen a *point d'appui* in a threatening world. Much of Bale's antiquarian labor (especially the bibliographical information he conveyed in the *Summarium* and the *Catalogus*) did help lay the foundation for the modern study of English literature, just as Archbishop Parker's Anglo-Saxon studies, undertaken with a similar polemical purpose, later contributed to modern critical scholarship as well.[126] But there was no disinterested spirit behind Bale's research, no imaginative desire to recreate the past simply for its own sake. His *historiarum dulcedo* and *literum cupiditas* were primarily facets of his yearning to discover and then communicate a vision of the past which illustrated what he felt the Bible said,[127] and which contemporary Englishmen could use as a lantern to guide their footsteps.[128]

V / The New English Saints

When Bale urged upon his countrymen a new interpretation of their nation's past, he naturally offered them
at the same time a new company of heroes to imitate and
honor. This was to be expected, and indeed the task was
forced on Bale. If he were to argue—as he did—that from
the time of St. Augustine's mission in 597 to the
repudiation of the papacy in 1533 the institutional English
Church had been corrupt, then first he had to dispose
somehow of all the saints whom that Church had produced
and had venerated. An attack on the traditional English
saints, the inhabitants of John Capgrave's popular *Nova
Legenda Angliae*, had of course been official policy under
Thomas Cromwell, before Bale had evolved a systematic
historical rationale to explain it. The injunctions of 1536
and 1538 had undermined the cult of the saints as
mediators; the shrine of St. Thomas at Canterbury had
received its comeuppance in full public view; and it seems
in the late 1530s someone (perhaps Cromwell or one of his
agents) had had an English edition printed of Erasmus's
lampoon, *A Pilgrimage of Pure Devotion*, pressing home the
attack on the traditional saints.[1] There were many other
skirmishes in this campaign, too, among them Bale's
doggerel plays such as *A Comedye concernynge thre lawes.*
What Bale did in the 1540s and the 1550s was to fit this

repudiation of the old English saints into an historical framework—to show at what point in time the heroes of the institutional Church had ceased to be valid, at what point the nimbus of sanctity had withdrawn from the visible Church and settled upon the "few faithful in each age," the oft-persecuted remnant. But by the same token, Bale's dissemination of his new vision of English history also placed a burden on him to define (more clearly than Cromwell's destructive campaign had done) how the true faithful had differed in life and doctrine from the now-rejected saints in Capgrave and in Voragine's *Legenda Aurea*. There needed to be a positive side to Bale's labor as well. The success he later had in founding Protestant hagiography in England, as well as the importance of his role in stimulating and inspiring John Foxe, make it worth-while to take a close look at this facet of Bale's historical thought.[2]

Bale actually had two motives for supplying the English reading public with the lives of new-model saints, just as his audience fell into two broad categories. The first group (and in the early 1540s no doubt the minority) were the reformers in England. They were of differing backgrounds and convictions (on the Eucharist, for instance) but most of them were apt to agree with the vision of history which Bale enunciated in *The Image of bothe churches*. Bale sensed an obligation to satisfy the curiosity of these readers by offering them flesh-and-blood examples of the "faithful in each age" who had kept the lamp of pure faith burning ever since the pre-Constantinian Church or the pre-Augustinian Church in England. More importantly, in the uneasy years of Henry's later reign when sporadic prosecutions under the Six Articles Act were keeping Protestants edgy and fearful, Bale felt a call to revive the role of the early Christian martyrologists: to comfort the brethren, as well as to encourage and instruct. The temporary ascendancy of the conservatives at court after 1540 increased the need among Protestant Englishmen for inspiring stories, tales of how God had strengthened and upheld His faithful under persecution. Adversity may also have made more poignant the search for models of piety to emulate and the hunger for teaching—needs which (along with the craving for entertainment) the traditional medieval saints' lives had more typically fulfilled. So the problem of building up the faithful at home was on Bale's mind as he thought and wrote at Antwerp in the early 1540s.[3]

There was also, to be sure, the second and much larger group among his potential audience in England: the not-so-faithful Christians (by Bale's new standards) and the downright unreconstructed papists. *The Image of bothe churches* was not going to convince men who repudiated Bale's very authority to interpret the Book of Revelation, let alone the scheme of history he deduced from it. Nor were specific applications of his pattern, such as *The Actes of Englysh votaryes*, likely to win over the hard-core opposition (though Bale no doubt hoped for the best). But the first-hand testimony of real, flesh-and-blood, English Protestant martyrs might do the job. The Church in the second and third centuries—also urging a new faith on a hostile population and government—had after all found that the witness of the martyrs, sealed with their blood, had a powerful effect on sceptics.[4] Bale then had the conversion of his conservative English countrymen on his mind as well, as he cast around for suitable Protestant heroes.

Bale's many years of work as a Carmelite hagiographer, in his younger days, had prepared him to answer the need for a new and reformed martyrology, the need which the earliest English Protestants such as William Tyndale had recognized. One might of course find surprising the ease with which Bale was able to adapt the older medieval tradition to Protestant uses. After all, in the mid-1530s he had violently repudiated the cult of saints. In his preaching he had sternly opposed their invocation as mediators, and rejected the notion that they had any merit except insofar as they were "canonysed in cristes blood."[5] One might have expected Bale to have thrown out the whole idea of sainthood altogether, as too touchy, given his particular background. But his interests as an historian and antiquary kept him from doing that. Bale was no theologian, no abstract thinker. As an historian he was interested in human beings (though still mostly as types, not as individuals—Bale was no humanist). God's "grand design" for history, as Bale came to understand it in the 1540s, had obviously been worked out through particular men and women who had fulfilled the type of sainthood established in the New Testament. And the specific ways in which the bona fide saints of God had fulfilled the pattern in each age was surely of interest to Protestant Englishmen who aspired to do likewise now in their own time. So Bale's historical interests and apologetic needs kept him from throwing out the saint's life along with the rest of his Carmelite piety. The genre simply needed to be purified of late-medieval anthropocentricity, so that all the glory might be given to God. It was during his first exile, then, that Bale proceeded systematically to redefine sainthood from a Protestant point of view.

In the course of Bale's dramatic activity during the later 1530s, he had already hit upon one potential Protestant saint—King John. But that monarch had posed problems as a subject for Protestant hagiography. True, he had suffered for resisting Pope Innocent III, and this had been virtuous. He had tried to stem the tide of Romish political subversion. But Bale lacked (not surprisingly) any first-hand material which would have depicted King John as a zealous Protestant.[6] What Bale needed was a figure who could edify the faithful, and persuade the unbelievers in England both by his actions and his beliefs. Bale found such a model (or so he thought) in the fifteenth-century Lollard rebel, Sir John Oldcastle.

There were two sources which Bale, in exile in the early 1540s, was able to use in forming his picture of Oldcastle as a Protestant saint. One was the English Church's official account of Oldcastle's examination for heresy by Archbishop Arundel in 1413. Bale had a copy of this with him in exile, in the fifteenth-century Carmelite collection of information about the Lollards known as *Fasciculi Zizaniorum*. He had evidently got this manuscript from the library of his old Carmelite house at Norwich when the latter was dissolved in 1538,[7] and had taken it with him when he fled into exile in the Low Countries.[8] This was one source for Oldcastle's story.

Bale also had at Antwerp a pamphlet which had been published about 1530 by the same "Marburg" press (in Antwerp) which had done many of Tyndale's works. This little volume, containing *The examinacion of Master William Thorpe preste* and *The examinacion of syr Ihon Oldcastel*, offered an account of Oldcastle's interrogation before Arundel which differed in many respects from the version in *Fasciculi Zizaniorum*.[9] Where the editor (whether it was Tyndale or another of that circle of early exiles) had found this material there is no way of telling.[10] The pamphlet reproduced Oldcastle's words simply, with little polemical or explanatory material which might have given a clue as to where the information had been found. It is possible that this little tract by itself had inspired Bale to write Protestant saints' lives.[11] But the creation of a Protestant martyrology followed naturally from Bale's emphasis on the "faithful in all ages" in *The Image of bothe churches*, on which Bale had been working since his flight into exile. One need not conclude that discovery of the "Marburg" pamphlet had first put the idea into his mind. In any case, Bale now had two first-hand accounts of a potential Protestant martyr's interrogation, the sort of material which had been so effectively used in the saints' lives of the early Church. Bale resolved to take these dialogues and bare narratives relating to Oldcastle, and turn them into hard-hitting polemic—showing the English reading public precisely what a true (that is, Protestant) saint was like, and by contrast who the real villains of English history had been. The resulting pamphlet was published at Antwerp in 1544 as *A brefe Chronycle concernynge the Examinacyon and death of the blessed martyr of Christ syr Johan Oldecastell*.

Unfortunately for Bale's project, there were two uncomfortable difficulties with the selection of Sir John Oldcastle as a model of Protestant virtue. In the first place, the man had been a notorious rebel and a traitor. In January 1414, Oldcastle had led an abortive coup against Henry V at St. Giles' fields outside London. Upon the embarrassing collapse of this plot, Oldcastle had fled to the West Country, where he was apprehended in 1417 and whence he was dragged to London for execution as an heretic and a traitor.[12] Clearly Bale was going to have to repair Oldcastle's unsavory reputation for treason, since according to his understanding of the "faithful in all ages," God's elect had always obeyed their divinely-appointed rulers and had resisted only the overweening pretensions of the Church. Moreover Bale wanted to portray Oldcastle not merely as a Christian martyr (who had fulfilled the types of Sts. Peter, Andrew, Barnabas, and so on) but also as a patriot, a postfiguration of those heroes in Hebrew, Greek, and Roman history who had died for their nations.[13]

Obviously, something had to be done to set the story straight, as Bale saw it. If Oldcastle really had fulfilled those godly and patriotic types, then he certainly must have shared their virtues, and the story of his rebellion must have been a wicked papistical invention aimed at discrediting one of God's faithful. As a matter of fact, Bale had a pretty good idea whom to blame for the presumed fabrication: Polydore Vergil, who—like all the other clerical writers on England's past, Bale thought—had completely mistaken the sinners for the saints.[14] Bale wanted to set Polydore and the older tradition right about English history, beginning with the Oldcastle episode. In the process he did have to twist and turn a bit. To begin with, Bale was able to find a tiny error in Polydore's account, and he turned this into an enormous red herring. According to the Italian's history, Oldcastle's revolt had taken place *after* news had reached England that John Hus and Jerome of Prague had been burned at Constance. As Bale correctly pointed out, these executions had taken place in 1415 and 1416 respectively. However, Bale continued, the supposed rebellion which Polydore was wickedly trying to pin on Oldcastle had occurred (even in Polydore's history) in 1414. Bale concluded in disgust, "Nowe reken these nombres and yeres and marke the proper conveyance of the Romish gentleman, the Popes collectour, to clought up that crooked kingdom of theyrs. He can by such legerdemaine both please his friends in Ingland, and also at Rome."[15]

Obviously, thought Bale, a man who could make that kind of mistake was not be be trusted about anything. So the Oldcastle rebellion (despite the fact that several reliable fifteenth-century chronicles mentioned it) must have been a Romish fabrication.[16] Why then had Oldcastle been interrogated and eventually executed? Clearly, Bale thought, it had been because Oldcastle had adopted Lollard beliefs, had sent Wyclif's works overseas to Hus, and had supported *Praemunire* legislation under Richard II to which the English clergy objected.[17] Oldcastle, in other words, had been a patriotic and protoprotestant Englishman done to death by wicked churchmen in the service of Rome. The lineaments of the new-model saint were beginning to emerge. Having demonstrated all of this to his satisfaction in the introduction to the pamphlet, Bale could now proceed to print what the valiant knight had said to his examiners in defense of the Protestant truth.

Here, regrettably, Bale ran up against the second difficulty in using Oldcastle as his prototype of the Protestant saint. It appeared that Olcastle had held certain beliefs—in purgatory, for example—which Bale had renounced, and that he had been dangerously vague on certain other points of doctrine. If Oldcastle had really been one of the "faithful in all ages," the surviving records must obviously have misrepresented his opinions, and the necessary corrections would have to be made in order that the English reading public should be properly edified. How Bale did this becomes apparent when one compares the version of a declaration of faith which Oldcastle made, as published in the 1530 "Marburg" edition, with the similar declaration in Bale's pamphlet of 1544. This particular declaration does not appear in Arundel's official account, so the changes in the 1544 version would seem to have been Bale's own work. On purgatory, for instance, the two tracts differ. The 1530 edition says, "The .ii. parte is in purgatory abiding the mercy of god /&purging them there of their sinnes. . . ," while Bale wrote, "The second sort are in purgatorye (yf any soche be by the scriptures) abydynge the mercye of God and a full delyveraunce of payne."[18] Bale evidently felt that for the purpose of edification (and of rectifying the historical record) the *sola scriptura* qualification needed to be added, and the suggestion removed that sins might be purged otherwise than through the blood of Christ. In much the same way, Bale felt that Oldcastle's statement on the Eucharist ("I believe verely that the most blessed sacrament of the altare is very Christes body in forme of bread. . . .") was confusingly imprecise, and needed correction as follows: "I believe in that sacrament to be contayned verye Christes bodye and bloude undre the symylytudes of breade and wyne. . . ."[19] Bale's formulation may not have been very precise either, but it did make clear that the elements were "symylytudes" and not Christ's body and blood in substance.[20]

This technique of revision and correction may be found in several other places in Bale's version of Oldcastle's "passion." To point this out is not to blame Bale for failing to observe canons of historical accuracy which he himself would have rejected. For Bale believed that the truth (eternal and unchanging) was the truth, and that whatever interfered with its expression needed to be set right—especially when the eternal destiny of his fellow Englishmen was at stake. This was the same sort of assumption with which Bale had grown up as a fashioner of Carmelite saints' lives. Conversion had not altered in the least his belief in the superior authority of revelation (be it through tradition or through the Bible) over the historical data. The significant point here, however, is that out of the intractable material of Sir John Oldcastle, Bale was creating a new model of sainthood. The Protestant saint, in the first place, questioned traditional doctrines such as that of purgatory which implied that Christ's sacrifice had not been sufficient to atone for man's sins. Similarly, he took the Bible for his only standard in matters of belief. He resisted doctrines which suggested that the sacraments were effective *ex opere operato*. The Protestant saint was more notable for his courage and his faith in God than for any wonder-working powers. And finally, he attacked the pretensions of the clerical caste (in particular, the claims of the papacy to world dominion) and he supported the English monarch, both as God's anointed representative and as the nation's only bastion against political and spiritual subversion from Rome. Here was Bale's reconstructed saint. The need for new heroes such as Oldcastle was a natural consequence of the Reformation in England, though before 1544 no Englishman had seen this as clearly as Bale now did. The former Carmelite hagiographer was in fact the most well-equipped of the early reformers to bridge the gap between Capgrave's *Nova Legenda Angliae* and Foxe's *Actes and Monuments*.

But for Englishmen in the 1540s, Bale's Oldcastle must have evoked hardly a vague recollection of the man and of the age in which he had lived. In a way this was an advantage, of course—the distance between Oldcastle's day and the present did allow Bale a certain protection from criticism when he had to retouch his saint's likeness with more Protestant and patriotic colors. But this distance was a drawback, too. Oldcastle's martyrdom, his faith and constancy, were less moving to the average Englishman in 1544 than the story of some contemporary saint would be. And indeed, although a second edition of the Oldcastle tract appeared in London in 1548, the work was by no means as popular as some of Bale's other books. Since the average Englishman in the 1540s was not at all convinced (as Bale well knew) that the Protestants were in the right,

Bale needed in addition to Oldcastle the figure of some attractive and contemporary Protestant martyr, some really powerful and convincing personality. Bale found the answer to his need in the papers of Mistress Anne Askew, who was burned at Smithfield for heresy in July 1546. By publishing Anne Askew's interrogations and her confessions of faith, as he did in 1546 and 1547, Bale both established the genre of Protestant hagiography on firm grounds, and pointed out the way which Foxe would take with his lengthy *acta* of present-day martyrs whom many Englishmen had seen and heard personally.

Anne Askew, born about 1520, was the daughter of Sir William Askew (or Ayscough) of Stallingborough in Lincolnshire. The family was a prominent one in the county and had good connections at court. Her recently knighted brother Francis was sheriff of Lincolnshire in 1544, and her brother Edward was one of Henry VIII's gentlemen pensioners. She had a streak of wilful independence in her character, however, and refused to cooperate in the family's rising fortunes. Her Protestant convictions estranged her from the husband whom she had accepted under family pressure, and she resumed her maiden name. Early 1545 found her on her own in London and on familiar terms with several Protestant ladies at court. Anne made no attempt to hide her radical beliefs, particularly concerning the Mass. Consequently in March 1545 she was arrested under the Six Articles Act, and examined by various notables including Bishop Bonner of London. Either Anne made some capitulation regarding her views on the Mass, or family influence got her off the hook; in any case, by June 1545 she was free. Her brush with the law had evidently not tamed her at all. Anne continued to spread Protestant ideas among the ladies at court—dangerous business in the tense and faction-ridden atmosphere of Henry VIII's last years. On May 24, 1546, the Privy Council, rounding up Protestants implicated by the unfortunate Dr. Edward Crome, summoned Anne to appear as well. After trying unsuccessfully to hide, she came before the council on 19 June. Under pressure, Anne still clung to her sacramentarian beliefs. So on 28 June she was arraigned, tried and condemned at the Guildhall, and automatically sentenced to the stake. But the conservatives on the Privy Council were interested in more than Anne's personal beliefs. Thinking that she might be brought to implicate her friends at court (and perhaps even Queen Catherine Parr), Sir Richard Rich and Lord Chancellor Wriothesley had Anne taken to the Tower on June 29, where she was brutally tortured. She refused to talk, however, and eventually Rich and Wriothesley gave up. Broken in body but emphatically not in spirit, Anne was burned at Smithfield on July 16, 1546.[21]

Bale lost no time in publishing the documents connected with Anne's interrogations and death. *The first examinacyon of Anne Askewe* (describing the events of March 1545) came from the press of Dirik van der Straten in November 1546, and *The lattre examinacyon of Anne Askewe* appeared from the same press the following January.[22] Bale had developed connections with England through German Protestant merchants, so that he was able to receive not only information and printed books from home, but also manuscripts such as Anne's.[23] While the execution of this prominent young gentlewoman was still fresh in the public memory, Bale resolved to avenge her death by using her story to reinforce the image of the Protestant saint which he was urging upon the English public.

In the pungent comments with which Bale interlarded the paragraphs of Anne's own text, and especially in his introduction to her second examination, Bale took pains to define true martyrdom absolutely clearly. Looking back over English history, he remarked that up until the mission of St. Augustine, when the faith in England had been tolerably pure, all the people who had died in its defense had been bona fide martyrs because the cause for which they had died had been valid. After the influx of Roman superstition in 597, however, the saints then produced by the English Church had been idolaters, lechers, and traitors, even the best of them. Bale was in no frame of mind to be charitable: "Yea, brynge saynt Edmonde of Burye, S. Fremunde of Dunstable . . . and Saynt Wynstave of Evesham (whych are the best of the Englysh martyrs) to the touche stone of Gods worde & ye shall fynde their martyrdomes and causes full unlyke to theirs whom the Byshoppes murther now apace in Englande."[24] Those who had died for the Roman faith had in fact been heretics, not true martyrs, since their beliefs had deviated from the "plain sense" of the Scriptures. The main point of Bale's commentary was to show that Anne Askew's faith had been biblical and her martyrdom valid, and therefore that her judges and interrogators had been agents of the devil.

One way of establishing the image of Anne as a true martyr in the popular mind was to link her typologically with the valid martyrs of the early Church. As Bale had done with his Carmelite saints and recently with Oldcastle, he depicted Anne as the fulfillment of a type established in the Bible (in this case, the godly and courageous young woman) which recurred time and again in the history of the Church. In his preface to Anne's first examination, Bale compared her at length with Blandina, a young martyr in second-century Gaul whom Eusebius of Caesarea had described. As Blandina had been young and tender, so was Anne. As Blandina's spirit had never wavered under torture, neither did Anne's. As Blandina had confidently rebuked the pagan priests for their errors, so Anne from the stake spoke bluntly to Nicholas Shaxton (the former bishop of Salisbury, who had been condemned with Anne but had since recanted). And so on. As was appropriate to the description of Protestant sainthood, Bale emphasized in Blandina and Anne the qualities of courage and faith in Christ, rather than those of ascetic virtuosity or wonderworking power.[25] So both Anne's beliefs and her virtues impressed on the English reading public the model of Protestant sainthood which Bale had sketched out in Sir John Oldcastle.

When one notices in Bale's treatment of Anne Askew much the same sort of typological thought patterns which had characterized his earlier Carmelite saints' lives, one naturally wonders whether the habit of subordinating the individual to the type did not continue to operate here, and whether Bale did not retouch the Askew documents to make his heroine conform more closely to the type she represented. Was Bale's version of Anne's passion an accurate one? At least one contemporary thought not— Bishop Stephen Gardiner, who called Bale's account "utterly misreported."[26] Unfortunately it is difficult to check Gardiner's statement, since (aside from the very brief notes in the records of the Privy Council) Anne's version of her examinations, as Bale published them, offers the only first-hand source which has survived. One consideration does speak in favor of Bale's general faithfulness to the manuscripts he received from Anne, though to be sure it is difficult to get behind these to the question of Anne's own accuracy in reporting her trials. In Bale's published version, the tone and the style of Anne's words ring true. The words are simple, terse, and moving. Even when Anne described her torture, she scarcely raised her voice.

> Then they ded put me on the racke, by cause I confessed no ladyes nor gentylewomen to be of my opynyon, and thereon they kepte me a longe tyme. And bycause I laye styll and ded not crye, my lorde Chauncellour and Mastre Riche toke peynes to racke me their (*sic*) owne handes tyll I was nygh dead. . . . Then the lyefetenaunt caused me to be loused from the racke. Incontynentlye I swounded, and then they recovered me agayne. After that I sate ii. longe houres reasonynge with my lorde Chauncellour upon the bare floore. . . .[27]

In all of Bale's other works he never achieved or even really attempted this restraint, this self-control. He was capable of creating earthy burlesque or gutter-polemic seething with rage. But nowhere in his works can one find duplicated Anne Askew's patient simplicity. This is not to state categorically that Bale could not have invented her words in a wholesale fashion, but the possibility seems remote.[28]

Though Bale may have been faithful to Anne's words in general, what about the correction of minor points? This was after all what Bale had done in publishing the Oldcastle documents. Two small considerations arouse suspicion in this regard. The first involves a phrase which Anne used at one point to describe the Eucharist. In a letter to an anonymous friend Anne says, "The breade and wyne were left us, for a sacramental communyon, or a mutuall pertycypacyon of the inestimable benefyghtes of hys most precyouse deathe and bloud shedynge."[29] These particular words were compatible with Anne's sacramentarian beliefs, expressed elsewhere in the pamphlets—that the Eucharist was a service of remembrance and thanksgiving, whereby Christians were knit to Christ in a communion of love.[30] But the specific words "mutuall pertycypacyon" raise a small question. They happen to be words which Bale himself used rather frequently in speaking of the Eucharist,[31] and which otherwise do not seem to have been especially common. Anne Askew might of course have picked up the phrase elsewhere and used it herself; but the coincidence does raise the question of whether here at least, Bale did not put his own words into Anne's mouth.

The other question mark concerning Bale's veracity stems from a detail in Anne's account of her first examination. On March 20, 1545, Bishop Bonner interrogated Anne on the matter of the Mass. He wrote out a statement categorically affirming the Real Presence, which he demanded that Anne should sign. According to Bale's published version of the incident, Anne affixed to the document not her signature alone, but the statement, "I Anne Askew do beleve all maner thynges contayned in the faythe of the catholyck churche."[32] An entry in Bishop Bonner's register, however, claims that Anne signed the statement without reservations.[33] Whom should one believe? On the one hand, the entry in Bonner's register was clearly placed there *after* Anne's execution, in order to justify her punishment and to demonstrate that she was a relapsed heretic, not a first-time offender (and perhaps also, in the atmosphere of faction-strife in 1546, in order to clear Bonner of having let a dangerous Protestant agent slip away unrepentant a year earlier). The need for this special pleading might be taken to support Anne's version of the incident. On the other hand, it seems unlikely that Bonner would have released her in March 1545 without some plain statement of her orthodoxy—even considering Anne's important family connections. The truth is elusive here, but the matter does raise again the question of Bale's (if not Anne's) trustworthiness.

With these two small exceptions, the overall impression which one receives is that Bale reproduced Anne's documents much as he had found them, though his own interlarded comments sometimes drew more out of Anne's words than was actually there. Though Bale would hardly have stuck at altering the text in the interests of edification, such modifications were less necessary here than with the Oldcastle material. Anne Askew was closer in her beliefs and in her actions to Bale's ideal of the Protestant saint; and of course since she had been a prominent lady in London and Lincolnshire society, a really gross fabrication would have been quickly exposed. It is interesting that Wriothesley and Rich apparently never gave Bale the lie.[34] But though it is of interest to a modern historian to evaluate Bale's fidelity to his sources, his importance in the 1540s did not rest on such considerations. Totally accurate or not, the Askew tracts were extremely popular. After the initial Wesel editions of the two separate examinations, four further combined editions were printed in England during the reign of Edward VI (a total, one may imagine, of some thirty-five hundred copies in all).[35] The story of Anne Askew's martyrdom was something of an early best-seller. With the Askew papers, more so than with the Oldcastle documents, Bale had answered a need on the part of English Protestants to see a flesh-and-blood model of the beliefs and virtues they were coming to respect. And Anne Askew's quick wit and vibrant personality made her words an effective apology for her cause, to wear away the resistance of those Englishmen who still struggled against the "plain truth" of the Bible.

By 1548 Bale's role as intermediary between the late medieval and the Protestant traditions of hagiography had been largely fulfilled. In that year Bale, back from exile, met John Foxe at Mountjoy House in London, the residence of their patroness, the duchess of Richmond. Bale probably had a good deal to do with Foxe's decision to develop an elaborate Protestant martyrology, of which the first fruits appeared in 1554 with *Commentarii Rerum in Ecclesia Gestarum*. But Bale had not wholly given up the hagiographic genre, nor passed it on entirely to his younger friend. For at the end of 1553 he published a curious and interesting little pamphlet—a sort of Protestant saint's life penned by the "saint" himself—called *The vocacyon of Johan Bale to the Bishoprick of Ossorie in Irelande*. Bale had been promoted (more likely deported) in August 1552 to the see of Ossory—the Tudor equivalent of a Siberian salt-mine, and a post which Edward VI had been having difficulty filling.[36] Bale and his wife Dorothy landed at Waterford in January 1553 and reached Kilkenny in time to preach in the cathedral there every Sunday and holy day in Lent. Bale's radical views did not sit well with most of the townspeople and the diocesan clergy. And after Edward VI had died in July and Queen Mary had been proclaimed at Kilkenny in August, Bale found his cathedral quite unsafe. Unfortunately his episcopal estate in the country was no more secure. When five of his servants were murdered in early September, Bale resolved to flee for his life (he never mentioned what he did about Dorothy, though she was certainly with him ten years later in Canterbury). He found no safety in Dublin, and decided to pass over to Scotland and wait for an auspicious moment for reclaiming his diocese. Unfortunately for this stratagem, Flemish pirates seized him from his hired "pyckarde" as he awaited the tide in Dublin harbor. Sometimes Bale seemed to have a magnetic capacity for attracting misfortune. But his energy never failed him. When the pirate captain put

Bale ashore at St. Ives in Cornwall and sailed off with the bishop's money, Bale hired a rowboat and chased the privateer, reboarding it in a mile or two. The captain (at his wits' end, perhaps) soon hit on the notion of selling Bale to Queen Mary's authorities ashore. But Bale offered him fifty pounds (which he didn't have) if the pirates would set him free in the Low Countries. With the bargain struck, off they sailed. Somewhere in Flanders the owners of the privateer held Bale captive for three weeks while the ransom money came in from the bishop's friends in exile. Then Bale made for Wesel, where in December of 1553 he published *The vocacyon*—venting his spleen against Irishmen, Flemish pirates, and papists in general.[37]

There are some elements in *The vocacyon of Johan Bale* which link it with the nascent tradition of auto-biography in Renaissance England, rather than with the late medieval saint's life.[38] The unselfconscious gusto with which Bale narrated his own adventures (without resorting to allegory or to the medieval convention of the dream-vision) might seem at first glance to point forward in time to the efflorescence of *res gestae* in seventeenth-century England, even though the chronological span of *The vocacyon* was scarcely more than a year.[39] Likewise Bale's zest in relating colorful but non-essential details for their own sake might seem considerably removed from the typological world-view of his Carmelite (or even his Protestant) saints' lives, in which details were apt to be examples of abstract truth. There is not much in the following except pleasure in spinning a thumping good yarn:

> In the mean tyme they (the Flemish pirates) went a roavinge by a whole wekes space and more. And first they toke an Englishe shippe of Totnes / going towardes Britaine and loaden with tinne / and that they spoiled both of ware and moneye under ye colour of Frenche mennis goodes. The next daye in the afternone / behelde they .ii. English shippes more / whome they chaced all yt night longe / and the nexte daye also till .x. of the clocke / & of them they toke one by reason yt his

topsaile brake / and that was a shippe of lynne. In this they
had nothinge but apples / for he went for his loadinge. After yt
traced they the seas over / more than halfe a weke / and
founde none there but their owne countray men / beinge men
of warre and sea robbers as they were.[40]

But despite hints of purely this-worldly interests, the
traditional elements in *The vocacyon* are much more
striking, and in fact the book lay squarely within the
tradition of hagiography which Bale had already exploited
for Protestant purposes.

In the preface to the work, Bale declared his
intentions quite plainly. The story of his year in Ireland, he
said, was meant to supply an example of the following
truths: that the duty of a Christian bishop is to preach the
Gospel, not to "loyter in blasphemouse papistrie"; that
continual persecution afflicts the bishop who lives up to his
duty; but that God may always be trusted to deliver the
faithful servant in the end.[41] And as an example of the
latter truth in particular, Bale intended the tale of his
misfortunes and his deliverance to comfort the persecuted
Protestants in Marian England.[42] The significance of Bale's
story, in other words, was extrinsic to the story itself—it
lay in the realm of theological and moral truth. Further-
more, Bale made clear that his individual life derived its
meaning from the way in which it fulfilled the type of the
few "faithful in each age." Like Bale, the Old Testament
prophets had been "first called / than afflicted / and
gracyously alwayes in the ende delyvered."[43] Christ Himself
had been sorely persecuted by the "clergie."[44] So had the
Apostles. But Bale felt that he had most clearly fulfilled
the type which St. Paul had embodied. For one thing, St.
Paul had supplied a scriptural precedent for "boasting"
(which was how the medieval friar in Bale evidently
regarded autobiography) in II Corinthians 11:16-33. For
another thing, Paul's experiences on his last journey to
Rome did on several points (the tempest, for instance)
seem to have parallelled Bale's adventures during his voyage
from Dublin to Flanders.[45] So in both its didactic concern

and in its typological thought patterns, *The vocacyon* stood clearly within the tradition of Protestant saints' lives which Bale had been developing.

It is interesting to note in passing that in *The vocacyon* Bale chose to identify with the external aspects of Paul's career—with his outward misfortunes—rather than with Paul's internal conversion experience on the Damascus road, that experience which would so fascinate seventeenth-century spiritual autobiographers.[46] There were several reasons for this. In the first place, Bale's conversion had occurred some two decades before the year which *The vocacyon* described, and that experience was not at issue in the pamphlet. Likewise, the causes of Bale's conversion had all been of an outward and objective nature: Henry VIII's breach with Rome, the patent weakness of the Carmelite order in the early 1530s, and the persuasion of Thomas, Lord Wentworth. If Bale went through any sort of inner spiritual crisis, he left no note of it in any of his writings. And indeed the *argumentum a silentio* is probably accurate in this one instance. For Bale the first-generation reformer was never affected by the Calvinist propensity to internalize spiritual struggle, to locate the forces of evil within the soul rather than outside it, in allegorical form.[47] So it is not really surprising that *The vocacyon* stands within the tradition of *res gestae*, particularly that genre which had emphasized the outward events of a saint's life, rather than within the tradition of spiritual autobiography in the pattern of St. Augustine's *Confessions*. Bale was a total extrovert. He thumped his enemies (verbally, to be sure), not his own breast.

Mention of Bale's polemical bent raises another point: one misses the full medieval flavor of *The vocacyon* if one considers merely its place within the saint's-life tradition. For Bale's purpose in writing the work was not merely to edify and console the faithful by offering them an example of God's ways with men. He was equally eager to blacken the reputation (or as Bale would have put it, reveal the depravity) of his enemies, the conservative clergy in

England and Ireland. Although hagiography (especially in the early Church) had sometimes served to defame the persecutors, from this point of view *The vocacyon* had its roots as much in the earthy literature of late medieval satire and complaint as it had in the saint's-life genre. G. R. Owst has pointed out how much the mordant attacks by late medieval preachers on clerical vice prefigured and influenced the scurrility of humanist and Protestant invective.[48] It is instructive to remember the ripe heritage of mendicant vituperation to which Bale the former Carmelite was heir. He was after all not merely a hagiographer, antiquary, dramatist, and historical thinker—in the very core of his being he was a preacher, too. And some of the passages in *The vocacyon* are quite consistent with what the good people of Doncaster, Thorndon, and Bishopstoke must have put up with (or delighted in, according to taste) when Bale was their preacher. At one point, for example, Bale lampooned the parish priest of St. Ives in Cornwall, with whom Bale and some unnamed gentleman had conversed of a Sunday evening:

> And the seyde Gentilman brought him into an other talke of
> olde familiaritees. Wherein he confessed / that he had in one
> daye / bygetten .ii. mennis wyves / of that parishe with childe /
> to encrease the churches profyght in crisyms and offeringes /
> where as their husbandes were not able to do it. Yea / marry
> sir James / sayth the Gentilman / & ye have done more
> miracles than that. Went ye not one daye a fishinge? sayth he.
> Yes by ye masse ded I /sayde the preste againe / and made the
> fyshes more holye than ever the whoresons were afore. For I
> sent out my maker amonge them / whome I had that daye
> recyved at the aulter. By the masse (quoth he) I was able to
> holde him no longar. Sens that daye / I am sure (quoth he) that
> our fyshars hath had better lucke / than ever thay had afore.[49]

This was burlesque—effective, because it was probably true—in a fine old tradition, stretching back into the fourteenth century and also forward, through the Marprelate tracts, into the age of the Civil War. The interesting point is that Bale saw the conservative clergy not merely (or even primarily) as his own enemies, but as the foes of God and the truth. They provided a foil for Bale's good example. Their importance, in other words, lay outside themselves; they were representatives of satanic types, just as they were agents of the devil in the sixth and final age of the world. Indeed, Bale repeated in *The vocacyon* the apocalyptic interpretation of English history which he had sketched out in *The Actes of Englysh votaryes*, just to make sure that the cosmic backdrop to his struggles was manifest.[50] So however individualized Bale's enemies appeared, their significance still lay in the pattern which they represented.

Despite all these traditional characteristics of *The vocacyon*, one is still confronted with the fact that the work was a fragment of autobiography. Bale cast himself as a Protestant saint, and he drew on his own experience for examples of good and evil. Now spiritual autobiography had been quite rare in the Middle Ages. In England perhaps *The Book of Margery Kempe* had come the closest, and even this work had been written by a third party. Similarly it had been uncommon for medieval preachers to draw on autobiographical material for their sermons.[51] In *The vocacyon* Bale actually began to shatter these conventions. The little book was hardly the story of his whole life, but it did demonstrate a concentration on the data of his personal experience which had been foreign to medieval hagiography and to mendicant preaching. What had encouraged Bale to write about himself?

For one thing, Bale had already written at least three brief sketches of his own life before he composed *The vocacyon*, and these may have made his excursion into autobiography more natural. Two of these were in manuscript surveys of Carmelite writers, and one in the *Summarium*.[52] Bale had had a two-fold purpose in preparing these painstaking surveys of English authors. First, he had wanted to demonstrate the glorious literary past, originally of the Carmelites and then later of England as a whole. But especially when he came to gather the

material which would form most of the *Summarium*, Bale
knew that he was racing against the effects of the whirl-
wind which was dispersing the English monastic libraries in
the later 1530s. So the preservation of information was his
second purpose. Bale realized that in the social upheaval of
his time, England's precious heritage of manuscripts might
be lost forever, so in haste and in desperation he wrote to
inform his countrymen what they had possessed, and what
they might never see again.[53] It was with this desire to
inform, to present a complete record of English literature,
that Bale had sketched his own life and listed his own
writings. Does one nevertheless detect a hint of simple
boasting in Bale's words? "Among the others I insert
myself—though I am the least of all—so that posterity may
know that I (like them) have not always been idle."[54] It is
hard to be sure. In any case, the pressing need to preserve
an account of English literature indicated to Bale that in
this context, his life and letters had an intrinsic significance. This was an interesting deviation from the
hagiographic tendency to subsume individuals under general
types; these autobiographical passages did supply precedent
for Bale's concentration on his own life in *The vocacyon*.

But still Bale reverted to the viewpoint *sub specie
aeternitatis* in *The vocacyon*, and the second reason for his
decision to use the autobiographical mode was probably the
stronger one. This was simply that Bale had seen how
successful Anne Askew's accounts of her examinations had
been. The literate and aggressive Protestant minority in
England needed this sort of first-hand testimony in its
struggle to convince the largely conservative nation and
Church that its new definition of the Christian life was
right. And precisely because the Protestant conception of
true sainthood was new, it was easier for the saint's own
personality to stand out—the conventional weight of
standard virtues and stock incidents was much less in force
here than in medieval hagiography. There was room for
innovation—in the case of *The vocacyon*, for experimenting
with autobiography. So as Bale recuperated in Wesel from

his nautical adventures and cast about for ammunition, what could have been more natural for him than to write his own testimony, his own account of what God had done for and through him? Given the empathy which he had felt during his first exile for St. John the Evangelist on the island of Patmos, that personal involvement which had fueled his study of Revelation, it is not at all surprising that Bale should now have included himself specifically in the company of the faithful in all ages.

The vocacyon of Johan Bale appeared in only one sixteenth-century edition, which was nevertheless enough to provoke an irate riposte from one of Queen Mary's literary defenders, James Cancellar, in 1556 or so. Cancellar's *The pathe of Obedience* attacked not only Bale's character and beliefs but also (as one might expect) his "boasting" and his self-identification with St. Paul.[55] Otherwise Marian England seems not to have noticed *The vocacyon*, nor was there evidently sufficient demand under Elizabeth for this sort of testimony to stimulate a further edition. Perhaps from Bale's point of view this would have been superfluous; the immediate need for consolatory tracts had passed, and there were after all many more striking heroes now, like Archbishop Cranmer, to fill the pages of a new English martyrology. Still *The vocacyon of Johan Bale*, along with the Oldcastle and Askew pamphlets, had at least marked out the way for Foxe's *Actes and Monuments*. The first edition of the "Book of Martyrs" appeared in 1563, the year in which Bale died.

VI / The Last Years

When Bale returned from exile in Basel during the summer of 1559, it was not to shoulder once more his episcopal duties at Kilkenny. Perhaps both Bale and his young queen agreed that sixty-three was too advanced an age for such a hardship post. In any case there was still some writing which Bale hoped to do—perhaps the final two parts of his *Actes of Englysh votaryes*. The desire for leisure may explain his acceptance of a canonry in Canterbury Cathedral, to which he was admitted on February 10, 1560.[1] The living—forty pounds a year, with a house thrown in[2]—was not bad by ordinary clerical standards, but a bit meager for one who had exercised a bishop's office, however briefly. Bale wrote, in fact, to Archbishop Parker in the summer of 1560 complaining of his "miserable state and poverty."[3] What made the problem really acute was that Bale could not afford to retrieve his library from Ireland which he needed before beginning to write in earnest. Though both Parker and the Privy Council made gestures toward helping Bale secure the library from the Sellenger family and others in Ireland who apparently had taken some of the books, the old man never saw much of his collection again.[4] Nevertheless he refused to let disappointment beat his spirit down. Even if he could not write his history, there were other ways in which Bale could strike a blow for the forces of truth. The surviving records at Canterbury make clear that even in old age, Bale was still in fighting trim. There is perhaps no monumental significance in the story of his strife at Canterbury against the tenacious forces of papistry, but glimpses of Bale's daily life are both rare and useful. A couple of incidents remind us that behind all Bale's historical and antiquarian scholarship there stood the Carmelite friar's need to preach.

It seems that in 1560 the town of Canterbury was controlled by a conservative group of men who were not in the least reconciled to any reversal of Queen Mary's attempt to rebuild Catholic England. One prominent member of this faction was the antiquary John Twyne, headmaster of the King's School, former mayor (in 1554) and now alderman of Canterbury. Another was John Okeden (or Ugden), also an alderman and a person of notoriously choleric disposition. Against this loose conservative group, there stood at least one alderman of Protestant sympathies, a man named George May. He was seconded by some of the cathedral preachers, but otherwise seems to have had few friends among the leading citizens of the town. Bale seems to have fallen in with May almost as soon as he arrived in Canterbury, and fallen out with the conservatives almost as quickly. On Friday, May 24, 1560, when Bale had been in the town scarcely three months, one of the traditionalists—Robert Okeden, son of the alderman—flew into a rage at some of Bale's activities and apparently uttered slanderous words about the old man. One may regret Okeden's lack of Christian charity, but be grateful that he did stimulate a written account of the tiff which survives in the diocesan consistory court's record of depositions.

Apparently that Friday afternoon several men were standing around the shop of Hugh Johns, a tailor, inside the cathedral close. Besides Johns there seem to have been four other young men passing the time—a servant of Johns's named John Poole, another young tailor named Philip Hall, and two passers-by, Robert Okeden and Robert Barnes.

Sometime in the afternoon Hall's former master, Hugh Pilkington, came by the shop and asked Hall if he were interested in doing some work.

"Yea," Hall replied, "have you cut any work?"

"No," said Pilkington, "I will by and by cut out a friar's garment on which you shall work." This sounded a little strange, since obviously there were no friars left in England. But Hall apparently shrugged it off.

"Well," he said, "I am clear."

At this point, however, Robert Okeden broke in. He obviously smelled something fishy in this business. "Countryman," he said to Hall, "make it not. If thou make a friar's coat thou shalt be my countryman no longer."

Hall was not going to miss some extra pocket money for nothing. "What will you give me, then?" he asked Okeden.

"I will give you twopence." At this point Pilkington evidently objected to Okeden's interference. The two of them fell to arguing, and Okeden (according to the witnesses) called Pilkington "knave" several times. After a while the former cooled down a bit, and his curiosity about the friar's robe grew. "Wherefore shall this friar's garment be made?" he inquired.

"Mr. Bale setteth forth a play wherein there's a priest," Pilkington responded. "It shall be played in Mr. May's house."

At this (so the bystanders said) Okeden smiled, no doubt a bit ironically. "Now Mr. Bale can preach no more, he setteth forth plays," he said, rather perceptively. Then his thoughts turned to the forthcoming performance in Alderman May's home. "How say thou, will they take any money? I will be there." But at the idea his blood pressure rose, and he exploded, "Nay, by God's blood, I will not come there—I will go to Romney where there is a good play! Mr. Bale doth well to occupy himself with such trumpery, and speaking against friars, yet the knave was a friar himself and knew their knavery well enough." Strange words from a defender of the traditional piety. Okeden was getting confused. Pilkington in any case chose to respond mildly.

"I knew not him to be such a man," he said.

"Yes, by God's blood," Okeden stormed, "he is as the rest are, knaves all the many of them."

Young Barnes by this time was not sure where Okeden stood vis-à-vis the old religion. "All priests be not knaves," he broke in.

"I do not mean priests, I mean ministers," Okeden answered, not clarifying the discussion particularly. He went on to reiterate that Bale was indeed a "railing knave" and a drunken one, too—at least according to the testimony of Pilkington, who did lack a certain spirit of objectivity. Poole and Barnes for their part later claimed in court that they had forgotten what Okeden had said about Bale. In Barnes's case this lapse of memory may have been encouraged by the father of the accused, John Okeden, and his fellow alderman George Bingham who had got hold of Barnes over the weekend and grilled him on what he meant to say in court. Philip Hall, the other witness, said he had conveniently left the scene of the quarrel early and had gone across the way "to see legs of sliver made for a game" (perhaps he meant cricket stumps). The consistory court took up the case on Monday, May 27, and evidently felt that the evidence against Okeden was inconclusive. Nothing in the court's act book shows that Bale succeeded in making the slander charge stick, this time at least.[5]

The incident is interesting because it points up not only Bale's irascible vigor in his old age (clearly he was a threat, or Okeden would not have felt so strongly) but also his urgent need to preach. Since Bale's duties as a canon of the cathedral did not include preaching, he had to pour his energy into other channels, of which the production of plays was one. Bale was not simply an antiquarian (despite his abilities in that direction) but in his heart a former friar turned "godly preacher."[6] The play in question may well have been *King Johan*, for Bale revised his earlier draft about this time,[7] and the friar's robe would have served for the character Dissimulation, who represented the mendicant orders. But other plays of Bale's called for a similar garment—*A Comedy concernynge thre lawes,*[8] for instance, which was reprinted in 1562—so one cannot really tell which of Bale's verse-plays he had chosen on this occasion for edifying the citizens of Canterbury.

In any case, Bale's dramatic activity continued to annoy the conservative group, for soon he was the object of slanderous words once more. This time it was the father of Robert Okeden, John Okeden the alderman, but now Bale succeeded in proving his charge. One Friday evening in early October 1560, Bale's son John (who must have been in his twenties by this time) was sitting and drinking in the parlor of John Twyne. This Twyne was a man of substance and influence in Canterbury, as he was master of the King's School there and had served as mayor of the city in the 1550s. He was also a distinguished antiquarian, which may explain how the younger Bale happened to be acquainted with him. On the other hand, Twyne was a religious conservative and a friend of the Okedens. That Friday evening he was entertaining not only young John Bale but also Thomas Pawlyn, the usher at the King's School, and a fletcher named John Richardson. As they sat and talked, in burst John Okeden. He and Twyne evidently talked about one thing and another, and then Okeden said vehemently that he hoped to see the crucifix set up in the cathedral again within the next month. Twyne was obviously a more cautious man than his friend, and for the sake of appearances he gently chided Okeden for meddling in matters of royal policy. Richardson the fletcher was more forthright in his disapproval. "No," he said, "I trust God never to see that day."

Okeden rounded upon him at once. "Thou art damned into hell as black as my cap!" he cried. At this point Twyne the host interposed, and drew Richardson and Pawlyn over to the far side of the room to play backgammon. This left Okeden alone with young Bale—a volatile combination. Okeden, his temper still up, began to rail at his enemy's son.

"By God's soul," he exclaimed, "every man saith thy father is an heretic and an Anabaptist, and thou art not his son. Mr. Bale is a tall man, and thou art but a little light knave. Some friar leapt in when he was away and begat thee." All this was accompanied by oath upon oath according to Richardson the fletcher. Okeden continued, "If thy father will come home to my house, I will lodge him and make him good cheer and will confute him with four words." Pawlyn the usher had his doubts as to whether even Okeden could make any headway with the elder Bale.

"No, Mr. Okeden," he countered, "he will then convict you."

"Nay, by God's blood," the alderman cried, "I will rather cut his throat!" And so on, apparently, in this vein. How the evening finally ended does not appear in the records. The next day, young Bale came and complained to Twyne that Okeden had called his father an Anabaptist heretic, and a day or two later the offending alderman (apparently unrepentant) assured Twyne that he had indeed used those very words. So it was a pretty open and shut case.[9] Bale the elder initiated a suit in the archbishop's consistory court on October 30. The case dragged on for eight months—which was actually not bad, given contemporary standards of judicial expedition, and also (perhaps) considering the local influence of the defendant. The verdict came through in Bale's favor on June 17, 1561, though whether this pacified relations between Bale and the conservatives is not at all clear.[10]

So this was the environment in which Bale spent the last four years of his life: scarcely a Sabbath rest from his labors. Though his scholarly activity was necessarily inhibited by the loss of his library in Ireland, the historical dramatist and activist reformer in him found expression up to the very end. Bale was just ten days short of his sixty-eighth birthday when he died on November 15, 1563.[11] The dean and chapter of Canterbury paid homage to the old warrior by ordering his burial in the nave of the cathedral. And six years later his widow Dorthy, still living in the town, was receiving an annuity of £6.13s.4d. out of the cathedral's alms money, by order of the queen.[12] Bale's friends and allies seem to have been as loyal to his memory as his enemies were savage; and Elizabeth apparently found it in her heart somewhat to overlook the embarassing zeal with which Bale had pressed reform upon her nation. Yet as usual the reward was slender as compared to Bale's efforts and his real achievements.

Bale's plays and his propaganda tracts neither provoked imitators nor had much long-term effect on English thought, which was no doubt a blessing in the case of his riper tracts. But his antiquarian spade-work and his vision of English history were important and influential, as many have recognized. Together with his friend John Leland, Bale founded the modern tradition of British antiquarian studies.[13] In the *Summarium* and the *Catalogus* he had shown how the study of early British history (however wrong he had much of it) could serve the cause of the Reformation in England. Archbishop Parker and his scholars had their task defined by what Bale had done. And of course they found Bale's actual data indispensable as well. Bale's letter to Parker of July 1560—written in the absence of most of his erstwhile library—showed what a vast mine of information he possessed, partly in his memory and partly in his notes.[14] He was simply the most learned man in England in his own particular field of study.

It was as a source of data that Bale also influenced the monumental Lutheran history of the Church, Matthias Flacius Illyricus' *Magdeburg Centuries*. During the course of the 1550s Bale had received several letters from Flacius and his collaborators Alexander Alesius and Johannes Wigandus, asking for books and any other cooperation he could offer.[15] And Bale was in Basel in 1556, working closely with the printer Oporinus, when the latter issued Flacius' *Catalogus Testium Veritatis* and *Varia Doctorum Piorumque Virorum de Corrupto Ecclesiae Statu*. Bale in fact told Archbishop Parker that these two books had been "set fourthe by me and Illyricus."[16] He was boasting a bit there, it would seem; the two works embody none of Bale's historical ideas, though they do contain bits of information he had collected. The same is true of the *Centuries* themselves. Flacius cited Bale frequently (especially his *Acta Romanorum Pontificum*)[17] throughout the great work, but the structure and the periodization which he employed owed nothing to the Englishman. Where Bale looked to the Book of Revelation for his pattern, Flacius merely divided the past into hundred-year segments. Though Flacius naturally did refer to the Apocalypse, identifying the Antichrist-papacy with various of the monsters described there,[18] the Book of Revelation simply did not undergird his historical imagination in the way it did Bale's. Likewise, though Flacius (like Bale) did stress, for example, the pontificate of Boniface III as a crucial moment in the decline of the institutional Church, this was traditional Lutheran teaching and one need not suppose that Flacius needed Bale to convince him on that point. So what Bale gave Flacius seems to have been information rather than interpretation.[19] Bale's vision of history appropriately found its most able and eloquent exponent in his own native land, rather than on the Continent.

The crucial influence of Bale on John Foxe has been widely recognized,[20] though in some respects it is easier to infer than to prove. It is clear that the two men became very good friends when they met in the Duchess of Richmond's household in 1548. Thus when one sees Foxe studying Wyclif and the Lollards in *Commentarii Rerum in Ecclesia Gestarum* (published at Strasbourg in 1554) one assumes that Bale and not the earlier Tyndale circle had awakened him to this interest. Likewise, when one notes Foxe's emphasis on the thousand years of Satan's bondage, and his use of the dramatic medium in *Christus Triumphans* (Basel, 1556), one presupposes Bale's influence and not that of Thomas Kirchmeyer's *Pammachius*, for instance. This is not to quibble with previous scholarship, but merely to note the absence of any clear acknowledgement by Foxe of his early debts to his older friend. With the first edition of *Actes and Monuments* (1563), to be sure, the impact of Balian ideas on Foxe's thought is quite apparent. Foxe assumes the authority of the Apocalypse as the key par excellence to Church history (though he looks to the Book of Daniel, too).[21] He labors to paint in vivid colors Protestant saints who are specifically English, taking for granted that the English have a special part in God's plan. He incorporates the documents that Bale published regarding Sir John Oldcastle and Mistress Anne Askew—and indeed adopts from Bale the technique of publishing at full length the documents or *acta* of the new Protestant saints.[22] For all of this, Foxe was indebted to his older colleague more than to any other. Yet there were also differences in the two men's personalities and in their deepest concerns, and these led to differences between the ways each man interpreted the Apocalypse and used it to supply a framework for Church history. The influence of Bale on Foxe has been so often stressed that the divergence between them, on certain points, is worth dwelling on for a moment.

Foxe felt an abhorrence toward bloodshed—even the slaughter of animals—and this made him peculiarly sensitive on the subject of persecution. He urgently (if unsuccessfully) opposed the execution of heretics, and felt strongly that a persecuting church could not be a true church.[23] This anguished sympathy for the oppressed—perhaps one of the primary motives behind his labor in compiling the *Actes and Monuments*—induced Foxe to wrestle with certain verses in the Book of Revelation which Bale had passed over cursorily. In the twelfth and thirteenth chapters, St. John had spoken of certain periods of time (1260 days and 42 months) which represented exile and persecution. Bale had taken these to mean merely the tribulations of the true Church in every age.[24] Foxe was not content with this general application, however. At some point between 1563 and the appearance of his second edition of the *Actes and Monuments* in 1570, he concluded that the 42 months in Revelation 13:5 must mean 42 weeks of years, or the 294 years during which the early Church had suffered persecution. Counting forward from 30 A.D. this pointed to 324 A.D. as the end of the first age in which the beast had raged unchecked. And so Foxe concluded that the thousand years of Satan's subsequent bondage must have begun in 324, not at the Ascension as (following Bale) he had held in the 1563 edition. This computation, together with Foxe's innate horror of persecution, further led him to believe that the essential characteristic of the millennium had been an absence of open oppression by the forces of Satan against the godly.[25] Foxe thought, in other words, in terms of an outward security for the elect. This was quite at variance from Bale's definition of the thousand years as the period during which Satan had been unable to sit in men's consciences as God or to impose tyrannic and legalistic restrictions such as clerical celibacy upon them—which had happened, in fact, after Sylvester II loosed Satan from the pit in 1000 A.D.[26] Bale had had in mind an inner freedom, a Lutheran "liberty of the Christian man," as the outstanding feature of the millennium. This dissimilarity between the two men's understanding of the millennium was altogether comprehensible in terms of their different personalities and past experiences—Foxe the sensitive and irenic advocate of toleration, Bale the liberated (and married) ex-friar. It is important to note, though, Foxe's independence of mind here vis-à-vis the pattern of history which Bale had bequeathed to him.

This contrast between the two men's points of view had other consequences in the 1570 edition of *Actes and Monuments* as well. It became clear in this edition that Foxe thought a good deal more of the post-Constantinian Church than Bale had—that he believed in the validity of the Roman Church, as the "true" Church, down almost through the eleventh century. True, in the 1563 edition Foxe had already said something of the sort—that the Roman Church reached its "middle age" in the ninth or tenth century and began to decay in spiritual strength. But in the edition of 1570, Foxe explicitly declared that although the institutional Church had been declining somewhat since the seventh century, down to the time of Pope Gregory VII it was the true Church of Christ.[27]

Bale's view of the post-Constantinian Church, it will be recalled, was considerably more jaundiced. In *Acta Romanorum Pontificum* he had argued forcefully for the purity of the ante-Nicene Church, but had gone on to assert that from Sylvester I through the early seventh century, the popes had been "mitred pontiffs, preparing a seat for the great Antichrist with their canons and decretals."[28] And of course after Phocas and Boniface III, the devil had wholly infiltrated the institutional Church, lacking only the power to oppress the consciences of the faithful (which power became available with the loosing of Satan in 1000). So Foxe and Bale disagreed markedly over the significance of Constantine's reign. Both, it should be noted, approved highly of Constantine the man and looked upon him as a prototype of the godly Christian ruler.[29] But Bale thought that the actual *results* of his reign had been evil—agreeing on this point with the Lollards and radical reformers of his own time, as well as with later Elizabethan and Jacobean commentators on the Apocalypse like John Napier and Thomas Brightman.[30] Foxe's divergence from Bale in this matter arose partly from his particular interpretation of the millennium, and partly from the different circumstances under which he was writing. If the foremost characteristic of the thousand years had been the outward peace of the Church, then of course Constantine's reign would seem the dawning of a bright new era, and Foxe would naturally minimize the immediate theological and moral deviations from apostolic Christianity which Bale (with evangelical doctrine as his yardstick) had stressed. And likewise, Foxe was writing under Queen Elizabeth when he could argue credibly that a godly English Church had followed naturally upon the accession of a godly ruler—predisposing him to feel similarly about

Constantine's reign. For Foxe, in other words, the supreme headship and biblical Christianity wend hand in hand.

Bale, writing under Henry, Edward, and Mary, had not been so sure. In *The Image of bothe churches,* for instance, Bale had diligently upheld Henry's God-given authority over the kingdom, but had denied that anyone but Satan was head of an English Church which in the mid-1540s was still filthy with the dregs of Rome.[31] Henry's formal headship of the Church, in other words, had not automatically meant its purification. Admittedly this *cri de coeur* was an extreme statement, and on other occasions Bale did feel more positive and optimistic about Henry as a new Jehoshaphat, and Edward the new Josiah.[32] But still he was troubled by the fundamental ambiguity over authority in the English Church—the nagging tension between what the Bible seemed to say and what the prince often directed—in a way that Foxe was not. This too conditioned their disagreement about the reign of Constantine and about the Church in the centuries immediately following.

But one should not overemphasize the divergences between Bale and Foxe, nor deny the way in which Bale's reinterpretation of English history found its fulfillment in the *Actes and Monuments.* Bale's recasting of the medieval saint's-life genre in Protestant form, his stress on the need to rewrite English history in the light of the Reformation, his sense of a peculiar mission for England in the Last Days—all this certainly underlay Foxe's achievement. And perhaps more than anything else, Bale gave to Foxe and to the English consciousness in the sixteenth and seventeenth centuries that belief in the Book of Revelation as the key par excellence for understanding the past, the present, and the future. In *The Image of bothe churches* Bale showed that the Book of Revelation was "safe," that it need not render the explosive conclusions which the Muensterite Anabaptists had drawn from it. By pulling the chiliastic sting from Francis Lambert's interpretation, by placing the millennium firmly in the past, Bale appealed both to the

English magisterial reformers' preoccupation with order and their need nevertheless for some new understanding of England's historical relationship with the Roman Church—indeed, some grasp of England's role in history as a whole. Not until the next century, with the work of Thomas Brightman and Joseph Mead, was Bale's post-millennial interpretation seriously challenged.[33] But those were different times. If the Antichrist loomed large in the consciousness of sixteenth-century Englishmen,[34] and if speculation about the correlation between prophecy and history became a pastime which tempted many of them, Bale may be held responsible as the man who introduced to the English Protestant mind the Book of Revelation as the key to history.

Appendix I

The Dating of Bale's Manuscripts

The dating of Bale's manuscripts rests upon a consideration of both their form (in particular, the handwriting) and their content. With regard to the former, W. T. Davies has produced a lucid study of Bale's changing hand, which evolved gradually from a formal and scribal style in his early Cambridge years to a small and very cursive script in his later years.[1] Davies suggests five stages in the evolution of Bale's hand: (1) a very vertical, scribal hand—probably the style which Bale taught the younger friars at the convent in Cambridge— which Bale maintained through the early 1520s; (2) a more rounded, slightly more cursive hand which Bale used during the same period for personal notes and less formal writing; (3) a slightly more fluent style, beginning about 1523, in which the "r" dropped below the line, but which remained largely formal; (4) a graceful, cursive script with a distinct rightward-leaning tendency, which Bale used for all his writing from the late 1520s into the early 1540s, and (5) the same script with a continental ticked "u" which Bale adopted sometime after his flight into exile in 1540. The significance of these changes will appear in the discussion of the manuscripts below. From a study of Bale's handwriting, and from consideration of internal evidence, Davies offered a tentative chronology of Bale's manuscripts.[2] Honor McCusker, in her study of Bale, also included a chapter dealing with the dating of Bale's manuscripts,[3] which is slightly less trustworthy than Davies's handling of the subject. The following discussion rests largely on Davies's work, with a few corrections where appropriate. In the interests of mitigating tedium, only those manuscripts mentioned in the preceding chapters of this book are treated below. These do, however, include all the significant manuscripts.

1. *Cambridge University Library MS. Ff.6.28.* A collection of saints' lives and Carmelite offices which Bale compiled while a student at Cambridge. Written in hands (1) and (2). This MS.

must date from between 1514 and 1523, approximately the date at which hand (3) evolved.

2. *Bodleian Library MS. Selden supra 72.* Four loosely-bound signatures, containing what are probably scribal exercises which Bale set for young friars at Cambridge. Neither Davies nor McCusker discusses this MS. In places it looks as though Bale had written the first few lines of an exercise at the top of the page, and then turned it over to a pupil to be finished. See for example fol. 5, where one finds in Bale's hand "*Incipit cronica parva sive exordium sacrae ordinis Carmelitarum Beate Marie Virginis quem edidit quidam eiusdem religionis professor . . .*" after which the student took over. Bale must have retained these exercises in his possession, for in handwriting (3) he later identified the *quidam eiusdem religionis professor* as Robert Bale, fifteenth-century prior of Burnham (and no relation). On fols. 12-19 is found a work which appears to be Bale's own: a catalogue of Carmelite priors general, which begins "*Hic incipit Brevis Cathalogus priorum generalium ordinis carmelitarum a sancto Bertholdo primo usque ad Bernardinum de Senis priorem generalem modernum compositus per fratrem Johannem Baleum carmelitam minimum.*" Some unknown person at a later date crossed out "*fratrem Johannem Baleum*"; it would be hard to say why. This portion of the MS. must date from before 1523, since Bernard de Senis (spoken of as alive) died in that year. The MS. also contains three tracts by Walter of Coventry, O. Carm., in a student's hand with corrections by Bale.

3. *Bodleian Library MS. Bodley 73.* Notes on Carmelite authors and Carmelite history made by Bale in England and the Low Countries, and a selection of saints' lives. McCusker stated that the latest date in the MS. was 1533,[4] and implies that the MS. as a whole was completed shortly thereafter. Davies, however, correctly observes that the last five dates in the list to which McCusker referred were written in Bale's hand (3), whereas the earlier dates (and most of the rest of the MS.) are in hand (2). So Davies believed that most of the MS. dates from 1520-1529, with a few additions through 1533.[5] There is no reason, however, to place the *terminus ad quem* for the bulk of the MS. any later than 1527, since there are no traces in it of the research Bale began in France during that year. Bale probably

concluded *MS. Bodley 73* before he left, then, and started a new notebook (*British Museum MS. Harley 1819*) specifically for that trip. *MS. Bodley 73*, then, represents part of Bale's research notes during the years 1522/3-1527, most of which he spent away from Cambridge.

4. *British Museum MS. Harley 1819*. McCusker described this MS. adequately,[6] though she erred in believing that the latest date it contained was August 1527. For on fol. 183 Bale wrote "*telos huius in die sebastiani 1527*," i.e., January 20, 1528 (new style). The MS. throughout is in Bale's hand (3). One further note on the dating of this MS. is useful. On fol. 50-verso Bale (writing at Avignon) recorded the death of Johannes Diophilax, O. Carm., at Lyon the previous June 18. It sounds as though Bale had come to know the young friar when passing through Lyon earlier in the year, and heard about his death later on. If Bale had passed through Lyon before June 18, he must have left England for his research in France in the early part of 1527. So *MS. Harley 1819* represents essentially the notes Bale took in 1527. Curiously, Davies merely assigns the MS. to the years "c. 1520-1529."[7]

5. *Bodleian Library MS. Selden supra 41*. This is a difficult MS. to date, for it is made up of at least five distinct notebooks, later bound together. McCusker quotes the Bodleian Library *Summary Catalogue* to the effect that the volume "was probably written in 1540."[8] This is clearly incorrect, however, for sections of the MS. are in Bale's (1) hand, pre-1523 or so. Davies more properly dates various portions of the volume between 1512 and 1540, but with no discussion of his reasons for doing so.[9] In the interests of precision, and because this MS. supplies important information about Bale's intellectual development, it is useful to examine the MS. section by section and try to establish a date for each. Each of the major sections below (indicated by capital letters) represents a separate notebook, insofar as these can be distinguished.

(A) *Fols. 1-17*: notes and an index to various works of Arnold Bostius, O. Carm. These are in Bale's (5) handwriting, after 1543 or so. Bale evidently had a few blank leaves in this notebook, and filled them in at a relatively late date.

Fols. 18-39: this section begins in Bale's (2) hand, and

contains extracts from the poems and letters of various Carmelite authors, including the Italian humanist Baptista Mantuanus. The handwriting would place this section before 1523 or so.

Fols. 39-73: the "r" begins to dip beneath the line on fol. 39, and the handwriting evolves into Bale's (3) style. The subject matter continues as on the previous leaves, ending with various short poems or *disticha* by Bale himself on fol. 73. Davies gives "c. 1512-c. 1533" as a date for this section, but judging from the transitional nature of the handwriting, "1523-1524" would not be far wrong.

(B)   *Fols. 75-87*: a new notebook, again beginning in the (2) hand, before 1523 or so. The notebook contains tracts by two Carmelites (Johannes Oudewater and John Cartwright) on the history and privileges of the order. In the midst of the Cartwright tract, on fol. 88, the "r" dips below the line and the style becomes Bale's (3) hand.

Fols. 88-106: Cartwright's tract is concluded, and Bale continues with a dialogue by Johannes von Hildesheim, O. Carm., on the privileges of the order. Davies does not suggest a date for this notebook as a whole (fols. 75-106). Bale probably copied this material in about 1523-1524, judging from the transitional quality of the hand.

(C)   *Fols. 107-193*: again a new notebook. This is the biographical history of the Carmelite Order which Bale later referred to as his *Fasciculus Carmelitarum* (see for example *British Museum MS. Harley 3838*, fol. 112). He made entries in the notebook at different times, as he acquired information. The slope of the handwriting—generally Bale's (3) style—is not consistent, and the inks vary from entry to entry. Up through the middle of fol. 193, the latest date given is 1532 (fol. 192-verso), except for four later additions in Bale's (4) hand (fols. 160-161, 190, 191-verso, and 192). Davies correctly dates this section "c. 1527-1533, with additions up to c. 1540."[10]

Fols. 193-195: beginning with Bale's notes on George Browne (one of those who administered the Oath of Supremacy to the mendicant orders) the handwriting is consistently style (4) and continues thus to the end of the notebook. The entries in this hand are stridently Protestant in tone, contrasting sharply with the spirit of

Carmelite piety pervading the earlier leaves of the book. It seems likely therefore that Bale finished the catalogue up to the top of fol. 193 in (or before) 1532, and that he later came back to the MS. after his conversion, to make additions concerning the breach with Rome and the eventual dissolution of the English Carmelite order.

(D)　*Fols. 197-220*: a new notebook, containing the lives of various Carmelite saints. The handwriting is style (2). Davies correctly assigns this section to "c. 1512-c. 1522."

(E)　*Fols. 221-366*: the first section of the final notebook. For the most part, this is made up of transcriptions from the work of Arnold Bostius, O. Carm. The script is Bale's (3) hand, much like the style of *British Museum MS. Harley 1819* (the notes from Bale's journey in France during 1527). So the section dates from between 1523 (the year his "third" hand evolved) and 1533, when Bale's interests began to turn more and more away from the Carmelite order. Neither McCusker nor Davies dates this section.

Fols. 366-395: the notebook concludes with various catalogues of Carmelite priors-general, drawn up both by Bale and by his friend John Barret; a catalogue of Carmelites who took the D.D. at Paris, by Barret, and a series of poems on famous Carmelites by Laurentius Burellus, O. Carm. All of this is in Bale's (3) hand. The latest date mentioned in 1526, in Barret's list of Parisian doctors; so the section probably dates from c. 1526-1533. Neither Davies nor McCusker mentions this part of the notebook.

6.　*British Museum MS. Harley 3838.* Perhaps the most important of all Bale's MSS., and as difficult to date precisely as *Bodleian MS. Selden supra 41. MS. Harley 3838* is composed of three distinct notebooks (distinguished by capital letters below).

(A)　*Fols. 3-112*: this is one of two copies of the (thus far unpublished) MS. of *Anglorum Heliades,* Bale's full-dress history of the Carmelite order in England, written in 1536 and dedicated to the antiquary John Leland. Unlike the rest of the MS. codex, fols. 3-112 are written in a scribal hand, not Bale's—though Bale corrected the MS. in places and added the *incipits* to a list of his plays (fol. 112). The history is divided into two parts: first a chronological sketch of the order's development in

England to the 1530s, and then a series of biographical entries on various English Carmelite writers. Although in his conclusion Bale asserted that he had written *Anglorum Heliades* in two months during 1536—and though the dedicatory letter to Leland was dated 1536, too—the MS. nevertheless bears several later dates. Bale's treatment of John Byrd, last Carmelite prior provincial, ends (for example) with the words, *"Fit Byrdus presul, Fitque Ordo Monasticus exul, Anno Domini 1538"* (fol. 43-verso). The biographical sketch of Byrd also contains references to his career after 1536 as well (fol. 110-verso). Likewise, in Bale's own autobiographical entry (fols. 111-verso to 112-verso), he referred to his rupture with the Carmelite order as though it were a *fait accompli,* whereas nothing in the chronological history of the order (fols. 3-43) suggests that Bale had already renounced his vows at the time he was writing. Finally, in a list of his plays which Bale appended to his autobiographical vignette, Bale included two plays (*thre laws* and *Kynge Johan*) which he did not write until 1538. Davies concludes that Bale wrote most of *Anglorum Heliades* in 1536; that he wrote his autobiography and drew up the list of plays and other works in the autumn of 1538 (since the list does include *thre lawes* and *Kynge Johan,* but not *the chefe promyses of God, the temptacyon of our lorde,* and *Iohan Baptystes Preachynge* which Bale also wrote in 1538); and that he revised the sections on Byrd in 1539 or 1540. At that point, says Davies, Bale gave the revised MS. to a scribe to have it recopied.[11] This is probably correct, though the list of plays may date from 1539 or 1540 as well—Bale was not always concerned about listing *all* his plays (see, e.g., *Bodleian Library MS. Selden supra 41,* fol. 195, where he names only seven) and the absence of certain titles is not a sure indication of the date when the list was compiled. McCusker agrees on 1539-1540 as the date of the scribal copy of fols. 3-112.

(B)   *Fols. 118-155*: a biographical history of the mythical, pre-twelfth century Carmelite order entitled *Perpaucorum carmeli scriptorum ab helia thesbite ad bertholdum primum eorum magistrum generalem, Cathalogus.* Davies feels that this was compiled in 1533, and McCusker implies that it was done thereabouts;[12] but the bitter invective against clerical celibacy and against religious vows in general which this tract contains (viz. fol. 118, right at the beginning) would argue for a later date— certainly after 1536, when Bale left the Carmelite order. The handwriting is all in Bale's (4) style. A reasonable guess at the date would be 1537-1539.

(C) *Fols. 156-249*: a history, similar to the one just above, covering the writers and theologians of the Carmelite order from the twelfth century to the 1530s. Bale called this *De Preclaris Ordinis Carmeli Scriptoribus ac Theologis Cathalogus*. The script is also Bale's (4) hand. Davies dates this 1533, but McCusker feels that Bale wrote this *after* he had done the companion-piece on the earlier order.[13] Davies is probably more nearly right, for this tract shows none of the anti-monastic fury which Bale vented in the history of the order before Bertholdus. Late 1520s or early 1530s is probably as close as one can come to dating this work.

7. *Public Record Office SP 1/111, fols. 183-187.* "The answer of John Bale pryst unto serten artycles uniustlye gadred upon hys prechyng" by the good folk of Thorndon, Suffolk. All in Bale's (4) hand. Obviously a product of Bale's arrest and incarceration in the porter's ward at Greenwich, this document must have followed on the complaints laid against him in January 1537 (see the letter of Sir Humphrey Wingfield to the Duke of Suffolk, January 8, 1537: *PRO SP 1/114*, fol. 54). Late January or early February 1537 would thus be the most likely date.

8. *Bodleian Library MS. Selden supra 64.* A notebook of information on early English authors, arranged alphabetically. This was published in 1902 by R. L. Poole and Mary Bateson as *Index Britannie Scriptorum*. The editors felt that Bale had probably begun the notebook in 1549 or 1550 and finished it at the end of 1557 or thereafter. Davies and McCusker both concur, and the dating seems reasonable.[14] The handwriting is Bale's (5) style.

9. *Trinity College. Cambridge MS. R.7.15.* A transcript by Bale of John Leland's *De Viris Illustribus*. Bale styled himself *"ossoriensi apud hibernos episcopo"* on the title page (fol. 1),

so the MS. must date from the period after the autumn of 1552, when Edward VI inflicted Bale on the diocese of Ossory, or vice versa. It would appear from the fly-leaves of the MS. that the *terminus ad quem* for its dating would be 1557, when Bale published his *Catalogus* of English authors at Basel. On fols. i-verso through iv-recto, Bale made many notes on the history of the papacy, which he later interpolated into the *Catalogus* (and published separately as *Acta Romanorum Pontificum*), and it looks as though he used these leaves for jottings as he organized his thoughts. So one would palce the MS. between 1552 (autumn) and 1557. The handwriting is Bale's (5) throughout.

10.   *British Museum MS. Cotton Titus D.X. fols. 101-194.* The latter half of a codex (unrelated to the first half) containing notes and jottings Bale made on books he read. The hand is (5) throughout. Davies dates the notebook "1549?-1557" but (as McCusker points out) the MS. contains the transcription of a letter to Bale dated November 1559.[15] Bale might have begun the notebook at any time after his return to England in 1548 or 1549, when he began doing research in English libraries again; and—as is clear—he was still adding things at the end of 1559. One might say 1548-1560 to be on the safe side.

Appendix II

Sixteenth-Century Editions of Bale's Works

The following is drawn principally from the soon-to-appear revised edition of the *Short-Title Catalogue* (STC) being prepared under the direction of Katharine Pantzer at Houghton Library, Harvard University; and from W. T. Davies, "A Bibliography of John Bale," *Oxford Bibliographical Society, Proceedings and Papers*, vol. 5, part 4 (1940), pp. 247-279 (cited below as "Davies").

1536

A Compendious letter which Ihon Pomerane sent to Englande. Southwark: J. Nicholson? Possibly translated by Bale (STC 4021; not listed in Davies). See Bale, *Summarium*, fol. 244: ". . . *Epistola Ioannis Pomerani ad anglos. . . .*"

1543

A Christen Exhortacyon unto Customable Swearers. Antwerp: widow of C. van Endhoven. (STC 1280; not listed in Davies). Possibly published the preceding year.

A dysclosynge or openynge of the Manne of synne. Antwerp: A. Goinus. (STC 1309, Davies #1).

1544

The epistle exhortatorye of an Englyshe Chrystyane. Antwerp: widow of C. van Endhoven. (STC 1291; not listed in Davies). Probably the work of Bale and William Turner in collaboration.

_____ . Antwerp: A. Goinus. (STC 1291a, Davies #2-i).

_____ . Antwerp: A. Goinus. (STC 1291a.5, Davies #2-ii).

A brefe Chronycle concernynge the Examinacyon and death of the blessed martyr of Christ syr Johan Oldecastell. Antwerp: A Goinus. (STC 1276, Davies #3-i).

1545

The Image of bothe churches. Antwerp?: S. Mierdman. (STC

1296.5, Davies #18-iii; only parts 1 and 2 have survived, but obviously part 3 appeared about the same time, as all three parts were banned by Bishop Bonner of London in September 1546: see Guildhall, London, MS. 9531/12, fol. 92-verso).

A Mysterye of inyquyte. "Geneva: Mychael Woode," i.e., Antwerp: A. Goinus. (STC 1303, Davies #4).

1546

The Actes of Englysh votaryes. Antwerp: S. Mierdman. (STC 1270, Davies #5-i).

The first examinacyon of Anne Askewe. Wesel: D. van der Straten. (STC 848, Davies #9-i).

Rhithmi Vetustissimi de Corrupto Ecclesiae Statu. Wesel: D. van der Straten. (No STC number; Davies #6). Translated by Bale.

The true hystorie of the Christen departynge of the reverende man, D. Martyne Luther. Wesel: D. van der Straten. (STC 14717, Davies #8). Translated by Bale.

1547

A brefe Comedy or enterlude concernynge the temptacyon of our lorde. Wesel: D. van der Straten. (STC 1279, Davies #13-i).

The lattre examinacyon of Anne Askewe. Wesel: D. van der Straten. (STC 850, Davies #10-i).

The first examinacyon of Anne Askewe; The lattre examinacyon of Anne Askewe. London: N. Hill or T. Raynalde. (STC 851, Davies #9-ii and #10-ii).

A Tragedye or enterlude manyfestyng the chefe promyses of God. Wesel: D. van der Straten. (STC 1305, Davies #11-i).

1548

The Actes of Englysh votaryes. London: T. Raynalde. (STC 1271, Davies #5-ii).

An answere to a papystycall exhortacyon. Antwerp?: S. Mierdman. (STC 1274a, Davies #17-i).

A brefe Chronycle concernynge the Examinacyon and death of the blessed martyr of Christ syr Johan Oldecastell. London: A. Scoloker and W. Seres. (STC 1278, Davies #3-iii).

A Christen Exhortacyon unto Customable Swearers. London: W. Hill. (STC 1280.5; not listed in Davies).

A Comedy concernynge thre lawes. Wesel: D. van der Straten. (STC 1287, Davies #14-i).

The Epistle Exhortatorye of an Inglyshe Chrystian. London: A. Scoloker and W. Seres. (STC 1292, Davies #2-ii).

The firste Examinacion of the worthy servaunt of God, Mastres Anne Askew; The latter Examination, of the worthye servaunte of God, mastres Anne Askewe. London: W. Hill. (STC 852, Davies #9-iii, #10-iii). This edition lacks Bale's commentary, but the contents were most likely exerpted from one of his editions.

A Godly Medytacyon of the christen sowle . . . compyled in frenche by lady Margarete quene of Naverre . . . translated into Englysh by the ryght vertuouse lady Elyzabeth. Wesel: D. van der Straten. (STC 17320, Davies #15). Edited by Bale.

Illustrium maioris Britannie Scriptorum . . . Summarium. "Ipswich: J. Overton," i.e., Wesel: D. van der Straten. (STC 1295, Davies #16a).

_____. Wesel: D. van der Straten. (STC 1296, Davies #16b). Variant title page.

_____. Wesel: D. van der Straten. (STC 1296, Davies #16c). Differs from STC 1296, Davies #16b only in including a leaf before sig. A1, with woodcut of Bale on the verso.

The Image of bothe churches. London: S. Mierdman for R. Jugge. (STC 1297, Davies #18-i).

A Treatyse made by Johan Lambert. Wesel: D. van der Straten. (STC 15180, Davies #7). Edited by Bale.

1549

A breve Chronycle of the Bysshope of Romes blessynge. London: S. Mierdman for R. Foster. (STC 11842a, Davies #20-i). Anonymous, possibly by Bale.

A dialoge or Communycacyon to be had at a table betwene two chyldren. London: S. Mierdman for R. Foster. (STC 1290, Davies #19).

The laboryouse Journey & serche of Johan Leylande. London: S. Mierdman for J. Bale. (STC 15445, Davies #21-i).

1550

The Apology of Johan Bale agaynste a ranke Papyst. London: S. Mierdman for J. Day. (STC 1275, Davies #22).

A Christen Exhortacyon unto Customable Swearers. (London: N. Hill for A. Vele. (STC 1281; not listed in Davies).

_____ . London: N. Hill for R. Kele. (STC 1282; not listed in Davies). Variant colophon.

_____ . London: N. Hill for J. Wyghte. (STC 1283; not listed in Davies). Variant colophon.

The first examination of A. Askew; The latter examination of A. Askew. London: J. Day. (STC 853; not listed in Davies).

_____ . London: W. Copland?. (STC 853.5; not listed in Davies).

The Image of bothe churches. London: S. Mierdman for J. Day and W. Seres. (STC 1298, Davies #18-ii).

_____ . London: J. Wyer. (STC 1299, Davies #18-iv).

1551

The fyrste part of the Actes of English votaryes. London: S. Mierdman for A. Vele. (STC 1271.5, Davies #23-i-b).

The first two partes of the Actes or unchast examples of the Englysh votaryes. London: S. Mierdman for A. Vele. (STC 1271.5 represents part I; STC 1273 represents Part II; Davies #23-i-a,b,c).

A lamentable complaynte of Baptista Mantuanus. London: J. Day. (STC 22992; not listed in Davies). Translated by Bale.

1552

An Expostulation or complaynte agaynste the blasphemyes of a franticke papyst of Hamshyre. London: S. Mierdman for J. Day. (STC 1294, Davies #24).

1553

Gardiner, Stephen. *De Vera Obediencia.* "Roane: Michal Wood," i.e., London: John Day? (STC 11585, Davies p. 277, #4-i). Probably translated and edited by Bale. See Leslie P. Fairfield, "The Mysterious Press of 'Michael Wood' (1553-1554)," *The Library*, 5th ser., 27, no. 3, (September 1972): 229-230.

_____ . "Roane: Michael wood," i.e., London: John Day?. (STC 11586, Davies p. 277, #4-ii). Type reset.

_____ . "Rome," i.e., Wesel: Joos Lambrecht? (STC 11587, Davies p. 277, #4-iii). For the printer and the location of this "Rome" press, see Leslie P. Fairfield, *"The vocacyon of Johan*

Bale and Early English Autobiography," *Renaissance Quarterly* 24, no. 3 (Autumn 1971), p. 331, n. 14.

The vocacyon of Johan Bale to the bishoprick of Ossorie in Irelande. "Rome," i.e., Wesel: Joos Lambrecht? (STC 1307, Davies #25-i).

1554

A Dialogue or Familiar talke betwene two neighbors. "Roane: Michael wodde," i.e., London: J. Day?. (STC 10383, Davies p. 278, #5). Probably written by Bale; see Fairfield, "The Mysterious Press of 'Michael Wood,' " pp. 230-231.

The Resurrection of the Masse. "Strasburgh," i.e., Wesel: Joos Lambrecht? (STC 13457; not listed in Davies). Possibly written by Bale; see Christina H. Garrett, *"The Resurrection of the Masse* by Hugh Hilarie—or John Bale?" *The Library,* 4th ser., 21 (1941): 143-159.

1557

Scriptorum Illustrium maioris Britannie . . . Catalogus. Basel: J. Oporinus. (No STC number; Davies #26, a & b). Two issues appeared in 1557, with slightly differing title pages.

1558

Acta Romanorum Pontificum. Basel: J. Oporinus. (No STC number; Davies #27-i).

1559

Acta Romanorum Pontificum. Basel: J. Oporinus. (No STC number; Davies #27-ii). A copy of this edition at the Houghton Library, Harvard University, bears the date 1559; another copy of what appears to be the same edition, at the University Library, Cambridge, is dated 1560. The latter is apparently a separate issue of the 1559 edition.

Scriptorum Illustrium maioris Britannie . . . Catalogus. Basel: J. Oporinus. (No STC number; Davies #26, c, d, & e). Three further issues of the 1557 edition appeared in 1559, differing from the 1557 issues in that they include a dedicatory epistle to Queen Elizabeth.

Scriptorum Illustrium maioris Britannie posterior pars. (Basel: J. Oporinus. (No STC number; Davies #28).

1560

The first two partes of the Actes or unchaste examples of the

Englyshe Votaryes. London: J. Tysdale. (STC 1274, Davies #23-ii).

1561

A Declaration of Edmonde Bonners articles. London: J. Tysdale for F. Coldocke. (STC 1289, Davies #29).

Les Vies des Evesques et Papes de Rome. Geneva: C. Badius. (No STC number; Davies #30-i). A translation of *Acta Romanorum Pontificum.*

_____ . No place; no printer. (No STC number; Davies #30-ii).

1562

A Newe Comedy or Enterlude, concernynge thre lawes. London: T. Colwell. (STC 1288, Davies #14-ii).

Les Vies de Evesques et Papes de Rome. Lyon: no printer. (No STC number; Davies #30-iii).

1566

Bepstliche Geschichte. Buedingen: Z. Muenster. (No STC number; Davies #31-i). A translation of *Acta Romanorum Pontificum.*

1567

Acta Romanorum Pontificum. Frankfort-am-Main: P. Brubachius. (No STC number; Davies #27-iii).

1570

The Image of both Churches. London: T. East. (STC 1301, Davies #18-v).

1571

Bepstliche Geschichte. Buedingen: Z. Muenster. (No STC number; Davies #31-ii).

1574

The Pageant of Popes. London: T. Marshe. (STC 1304, Davies #32). A translation of *Acta Romanorum Pontificum*, with various additions, by John Studley.

1575

A Christian exhortacion unto customable Swearers. London: J. Audley. (STC 1286; not listed in Davies).

1577

A *Tragedie or Enterlude, manifesting the Chiefe promises of God.* London: J. Charlewoode for S. Peele. (STC 1306, Davies #11-ii).

1585

The first examination of Anne Askew. London: R. Waldegrave. (STC 849; not listed in Davies).

Notes

Abbreviations

Catalogus   John Bale, *Scriptorum Illustrium maioris Britanniae
. . . Catalogus*, 2 vols. (Basel, 1557-1559).

Davies   W. T. Davies, "A Bibliography of John Bale,"
*Oxford Bibliographical Society, Proceedings and
Papers*, vol. 5, part 4 (1940), pp. 203-279.

Harris   Jesse Harris, *John Bale* (Urbana, Illinois, 1940).

L & P   *Letters and Papers, Foreign and Domestic, of the
Reign of Henry VIII*, ed. J. S. Brewer, et al., 21
vols. (London, 1862-1910).

McCusker   Honor McCusker, *John Bale: Dramatist and Antiquary* (Bryn Mawr, Pennsylvania, 1942).

STC   A. W. Pollard and G. R. Redgrave, et al., *A Short-
Title Catalogue* (London, 1926); now in revision
under the direction of Katharine Pantzer at the
Houghton Library, Harvard University.

Summarium   John Bale, *Illustrium Maioris Britanniae Scriptorum
. . . Summarium* ("Ipswich" [i.e., Wesel], 1548).

1 / The Carmelite Friar

1.   Bale gives his birthdate in Bodleian Library MS. Bodley 73, fol. i. In British Museum MS. Harley 3838, fol. 111-verso, he says he was born *in pago covensi*. The Latin name *Cova* applied in the sixteenth century both to Covehithe and the neighboring village of Cove (W. A. Copinger, ed., *County of Suffolk*, [London, 1904], 2:151, 155), but evidently the Bales lived in Covehithe. S.H.A. Hervey, ed., *Suffolk in 1524—Return for a Subsidy Granted in 1523* (Woodbridge, 1910), pp. 91-92, lists Bales in Covehithe and none in Cove.

2.   Joan Thirsk, ed., *The Agrarian History of England and Wales, Vol. IV: 1500-1640* (Cambridge, 1967), pp. 40-49, is useful for the agricultural history of sixteenth-century Suffolk.

3.   See Bodleian Library MS. Bodley 73, fol. i, where an entry —apparently referring to Bale—in the notebook lists four brothers and five sisters. If one's impression of family sizes in seventeenth-century England holds true for a century or so earlier, the senior Bales were unusually prolific: see Peter Laslett, *The World We Have Lost* (New York, 1965), p. 64. Bale's parents are named in British Museum MS. Harley 3838, fol. 111-verso. He refers specifically to their poverty (*inopia*) in his *Summarium*, fol. 242-verso.

4.   E. F. Jacob, *The Fifteenth Century* (Oxford, 1961), p. 297.

5.   John Bale, ed., *A treatyse made by Johan Lambert* (n.p., n.d. [Wesel, c. 1548]), fols. 304. See also *Catalogus*, 1:644.

6.   The starting-point for the history of the Carmelites in England is Bale's *Anglorum Heliades*, British Museum MS. Harley 3838, fols. 3-43 especially. For more modern studies see Keith J. Egan, "Medieval Carmelite Houses, England and Wales," *Carmelus* 16 (1969): 142-226; idem, "An Essay toward a Historiography of the Origin of the Carmelite Province in England," *Carmelus* 19 (1972): 67-100; L.C. Shepherd, *The English Carmelites* (London, 1943); and Dom David Knowles, *The Religious Orders in England*, 3 vols. (Cambridge, 1960-61), 1:196-199, 241-242; 2:144-148; 3:52-61. See also Philip Hughes, *The Reformation in England* (New York, 1963), 1:68-70; J.R.H. Moorman, *The Grey Friars in Cambridge* (Cambridge, 1952), passim (for information on the friars in general); F.R.H. duBoulay, "The Quarrel between the Carmelite Friars and the Secular Clergy of

London, 1464-1468," *Journal of Ecclesiastical History* 6 (1955): 156-174; and A.G. Little, "Corrodies at the Carmelite Friary of Lynn," *Journal of Ecclesiastical History* 9 (1958): 8-29.

7. Cambridge University Library MS. Ff.6.28, fol. i. In Bodleian Library MS. Bodley 73, fol. i-verso, Bale refers to a fire at the Carmelite convent in Cambridge in April 1513, in such a way as to suggest that he might have seen the fire himself. In 1557 he did, however, state that he had gone up to Cambridge together with Robert Barnes in 1514: *Catalogus*, 1:666-667.

8. For Norwich in the early sixteenth century, see J. F. Pound, "The Social and Trade Structure of Norwich, 1525-1575," *Past and Present* 34 (July 1966): 49-69.

9. There is no evidence whatever that Bale ever became a member of Jesus College, as many historians have supposed. In his *Summarium* and *Catalogus* he claims he knew Thomas Cranmer and Geoffrey Downes, both of Jesus, during his Cambridge years, but this is no proof that Bale was a member of that college, too. All previous lives of Bale have erred on this point: see J. F. Crompton, *"Fasciculi Zizaniorum," Journal of Ecclesiastical History* 12 (1961): 40.

10. J. H. Gray, *The Queens' College* (London, 1899) pp. 13 and passim. For Cambridge in general during Bale's years there, see H. C. Porter, *Reformation and Reaction in Tudor Cambridge* (Cambridge, 1958), chapter 1.

11. Viz. J. R. Hale, *Renaissance Europe* (London, 1971), pp. 41-43, for comments upon the sixteenth century's lack of interest in the aesthetic qualities of landscape.

12. K. B. McFarlane, *Wycliffe and English Non-Conformity* (Harmondsworth, Middlesex, 1972), p. 9.

13. See *Victoria County History, Cambridgeshire* (London, 1948), 2:284; and Moorman, op. cit., p. 120, for these dispensations. For the curriculum at Cambridge in general, see Porter, op. cit., pp. 4-5; S. E. Morison, *The Founding of Harvard College* (Cambridge, Massachusetts, 1935), pp. 26-35; and Craig R. Thompson, *Universities in Tudor England* (Ithaca, New York, 1964), pp. 8-17. For the regulations given the Carmelite order regarding study towards the D.D., see Knowles, op. cit., 2:145, n. 1.

14. See for example British Museum MS. Harley 3838, fol. 111-verso. For Bale's grace, see *Grace Book* Γ, W. G. Searle, ed.,

(Cambridge, 1908), p. 241: "*conceditur fratri Ball ordinis Carmelitarum ut studium decem annorum in theologie facultate hac in universitate et in partibus ultromarinis. . . .*" Bale's grace is listed under the year 1528-1529 (which ran from Michaelmas to Michaelmas: see Searle's introduction, p. xvii) and Bale is scheduled to have all the requirements—including preaching at Paul's Cross—completed by St. Martin's Day. This was probably July 4 among the various feasts of St. Martin (C. R. Cheney, *Handbook of Dates* [London, 1970], p. 55) since early July was the normal time for inception. This would mean, then, that Bale took his degree in 1529 rather than 1528.

15.   Borthwick Institute, York, Reg. Lee, R.I.28, fol. 85-verso.

16.   Bodleian Library MS. Selden supra 72, fol. 41: *frater Johannes Bale, iuvenum informator.* See Appendix 1 for the dating of Bale's early manuscripts.

17.   Cambridge University Library, Ely Diocesan Records AG 1/7, fol. 82.

18.   The notebooks in Bale's hand which have survived from his Carmelite days before 1530 or so are as follows: Cambridge University Library MS. Ff. 6. 28; Bodleian Library MSS. Selden supra 41, and Bodley 73; and British Museum MS. Harley 1819.

19.   Bodleian Library MS. Bodley 73, fols. 9-38. The latest date in this handwriting in the MS. as a whole is 1522, on fol. 82-verso.

20.   Ibid., fol. 39.

21.   J. Bale, *The Actes of Englysh votaries* (London, 1551), part 2, fol. ix-verso.

22.   British Museum MS. Harley 3838, fol. 111-verso.

23.   J. F. Crompton, loc. cit., p. 161.

24.   Bodleian Library MS. Bodley 73, fols, 56-58.

25.   British Museum MS. Harley 1819, fol. 87-verso.

26.   British Museum MS. Harley 1819. The itinerary is apparent from Bale's marginal notes, indicating where he had discovered the information he was recording. A cross-check is supplied by the chapter headings to a life of St. Anne, the mother of the Virgin, which Bale seems to have composed or copied en route (fols. 17-40). Each chapter seems to be dedicated to a particular Carmelite house which Bale visited, and the list of convents thus supplied coincides

roughly with his marginal notes. Concerning the dating of the manuscript, see Appendix 1.

27. Ibid., fol. 123-verso. For Bale's reference to William Gregory, see, for example, *Summarium*, fol. 218-verso.

28. Bale's later claim that he had "studied" at Toulouse—British Museum MS. Harley 3838, fol. 111-verso—is hard to reconcile with the admission that he had stayed there for only a few weeks in 1527 (*Summarium*, fol. 218-verso). There is no evidence that Bale was at Toulouse on any other occasion.

29. The last date recorded in British Museum MS. Harley 1819 is 20 January 1528, new style—*in die sebastiani* 1527—fol. 183.

30. Porter, op. cit., pp. 23-24.

31. For biographical data on Mantuanus, see the introduction to his *Eclogues*, ed. W. P. Mustard (Baltimore, 1911).

32. Bodleian Library MS. Selden supra 41, fols. 29-verso, 30.

33. Ibid., fol. 44 ff.

34. British Museum MS. Harley 1819, fol. 144-verso. Roughly translated, the poem reads: "O Virgin whom Carmel nurtured in the city of Toulouse, make atonement for my sin. Grant that I may please Christ, that I may serve the Thunderer; and do not let Time destroy the great gifts of God. O holy Joanna, grant that I may grow more apt in letters; grant that I may grow in zeal within the religious life, and merit the life to come."

35. Cf. especially E. G. Rupp, *Studies in the Making of the English Protestant Tradition* (Cambridge, 1966), chapter 1.

36. For Barnes, see *Summarium*, fol. 226, and *Catalogus*, 1:666-667. On Cranmer, see *Catalogus*, 1:632. Bale's words here about Jesus College have led many scholars to suppose erroneously that Bale himself belonged to that college, though the passage says nothing of the kind. See above, n. 9.

37. Bodleian Library MS. Bodley 73, fols. iv-v.

38. Ibid., fol. 121.

39. *Catalogus*, 1:702, cf. Bale's comments in the *Summarium*, fol. 243.

40. *Summarium*, fol. 228-verso; *Catalogus*, 1:668-669.

41. John Bale, *A Mysterye of Inyquyte* ("Geneva," i.e., Antwerp, 1545), fol. 40.

42. See Lambeth Palace Library, MS. 2001, an unpublished pamphlet which Bale wrote in 1561: "A Returne of James Cancellers raylynge boke upon hys owne heade, called the pathe of obedyence." This little tract—no less "raylynge" than the one it attacks—proceeds in the usual, almost sentence-by-sentence fashion.

43. Otto Scheel, ed., *Dokumente zu Luthers Entwicklung* (Tuebingen, 1929), p. 141.

44. Cf. A. G. Dickens, *The English Reformation* (London, 1964), pp. 5-6.

45. See Eamon Carroll, "The Marian Theology of Arnold Bostius (1445-1499)," *Carmelus* 9 (1962): 197-236. Bale was naturally familiar with Bostius's work; he copied the latter's major tract, *De Patronatu et Patrocinio Beatae Virginis Mariae in ... Carmeli Ordinem* into Bodleian Library MS. Selden supra 41, fols. 221-315.

46. Cambridge University Library MS. Ff. 6.28.

47. Ibid., fol. 2.

48. Ibid., fol. 4: *"Deo tu propinquior sanctisque celerior mater ad dandum munera vite...."*

49. Ibid., fol. 4-verso: *"Felix Carmeli domina et patrona qui ... in gregem suum carmelitarum hostem sevire non sinit...."*

50. Ibid., fol. 5: *"O beata celorum domina flos virginum ... castitatis lilium...."*

51. British Museum MS. Harley 1819, fols. 87-verso to 88: "Hail flowering blossom of Carmel, the Father's pious daughter, Mother of Emmanuel, happy above thousands; O Virgin, give aid, as You are wont, to your brothers...." For other examples of this spirit, see in the same manuscript fols. 140-144.

52. Cambridge University Library MS. Ff.6.28, fol. 17-verso: *"Per tua sancta merita dele nostra debita...."*

53. Bodleian Library MS. Bodley 73, fol. 59: *"mendacia sunt ... ecce mendacem...."*

54. Ibid., fol. 45-verso, where he quotes with approval his fellow Carmelite John Bloxham to the effect that *"ea ad quae non possumus venire naturali ratione revelat et revelavit deus virginibus,"* and so on.

55. British Museum MS. Harley 1819, from a short collection of monastic maxims, fol. 123: *"In cella invenies quod foris saepius ammittis."*

56. See Bodleian Library MS. Bodley 73, fols. 24, 34.

57. Johann Huizinga, *The Waning of the Middle Ages* (Garden City, New York, n.d.), p. 233.

58. See Bodleian Library MS. Bodley 73, fol. 34 and 34-verso for miracle-stories Bale recorded, including one in which a healing was accomplished simply by putting on the scapular.

59. See Keith Thomas, *Religion and the Decline of Magic* (New York, 1971), chapters 2 and 3 especially.

60. Brother Johannes Soreth, in Ghent.

61. Bodleian Library MS. Bodley 73, fol. 14: *"Alia quaedam obcessa erat a demonio, cuius amici votum emiserant ut cum eadem et uno luminari xii librarum sancti huius viri sepulchrum visitarent, quo peracto statim liberata est."*

62. See also for example British Museum MS. Harley 1819, fols. 85-97.

63. See for example ibid., fols. 140-144, and Bodleian Library MS. Bodley 73, fol. 87-verso for the latter.

64. On the subject of hagiography in general, see René Aigran, *L'Hagiographie* (Paris, 1953); and Hippolyte Delehaye, *The Legends of the Saints* (South Bend, Indiana, 1961).

65. For this literature see Pierre Janelle, *L'Angleterre Catholique à la Veille du Schisme* (Paris, 1935), pp. 13-20.

66. Cambridge University Library MS. Ff.6.28.

67. Bodleian Library MS. Selden supra 41, fols. 197-220. The handwriting is quite rounded—rather schoolboyish—and could date from almost any time between 1515 or so and 1522. It is definitely more mature, however, than the hand in Cambridge University Library MS. Ff.6.28.

68. British Museum MS. Harley 3838, fol. 112.

69. Compare for example the following excerpts from the life of St. Cyril, the first from Bodleian Library MS. Selden supra 41, fol. 202-verso, the second from the office which Bale copied into Cambridge University Library MS. Ff.6.28, fol. 15: *"Hic angelus*

virgam afferens liliatam et tabellam argenteam pendentem in dextera: et aliam argenteam in sinistra litteris grecis scriptis: ait cirillo Has tabellas misit tibi deus omnipotens tanquam familiari suo famulo et fideli preconi. . . ." The office from Bale's earliest manuscript (which he had obviously copied from some other source) reads quite similarly: *"Hic autem angelus attulit virgam liliatam et duas tabellas argenteas / unam in dextera pendentem et alteram in sinistra litteris aureis grecis descriptas futuri status seculi continentes / Qui beato cirillo sic ait / has tabellas devote cirille misit tibi deus omnipotens tanquam familiari suo famulo et fideli preconi. . . ."*

70. Bodleian Library MS. Selden supra 41, fols, 198, 202-verso to 203.

71. Huizinga, op. cit., pp. 215-216.

72. For all of this, see Delehaye, op. cit., pp. 12-39, and also Mircea Eliade, *The Myth of the Eternal Return* (Princeton, New Jersey, 1971), pp. 3-48.

73. Jean Daniélou, *From Shadows to Reality: Studies in the Biblical Typology of the Fathers* (Westminster, Maryland, 1960), pp. 160-161; see also Erich Auerbach, *Scenes from the Drama of European Literature* (New York, 1959), pp. 28-60, and Auerbach, *Mimesis* (Garden City, New York, 1957), pp. 63-66.

74. Auerbach, *Scenes*, pp. 52-53; Daniélou, op. cit., pp. 287-288.

75. Auerbach, *Mimesis*, pp. 64-65, argues that a preoccupation with the timeless was implicit in the typological view of history from the very earliest days of the Church—that each of the "moments" depended upon God's overall plan, outside of history, for its significance. Thus, Auerbach continues, "The horizontal, that is the temporal and causal, connection of occurrences is dissolved; the here and now is no longer a mere link in an earthly chain of events, it is simultaneously something which has always been, and which will be fulfilled in the future; and strictly, in the eyes of God, it is something eternal, something omni-temporal, something already consummated in the realm of fragmentary earthly event. . . ." (pp. 64-65). However, Oscar Cullmann (*Christ and Time* [London, 1951], esp. chapter 3) has argued strongly against the view that the early Church accepted a dichotomy between Time and Eternity, and believed that "real" reality lay in the latter. I find Cullmann convincing, and prefer to believe that the preoccupation with the timeless, the static *forma* in the mind of God, came with the invasion of Platonic and neo-

Platonic elements into Christian thought, and was not implicit in the figural view of history one sees, e.g., in St. Paul.

76. Auerbach, *Scenes*, pp. 42-43.

77. It was not surprising that the figural exegesis of the Old Testament gave way, by and large, throughout the Middle Ages to the generally ahistorical and "spiritual" four-fold exegesis of which Origen was the first major exponent: see Beryl Smalley, *The Study of the Bible in the Middle Ages* (South Bend, Indiana, 1964), pp. 1-26. See also Thomas M. Davis, "The Traditions of Puritan Typology," in *Typology in Early American Literature*, ed. Sacvan Berkovitch (Amherst, Massachusetts, 1972), esp. pp. 17-28.

78. See Carroll, loc. cit., for the principles of Mariolatry in the Carmelite tradition, which could as well be applied, *mutatis mutandis*, to the other saints. Especially important was the principle of "fittingness," that all virtues and perfections must *a priori* be ascribed to the Virgin, as are appropriate to her status as Mother of God and Mediatrix for the human race.

79. Jean Leclercq, *The Love of Learning and the Desire of God* (New York, 1961), pp. 201-203.

80. Delehaye, op. cit., p. 69.

81. See Herschel Baker, *The Race of Time* (Toronto, 1967), chapter 1.

82. It is difficult in this connection to suppress recollection of the apocryphal friar who allegedly remarked, "For humility, our order is tops."

83. Cf. his later comments on the relative authority of Bible and chronicles, in *The Image of bothe churches* (London, Richard Jugge, 1548), 1:sig. A4-verso.

84. Cf. McCusker, p. 123, where the author misses the essentially partisan nature of Bale's temperament.

85. Bodleian Library MS. Selden supra 41, fols. 107-195. This was evidently the *Fasciculus Carmelitarum* which Bale included in later lists of his works—see, e.g., British Museum MS. Harley 3838, fol. 112. Judging from the handwriting and the dates mentioned in the *Fasciculus*, most of the notes were made before the early 1530s. A few sections are in a later handwriting and express a Protestant spirit inconsistent with the earler entries: see Appendix 1.

86. See Bodleian Library MS. Selden supra 41, fol. 107 for the Carmelite historians Bale drew on; fol. 126 for Baptista Mantuanus; and Bodleian Library MS. Bodley 73, fols. 46-48, where it is clear that Bale was drawing on Vincent of Beauvais.

87. Bodleian Library MS. Selden supra 41, fol. 151-verso. But Bale went on immediately to repeat without comment the story that the English Carmelites received the site for their first convent in 1223.

88. Crompton, loc. cit., pp. 155-157.

89. For Bale's preaching in Suffolk, see John Foxe, *Actes and Monuments*, ed. George Townsend (New York, 1965), 8:581; and for Bale's grace, see *Grace Book* Γ, p. 241.

II / Conversion

1. Greater London Record Office, Vicar General's book, DL/C/330, fol. 267-verso. The entry actually reads "*Fr. Johēs Bale prior conventus de*," at which point the corner of the folio is torn, but Maldon was the only one of the houses Bale headed (the others being at Ipswich and Doncaster) which lay in the London diocese, so the entry must have referred to that convent. The date in the records is given as 16 February 1530 (old style). Bale later referred—in a book published in 1550—to having been at Maldon about twenty years previously: John Bale, *The Apology of Johan Bale agaynste a ranke Papyst* (London, S. Mierdman for John Day, c. 1550), fol. 23.

2. James E. Oxley, *The Reformation in Essex* (Manchester, 1965), pp. 27-28.

3. Benedict Zimmerman, O. Carm., "The White Friars at Ipswich," *Proceedings of the Suffolk Archaeological Society* 10 (1900): 199. Zimmerman cites no source for establishing 1533 as the year in which Bale became prior at Ipswich, but the date is reasonable. Bale says he headed the convents at Maldon, Ipswich, and Doncaster "successively" (*vicissim*): British Museum MS. Harley 3838, fol. 111-verso. He was certainly at Maldon in 1531, and clearly at Doncaster in 1534 (see below).

4. *Victoria County History, Essex*, 2:183.

5. John Strype, *Annals of the Reformation*, vol. 2, part 2 (Oxford, 1824), pp. 503-505, cited in Davies, p. 208. Cf. Public Record Office, SP 1/114, fol. 54 (a letter of Sir Humphrey Wingfield to the Duke of Suffolk, 8 January 1537) which refers to Bale as late prior of the White Friars at Ipswich.

6. Borthwick Institute, York, R.I.28 (Archbishop Lee's register), fol. 85-verso.

7. *Summarium*, fol. 246-verso: *"Nam cum certis argumentis praevidissem anno Christi M.D. xxxiii. Anglorum coenobiis iustissimam, ob nefanda inhabitantium scelera ac veritatis contemptum, imminere destructionem. Ad eorum statim singulari Dei dono, me contuli Bibliothecas, qui mihi tunc magis erant familiares ac benevoli, utpote Carmelitarum & Augustiniensium. Apud illos triennio fere laboravi in colligendis diversorum librorum autoribus & titulis, cum quorundam eorum initiis."*

8. See Philip Hughes, *The Reformation in England* (New York, 1963), 1:33.

9. John Bale, *A dysclosynge or openynge of the Manne of synne* ("Zurich" [i.e., Antwerp], 1543), fol. 55.

10. See Bodleian Library MS. Selden supra 41, fol. 191-verso: the latter part of Bale's *Chronica seu fasciculus temporum ordinis Carmelitarum*. An entry concerning prior general Nicholas Audet relates approvingly how he reformed the province of Scotland, recalled Carmelites throughout Europe to their former piety and studies, and in general revived the order. The entry concludes by mentioning a general chapter in Padua in 1532. Immediately following this note, in a different ink and later handwriting, Bale recorded England's breach with Rome in 1533 *"ob enormitates atque detestanda scelera quae fiebant in clero"*—a far cry from the spirit of piety and optimism in the note regarding Audet.

11. *Dictionary of National Biography* (London, 1949-1950), 20:1175 ff.

12. D. S. Bailey, *Thomas Becon* (Edinburgh, 1952), pp. 12-14.

13. *Dictionary of National Biography* (London, 1949-1950), 19:1290 ff.; M.M. Knappen, *Tudor Puritanism* (Chicago, 1965), p. 187. Bale's *Manne of synne* (1543) had as a superscription on the title page the phrase "Yet a course at the Romyshe foxe," a reference to Turner's *The Huntyng & fyndyng out of the Romishe Foxe* ("Basyl,"

i.e., Bonn, 1543). Bale and Turner probably collaborated in writing *The epistle exhortatorye of an Englyshe Christyane* ("Basyle," i.e., Antwerp, 1544). See below in chapter 4.

14. *Catalogus*, 1:702.

15. *Summarium*, fols. 229-verso to 230: "...*quod sim Evangelii regni Dei (ut spero) per eius administrationem particeps, cum ante illius in Romanum Pontificem edictum, obstinatissimus papista fuerim.*"

16. See Bale's comments on all this in British Museum MS. Harley 3838, fol. 41.

17. For the friars and the oath, see Dom David Knowles, *The Religious Orders in England* (Cambridge, 1961), 3:177-178.

18. For Bale's attitude toward the order by 1536 see British Museum MS. Harley 3838, fols. 40-43, and passim—e.g., fol. 212, re Prior General Johannes Soreth: "*carmelitici ordinis decus, gloria, splendor et reformator, qualem nostra raro viderunt secula, rarius cernent ventura.*"

19. Bale's statement in his *Acta Romanorum Pontificum* (Basel, 1559), fol. 5, that he had lived in the Carmelite order for twenty-four years, has sometimes been used in calculating the date of his conversion (viz. Harris, p. 22). The statement is useful for this purpose, however, only if one assumes that Bale put off his friar's habit at once after he was converted to Protestant theology—which he manifestly did not. Even as an indication of how long Bale remained formally a Carmelite, his words pose a problem: if he went up to Norwich in 1507 (as he said he did), and if he was still a friar in 1534 (as Archbishop Lee's register—see below—shows he was) then he was a Carmelite for rather more than twenty-four years. This is especially so if—as appears the case—he was still in the order in 1536 when he wrote his *Anglorum Heliades*. Either Bale was not adding properly when he made the statement or he meant "twenty-four years ago," in which case he should have used *abhinc* instead of *ante*: "...*ante viginti quatuor annos, in ea secta vixi, interfui & praefui, Papae miles non minimus. . . .*"

20. Borthwick Institute, York, R.I.28, fol. 85-verso.

21. Bale later recalled, for instance, an occasion at Ripon in Yorkshire where he was "ones bayted of his (i.e., Antichrist's) Basan bulles, for mayntaynynge the Kynges prerogative agaynst theyr

Pope. . . ." John Bale, *The Actes of Englysh votaryes* (Antwerp, 1546), fol. 43.

22. Borthwick Institute, York, R.I.28, fol. 91. The incident is also discussed in A.G. Dickens, *Lollards and Protestants in the Diocese of York* (London, 1959), pp. 140-143.

23. *L & P*, viii-1, 963.

24. Dickens, op. cit., p. 144. The letter is quoted and the incident described on pp. 144-145.

25. Anthony Blake: see J. Caley and J. Hunter, *Valor Ecclesiasticus* (London, 1810-1834), 5:45.

26. Dickens, op. cit. p. 143.

27. One of the others, Lawrence Cooke, was attainted for partici-pating in the Pilgrimage of Grace, though later pardoned: A. G. Dickens, *Thomas Cromwell and the English Reformation* (New York, 1969), p. 133; see also *L & P* xii-1, 854, and xii-2, 181. It appears that the northern Carmelites were a diverse lot, theologically and politically.

28. Bale, *Manne of synne*, fol. 86. For the same incident, see Bale's *Summarium*, fol. 228.

29. *Catalogus*, 1:702: "*ob editas commedias.*"

30. Professor Elton implies that Cromwell's enthusiasm was well under control: *Policy and Police* (Cambridge, 1972), pp. 185-186.

31. Bale, *Manne of synne*, fol. 86. Downes, later chancellor of York, had perhaps been Bale's respondent for the B. D. in 1529; cf. the *Catalogus*, 1:632, where Bale calls Downes "*olim in re theologica dignissimum patrem.*"

32. British Museum MS. Cotton Cleopatra E.V., fol. 397; cf. *L & P* ix, 230. The editors of *L & P* assigned the undated document to 1535. This is unlikely, not only because it would mean that Bale had been openly preaching Protestant doctrines as early as 1531, but also because the deposition mentions the Whitechapel bricklayer and preacher John Harrydaunce, who first made himself notorious in August 1537. Elton guesses that the deposition dates from 1538 or 1539, and this is no doubt correct: Elton, op. cit. p. 163, n. 1. This would then suggest that Bale was at Doncaster when he taught Broman the offensive doctrine, though all the other individuals mentioned in the deposition were from the south of England.

33. Dickens, *Lollards and Protestants*, pp. 19-23.

34. From Bale's *Anglorum Heliades*, (1536): British Museum MS. Harley 3838, fol. 111-111-verso. For Barret see also *Victoria County History, Cambridgeshire*, 2:285-286.

35. British Museum MS. Cotton Cleopatra E.V., fol. 397. Barret was probably at Ipswich in 1535 while he prepared to leave the Carmelite order. For his dispensation ("capacity") to wear the garb of a secular priest and to hold a cure, see D.S. Chambers, *Faculty Office Registers* (Oxford, 1966), p. 27. Bale said that by 1536 Barret had been appointed to a lectureship on St. Paul's epistles at Norwich: British Museum MS. Harley 3838, fol. 111.

36. Viz. his comments on Thomas Netter of Walden in *Anglorum Heliades* (1536), which sound pretty negative toward the Lollards even considering the ease with which Bale—when writing on Carmelite topics—lapsed into conventionally pious rhetoric: *"Cum sciret Anglie populum per quosdam Wycleffistas quam impie sentire de sacramentis nec quemquam esse qui manum apponeret, Londini ad Crucem Pauli Regem & alios regni proceres ut hereticorum fautores ad mortem sese obiciens increpabat."*

37. Hughes, op. cit. 1:315.

38. In the *Summarium*, fol. 225-verso, Bale said he had formed a friendship with the scholar Robert Wakefield at Doncaster and Greenwich in 1536. This was presumably after March 25, as Bale elsewhere followed convention in beginning the year on that date. Archbishop Lee, it will be recalled, was writing on January 24 when he mentioned that the "light fryer" had already been to London and back. There is one other sign that Bale may still have been in Yorkshire in January 1536. On January 20 a certain John Bale, who had married a woman named Anne six years previously in Norfolk, appeared before the Archbishop's Court of Audience in a matrimonial case. The same day his brother—also named John Bale—appeared in court, claimed that the first John was burdened with royal business, and had him excused until after Easter. (Borthwick Institute, York, R.VIII.3, fols. 3-verso to 4.) Our John Bale did apparently have a brother named "John junior" (Bodleian Library MS. Bodley 73, fol. i). If Friar Bale had recently returned from London, and if he had a brother in trouble with the law, he might possibly have convinced the court that the brother had some "royal business." In any event, there are no more references to the case in the Court of Audience records. The Bales, whoever they were, evidently made themselves scarce.

39. Of the Carmelites Bale mentioned as having done so in *Anglorum Heliades* (Summer 1536), Barret and Giles were the ones who had received their dispensations before the turn of the year: see Chambers, op. cit., pp. 27, 38.

40. Which leads one to be a bit skeptical about Bale's claim that Cromwell had saved him from Archbishop Lee *ob editas commedias: Catalogus,* 1:702. Perhaps it was so, but one doubts that Bale really had much access to Cromwell's attention as yet.

41. For Leland, see T. D. Kendrick, *British Antiquity* (London, 1950), pp. 45-64, and May McKisack, *Medieval History in the Tudor Age* (Oxford, 1971), pp. 1-11. For Bale's flattering words to Leland, see British Museum MS. Harley 3838, fols. 3-4.

42. The rector of Thorndon, Christopher Braunche—presented in 1508 by the Brandon family (see Norfolk and Norwich Record Office, REG/10, book xv, fol. 157)—was also master of the Hospital of St. Mary Magdalene at Thetford, twenty miles to the northwest in Norfolk. In 1535 the collector of rents for the guild of the Blessed Virgin there was a John Bale. Though this is unlikely to have been the same man as the contemporary Carmelite prior of Doncaster, it might have been his younger brother—which could explain how Bale came to know Christopher Braunche and take a post as stipendiary priest in the latter's parish of Thorndon. For the John Bale at Thetford and for Braunche at Thetford and Thorndon in 1535, see *Valor Ecclesiasticus,* 3:315, 480.

43. For these problems, see Joan Thirsk, ed., *The Agrarian History of England and Wales, Vol. IV, 1500-1640* (Cambridge, 1967), pp. 40-41, 49. For the general pattern of discontent in East Anglia in the 1530s, see Elton, op. cit., pp. 135-151; Oxley, op. cit., pp. 115-117; and J. J. Scarisbrick, *Henry VIII* (London, 1968), pp. 341-342.

44. The documents relating to Bale's three months at Thorndon are: Public Record Office, London, (henceforth PRO) SP 1/111, fols. 183-187 ("The answer of John Bale pryst unto serten artycles uniustlye gadred upon hys prechyng"); SP 1/114, fol. 54 (Humphrey Wingfield to the Duke of Suffolk); SP 1/115, fol. 63 (John Leland to Thomas Cromwell); and British Museum MS. Cotton Cleopatra E.IV, fol. 167 (John Bale to Thomas Cromwell).

45. For Wingfield's letter see PRO SP 1/114, fol. 54.

46. British Museum MS. Cotton Cleopatra E.V, fols. 395-396.

47. How potentially dangerous conservative sentiment could be, when provoked, may be seen from the Walsingham conspiracy later in 1537: Elton, op. cit., pp. 144-151.

48. British Museum MS. Cotton Cleopatra E.IV, fol. 167.

49. PRO SP 1/111, fols. 183-187.

50. For the continuity between the theology and the values of the early mendicants and those of the Puritan preachers of the sixteenth and seventeenth centuries—who are seen to have filled a gap left by the decay of the English mendicant orders in the later middle ages—see Irvonwy Morgan, *The Godly Preachers of the Elizabethan Church* (London, 1965), pp. 1-10, 138-174; and G.R. Owst, *Preaching in Medieval England* (New York, 1965), pp. 92-95.

51. PRO SP 1/111, fol. 184-verso.

52. Ibid., fol. 186: spelling and punctuation modernized here and in succeeding quotations from Bale's "Answer."

53. Ibid., fol. 186-verso.

54. G. Burnet and N. Pocock, *History of the Reformation of the Church of England* (Oxford, 1865), 4:283.

55. H. Gee and W. J. Hardy, *Documents Illustrative of English Church History* (London, 1910), p. 271.

56. PRO SP 1/111, fol. 186.

57. See William A. Clebsch, *England's Earliest Protestants* (New Haven, Connecticut, 1964), pp. 219-223.

58. The third in the triad of Lutheran assertions, *sola gratia* or *sola fide*, did not appear in the articles laid against Bale, but was of course implied throughout his "Answer."

59. PRO SP 1/111, fol. 184. For the background of the problem of doctrinal authority, as Englishmen wrestled with it, see E. Flesseman-van Leer, "The Controversy about Scripture and Tradition between Thomas More and William Tyndale," *Nederlands Archief voor Kerkgeschiedenis* 43 (1959):143-164; and H.C. Porter, "The Nose of Wax: Scripture and the Spirit from Erasmus to Milton," *Transactions of the Royal Historical Society*, 5th ser., 14 (1964):155-174.

60. PRO SP 1/111, fol. 183-verso.

61. Ibid., fol. 187.

62. M. M. Knappen, op. cit., pp. 61-71, traces the anti-ceremonial

polemics of later Elizabethan Puritans back to Bale and his friend William Turner in the early 1540s.

63.   Viz. PRO SP 1/111, fol. 185: his comments on fornication, etc., referring to St. Paul, the Book of Revelation, and so on.

64.   For the themes of earlier preaching, see J. W. Blench, *Preaching in England in the Late Fifteenth and Sixteenth Centuries* (New York, 1964), pp. 228-263.

65.   PRO SP 1/111, fol. 186-verso.

66.   Ibid., fol. 186.

67.   Viz. J.F.H. New, *Anglican and Puritan: The Basis of their Opposition, 1558-1640* (Stanford, California, 1964), esp. pp. 70-72.

68.   PRO SP 1/111, fol. 183-verso. "*Descendit ad inferna*" are the words Bale used.

69.   Ibid., fol. 185.

70.   Bale's reply to the seventh article laid against him repeats, more or less, the words reported of him in William Broman's deposition— that God is "essentially and personally" in heaven, though in every Christian by His Spirit and Word, and elsewhere by His power and grace. Bale took pains to deny in his "Answer," though, that he had said this in reference to the Mass: he had got on to the topic, he said, by preaching about prayer. (Ibid., fol. 185-verso.)

71.   British Museum MS. Harley 3838, fol. 112.

72.   PRO SP 1/111, fol. 183-verso. Bale was apparently referring to Erasmus's suspicion that the article in the Creed *descendit ad inferos* was added by St. Thomas Aquinas: see Erasmus, *A playne and godly exposytion or declaration of the commune Crede and of the x. commaundmentes* (London, 1533), fol. 79-verso. Other of Bale's general attitudes may of course have been influenced by Erasmus as well—viz. the Erasmian attack on hagiolatry in his colloquy "A Pilgrimage for Religion's Sake" (Erasmus, *Ten Colloquies* [New York, 1957], pp. 56-91).

73.   Cf. Erasmus's attitude in his exposition of the Creed. On the matter of the perpetual virginity of Mary, for instance, Erasmus concedes that Scripture does not witness to it, but that the Church declares it and therefore it is to be accepted. For Erasmus, Scripture and tradition are coordinate and complementary. See *A playne and godly exposytion*, fol. 61.

74. On the Eucharist see Frith's treatment in *The Whole Workes of W. Tyndall, John Frith, and Doct. Barnes* (London, 1573), 2:107 ff.; and Tyndale's also, ibid., I: esp. 451. On the matter of purgatory, see the belief of George Joye which Bale seemed to prefer in Edward Arber, ed., *An Apology made by George Joye* (Birmingham, 1883), p. 8; and cf. Tyndale's conflicting view, (ibid., p. xii). See also Frith in *The Whole Workes*, 2:32.

75. For comments on his eucharistic theology, see C.W. Dugmore, *The Mass and the English Reformers* (London, 1958), pp. 234-236.

76. British Museum MS. Cotton Cleopatra E.IV, fol. 167. For Leland's letter see PRO SP 1/115, fol. 63.

77. Harris, p. 103, rates Bale's importance in Cromwell's campaign too highly. For Cromwell's measures see Elton, op. cit., pp. 171-216 and especially p. 186 n. 1 for Bale. See also Scarisbrick, op. cit., pp. 367-368. Apparently it was noised abroad in 1537 that Cromwell was in the market for anti-papal playwrights: viz. PRO SP 1/116, fols, 158-159, a letter of 1537 from one Thomas Wylley, vicar of Yoxford in Suffolk, offering Cromwell plays against "the Pope's counselors," the "rude commonalty" (presumably the northern rebels), and so on.

78. Bale was certainly not married while he was at Thorndon, or the villagers would doubtlessly have mentioned the fact in their accusations. Davies (p. 207) says that the desire to marry was one of the reasons Bale left the Carmelite order; but Bale never linked the two acts causally himself—merely remarking that he had married in order to exercise Christian liberty (*Summarium*, fol. 242-verso and *Catalogus*, 1:702). Dorothy was probably a widow with children when Bale married her—at least, she had a son old enough to be apprenticed at Norwich in 1545: John Bale, *The first two partes of the Actes or unchast examples of the Englysh votaryes* (London, 1551), 2:fol. 83.

79. A. G. Dickens, *The English Reformation* (London, 1965), p. 170.

80. See Davies, pp. 209-213; Harris, pp. 60-109; and McCusker, pp. 72-96. See also Thora B. Blatt, *The Plays of John Bale* (Copenhagen, 1968).

III / A Pattern for Church History

1. There are problems involved in the dating of the manuscript—British Museum MS. Harley 3838, fols. 3-112—since it represents a copy which Bale had made (with a few additions) in 1538 or 1539. But the bulk of the chronicle (fols. 3-43; fols. 54-112 represent a biographical catalogue of English Carmelite writers) dates from 1536. See Appendix 1.

2. British Museum MS. Harley 3838, fols. 4-verso to 5.

3. Ibid., fol. 15.

4. See, e.g., Sacvan Bercovitch, ed., *Typology and Early American Literature* (Amherst, Massachusetts, 1972), pp. 11-45.

5. British Museum MS. Harley 3838, fol. 18-verso.

6. By 1532 these exiles had at least four works in print: See M. E. Aston, "Lollardy and the Reformation: Survival or Revival?" *History* 49 (1964): 149-174.

7. British Museum MS. Harley 3838, fols. 35-37.

8. Bale was the first to apply the epithet *stella matutina* to Wyclif: see *Summarium* fol. 154-verso, and *Catalogus*, 1:450. The phrase—originally from Ecclesiasticus 50:5—was a commonly-used one in Carmelite devotion to the Virgin (see, e.g., the poem quoted in L. C. Shepherd, *The English Carmelites* [London, 1943], p. 17). For Bale's contribution to the Reformation's understanding of Wyclif, see M. E. Aston, "John Wycliffe's Reformation Reputation," *Past and Present* 30 (1965): 24-26.

9. British Museum MS. Harley 3838, esp. fols. 5, 40-43.

10. Ibid., fol. 42: "*ac si in illis et non in sola spiritus libertate situs sit Dei optimi maximi cultus.*"

11. Ibid., fol. 19.

12. Ibid., fol. 42-verso. Cf. Hebrews 11: 37-38 (KJV).

13. British Museum MS. Harley 3838, fols. 118-155. The complete title is "*Perpaucorum carmeli scriptorum ab helia thesbite ad bertholdum primum eorum magistrum generalem, Cathalogus admodum brevissimus.*" (For the dating of the tract, see Appendix I.)

14. Ibid., fol. 118: "*. . . non erant tam atrociter astricti, illis*

papistici monachismi votis, quo sanctum matrimonium tam exosum . . . et obedienciam erga parentes ac principes tam nauseacam habeant."

15. Ibid., fol. 133: "*Non erant tunc cenobia ut nunc sunt, ociosum nebulonum prostibula.*"

16. For the dating see John Bale, *King Johan*, Barry B. Adams, ed., (San Marino, California, 1969), pp. 20-24; Davies, p. 209, as well.

17. Bale, *King Johan*, p. 76.

18. See McCusker, pp. 90-94; and especially Rainer Pineas, "William Tyndale's Influence on John Bale's Polemical Use of History," *Archiv fuer Reformationsgeschichte* 53 (1962): 79-96; see also the same author's "William Tyndale's Use of History as a Weapon of Religious Controversy," *Harvard Theological Review* 55 (1962): 121-141. A case for Tyndale's influence on Bale is also made by Glanmor Williams, *Reformation Views of Church History* (Richmond, Virginia, 1970), p. 27. For Tyndale's references to a "good" King John see, e.g., *The Whole workes of W. Tyndall, John Frith, and Doct. Barnes*, (London, 1573), 1:362-363.

19. Simon Fish, *A supplicacyon for the beggers* (Antwerp, c. 1528), fol. 3-verso; anon. (William Roy or Jerome Barlowe?), *A proper dyaloge betwene a Gentillman and an Husbandman* (Antwerp, ca. 1529), sigs. B1-verso to B2.

20. Robert Barnes, *A supplicacion unto the most gracyous prynce H. the .viii.* (London, 1534), sig. C1. Barnes's version differs considerably from Tyndale's account of John's reign; see *The Whole workes*, 1:362-363.

21. Bale, *King Johan*, pp. 81-82.

22. One vein which Bale most likely did *not* mine in compiling *King Johan*—contrary to what used to be thought—was the Latin "tragedy" *Pammachius*, published at Wittenberg by the German reformer Thomas Kirchmeyer in 1538. Though the latter's drama almost certainly did influence Bale's thought in the early 1540s, it was published too late to have any impact on *Kynge Johan*. The links between *Pammachius* and *Kynge Johan* were first suggested by C. H. Herford, *Studies in the Literary Relations of England and Germany in the Sixteenth Century* (London, 1886), p. 136. The hypothesis has been convincingly refuted in Thora B. Blatt, *The Plays of John Bale* (Copenhagen, 1968), pp. 164-181. For other studies of the back-

ground to *Kynge Johan*, see Herbert Barke, *Bales "Kynge Johan" und sein Verhaeltnis zur Zeitgenoessischen Geschichtsschreibung* (Berlin, 1937); and Bale, *King Johan*, esp. pp. 60-61.

23. Davies, pp. 212-213.

24. John Bale, *The Dramatic Writings of John Bale*, ed. John S. Farmer (London, 1907), p. 2.

25. For St. Paul and the three-age pattern, see, e.g., James Westfall Thompson, *A History of Historical Writing* (New York, 1942), 1:124, and John M. Headley, *Luther's View of Church History* (New Haven, Connecticut, 1963), p. 109. For St. Augustine and this scheme, see R. A. Markus, *Saeculum: History and Society in the Theology of St. Augustine* (Cambridge, 1970), pp. 17-19. On the use of the threefold pattern in *Speculum Sacerdotale*, see Blatt, op. cit., p. 68. The three-age scheme was used by early Protestant historians too: Johann Carion mentioned it in the opening of his *Chronica* (first published in 1532; see the first Latin edition, [Halle, 1537], sig. B1). Melanchthon also used the scheme in revising Carion's work: see J. W. Thompson, op. cit., p. 527.

26. Bale, *Dramatic Writings*, p. 59. Numerous entries relating to this Wharton in *L & P* during the 1530s make it appear that he was a local henchman of Cromwell's; but Bale, who had clearly had some trouble with the man, thought his loyalty to the minister questionable: see John Bale, *The Image of bothe churches* (London [Richard Jugge], 1548), 2: sig. I7-verso.

27. This is the gist of Act 5: Bale, *Dramatic Writings*, pp. 68-79.

28. Amos 3:7 (KJV).

29. Headley, op. cit., pp. 164-181; Williams, op. cit., pp. 16-20; and Fritz J. Levy, *Tudor Historical Thought* (San Marino, California, 1967), pp. 79-83.

30. Judas Nazarei, pseud. of Joachim von Watt, *Vom Alten und neuen Gott* (n.p., 1521), sig. C2.

31. Johann Carion, *Chronica* (Halle, 1537), sigs. B1-B2 ff.

32. Markus, op. cit., pp. 17-21; R. L. P. Milburn, *Early Christian Interpretations of History* (London, 1954), pp. 79-81; C. A. Patrides, *The Grand Design of God* (London, 1972), pp. 16-19; Peter Toon, ed., *Puritans, The Millennium and the Future of Israel* (Cambridge, 1970), pp. 10-15; Stephen Toulmin and June Goodfield, *The Discovery of Time* (New York, 1966), pp. 60-61.

33. Headley, op. cit., pp. 109-110.

34. I borrow the phrase from Robert W. Hanning, *The Vision of History in Early Britain* (New York, 1966).

35. Bale, *Dramatic Writings*, pp. 72, 74.

36. See especially Oscar Cullmann, *Christ and Time*, tr. by Floyd V. Filson (London, 1951), pp. 81-93.

37. Revelation 5:9 ff.

38. Revelation 20-21. For the background of the Book of Revelation, see *inter alia* H. M. Feret, *The Apocalypse of St. John*, tr. by Elizabethe Corathiel (London, 1958), esp. pp. 82-110; and Austin Farrer, *A Rebirth of Images* (Westminster, 1949), esp. pp. 170-177.

39. For the above, see Cullmann, op. cit., esp. pp. 81-106; Toon, op. cit., pp. 10-17; Norman Cohn, *The Pursuit of the Millennium* (London, 1970), pp. 24-30; Wilhelm Kamlah, *Apokalypse und Geschichtstheologie* (Berlin, 1935), pp. 10-12; Beryl Smalley, *The Study of the Bible in the Middle Ages* (South Bend, Indiana, 1964), pp. 6-14; and Ernest Lee Tuveson, *Millennium and Utopia* (New York, 1964), pp. 7-18.

40. For all this see Kamlah, op. cit., pp. 66-74, 99-104, 115-129.

41. Joachite and pseudo-Joachite works were being published in significant numbers in Venice, especially in the early sixteenth century. For the whole subject of Joachim's thought and influence, see the impressive work of Marjorie Reeves, *The Influence of Prophecy in the Later Middle Ages* (Oxford, 1969), esp. pp. 3-58, 76-125, and 295-305.

42. For the Sibylline tradition and the image of Antichrist in the later middle ages, see Cohn, op. cit., pp. 30-36; Headley, op. cit., pp. 152-155; Reeves, op. cit., pp. 295-319, 416-452; and Toon, op. cit., pp. 18-19. See also Christopher Hill, *Antichrist in Seventeenth Century England* (London, 1971), pp. 3-8; Pontien Polman, *L'Elément Historique dans la Controverse Réligieuse du XVIe Siècle* (Gembloux, 1932), esp. pp. 152-166; and Hans Preuss, *Die Vorstellung vom Antichrist im spaeteren Mittelalter* (Leipzig, 1906), passim.

43. See above, n. 22.

44. Blatt, op. cit., p. 164; for Bale's reference, see Bale, *Image*, 1: sig. R4-verso.

45. For Turner's edition, see Joachim Vadianus (i.e., von Watt), *A Worke entytled of ye olde god & the newe* (London [J. Byddell], 1534). Bale referred to von Watt's work in *A dysclosynge or openynge of the Manne of synne* (Antwerp, 1543), fol. 48-verso. Here he attributed the work to "one Hermannus a germane," evidently thinking of the 1523 Latin translation of von Watt's work by Hartmann Dulichius.

46. Viz. Bodleian Library MS. Bodley 73, fol. v.

47. Von Watt, sigs. F3-verso to F5-verso.

48. Viz. ibid., sig. K1.

49. J. F. Crompton, *"Fasciculi Zizaniorum," Journal of Ecclesiastical History* 12 (1961): 39-43. Crompton discusses the dating of Bale's annotations.

50. Bodleian Library MS. e Musaeo 86, fol. 33. It is pretty clear that the underlining was done by Bale, since marginal comments in his hand appear in the same ink.

51. See Wyclif's *De Solutione Sathanae*, in Rudolf Buddensieg, ed., *John Wiclif's Polemical Works in Latin* (London, 1883), 2:393: *"Sed in secundo millenario . . . amplius est solutus . . . etc."*

52. Bodleian Library MS. e Musaeo 86, fol. i-verso: *"movetur haec questio. . . . An substancia panis, essencialiter maneat post consecrationem, Ubi non solum confitetur manere panem cum Luthero, set et merum panem cum Oecolampadio et Zwinglio."*

53. For beliefs among later Lollards that the institutional Church was the Antichrist, see J. A. F. Thompson, *The Later Lollards* (Oxford, 1967), pp. 249-250 and passim; and Edwin Welch, "Some Suffolk Lollards," *Proceedings of the Suffolk Archaeological Society* 29 (1962): 154-165.

54. Though one cannot be sure that authors were resident in the cities where their books were published (which was wisely pointed out by M. M. Knappen, *Tudor Puritanism* [Chicago, 1965], p. 58 n. 10) the fact that Bale had books printed by two separate presses in Antwerp between 1543 and 1546 makes it sound as though he may have been living there. See Appendix 2 for his books published during these years.

55. Bale, *Image*, 1: sigs. A5-A6.

56. Viz. ibid., 1: sigs. A6-B1: Bale supplied a long list of com-

mentators on Revelation, from the Church Fathers on forward. He said that he had seen "almost so many, as have their beginnings here registered." Of the recent and/or Protestant commentaries which he listed, he supplied *incipits* only for those by Georgius Aemilius, Francis Lambert, Martin Luther, and Sebastian Meyer.

57. Luther's 1545 preface to the Apocalypse, which did accept the book as a key to history, appeared too late to influence Bale's thought, and in any case offered a periodic scheme which differed significantly from the one which Bale had adopted.

58. Bale, *Image*, 1: sig. L5, for example: Bale cites Meyer's commentary in support of the belief that the souls of the martyrs beneath the altar (in Revelation 6:9) represented all the true Christian believers since Christ's Ascension. Meyer, however, interprets these martyrs as representing the Old Testament faithful: Sebastian Meyer, *In Apocalypsim Ioannis Apostoli . . . Commentarius* (Zurich, 1539), fol. 23.

59. Ibid., fol. 80-verso for the loosing of Satan; fols. 21-22 for the first four seals.

60. For Lambert's career and work see Roy L. Winters, *Francis Lambert of Avignon* (Philadelphia, 1938).

61. Francis Lambert, *Exegeseos . . . in sanctam Divi Ioannis Apocalypsim Libri VII* (Marburg, 1528), fols. 117-verso to 149-verso, 232-234, 283-verso to 285.

62. Reeves, op. cit., pp. 464-465, suspects a Joachite origin for many of Lambert's ideas.

63. Viz. the collection entitled *Abbas Joachim Magnus Propheta* (Venice, c. 1516), fol. 55: a scheme from the *tractatus de septem statibus ecclesie* of Ubertinus de Casali, O.F.M., which divides Church history into periods very different from Lambert's, but does assume that the seven seals indicate clear-cut ages, and does look forward to a seventh age within history.

64. Winters, op. cit., p. 60.

65. Only the first two parts of this edition have survived. STC assigns them to the press of Stephen Mierdman, probably at Antwerp: STC 1296.5. All three parts must have been published and available in England by the summer of 1546, for they were banned by proclamation on September 26 of that year. See Bishop Bonner's register, Guildhall (London) MS. 9531/12, fol. 92-verso; the procla-

mation is also printed in John Foxe, *Acts and Monuments*, Josiah Pratt, ed. (London, 1870), 5:567-568. Bale had evidently almost finished the commentary by 1543: see Bale, *Manne of synne*, fols. 7-verso, 8, 40. References to *Image* will henceforth be to the first complete edition that survives: London (R. Jugge), 1548.

66.   Bale obviously made use of many previous commentaries besides Lambert's. "Of these commentaries," he said in reference to the ones he had listed in his preface, "have I taken both example to do thys thynge, and also counsell to understande the text, to none of them wholly addyct, but as I preceyved them alwayes agreynge to the scripturs. . . ." Ibid., 1, sig. B1. But it was Lambert's interpretation which he followed for the greater part of his historical exegesis.

67.   Here Bale followed Lambert in a periodization of world history which was different from St. Augustine's traditional scheme. For Bale and Lambert, the seven ages were the following: Adam to Noah, Noah to Abraham, Abraham to Moses, Moses to David, David to the Exile, the Exile to the birth of Jesus, the Incarnation to the end of the world. Bale and Lambert, in other words, split Augustine's third age (Abraham to David) into two. This meant that the period of Church history fell into the seventh age, not the sixth, for Bale and Lambert. Neither of them made much of this point; it does not seem to have affected their interpretations of Church history. See Ibid., 1: sig. H8, and Lambert, *Exegeseos*, fol. 232.

68.   Bale, *Image*, 1: sigs. A3-verso, A4-verso, I8.

69.   Ibid., 1: sig. A4-verso.

70.   See, for instance, *à propos* the white horse of Revelation 6:2, Bale's comment, "Suche a whyt horse to the glorye of God was Paule, whan he bare the name of Christe before the gentyles, the kynges, and the children of Israel." Lambert had written, "*Sic equus albus & gloriae dei fuit Paulus, qui nomen Christi portavit coram gentibus, & tribubus, & filiis Israel.*" (Bale, *Image* 1: sig. K1; Lambert, *Exegeseos*, fol. 118-verso.)

71.   Bale, *Image*, 1: sigs. K5-K8; Lambert, *Exegeseos*, fols. 122-123.

72.   Bale, *Image*, 1: sigs. K5-K8; Lambert, *Exegeseos*, fols. 122-123. Lambert includes scarcely any of the historical detail which Bale supplies. Bale on the other hand leaves out a section in which Lambert—in a vein of legalism which apparently was typical of him—emphasizes his belief that Christ came above all to fulfill the Old

Testament Law. Bale by no means slavishly copied Lambert when he disagreed with the man theologically.

73.   Cf. Williams, op. cit., p. 19.

74.   Von Watt, op. cit., sigs. F3-verso to F5-verso. For the use of this theme by other reformers, see Polman, op. cit., pp. 165-166, 176-177; and Williams, op. cit., p. 17.

75.   Bale, *Image*, 1: sig. L2; Lambert, *Exegeseos*, fol. 125.

76.   Bale, *Image*, 1: sig. L5: "at thys tyme so well as at all other tymes sens Christes ascensyon. . . ." Lambert, *Exegeseos*, fol. 127: *"quod tum fuit, est hodie, & erit usque in saeculi finem, nempe quod Antichristi & hypocritae, ad piorum interfectionem adnituntur. . . ."*

77.   Bale, *Image*, 1: sig. M1-verso; Lambert, *Exegeseos*, fol. 131-verso.

78.   Bale, *Image*, 1: sig. L8-verso: "The greate antychryste of Europa is the kynge of faces, the prynce of hypocrysye. . . ." Lambert, *Exegeseos*, fol. 130-verso: *"Magnus ergo Europae Antichristus, Rex facierum & Princeps hypocriseos. . . ."*

79.   Ibid., fols. 232-verso to 233, 283-verso to 285.

80.   Ibid., fol. 233: *"Ego, ut saepe dixi, puto omnino in ianuis esse, magni Antichristi adventum. . . ."*

81.   Bale, *Image*, 2: sigs. i6-verso to i7.

82.   Ibid., 2: sig. k7.

83.   Ibid., 1: sig. O3-verso.

84.   Ibid., 1: sig. O4.

85.   Ibid., 3: sig. Gg3.

86.   Ibid., 2: sigs. i6-verso, r6.

87.   Ibid., 3: sig. Gg4.

88.   Ibid., 3: sig. Gg7-verso; for this sentiment in general, see, e.g., Tuveson, op. cit., pp. 22-30.

89.   See below, Chapter 4.

90.   Bale, *Image*, 2: sigs. s1-s2.

91.   Ibid., 1: sigs. K2 to K4-verso.

92.   Ibid., 1: sig. S4-verso.

93.   Viz. Polman, op. cit., pp. 183 ff.

94.   See V. Norskov Olsen, *John Foxe and the Elizabethan Church*

(Berkeley, California, 1973), Chapter 2; and H. F. Woodhouse, *The Doctrine of the Church in Anglican Theology, 1547-1603* (London, 1954), especially chapters 1, 2, and 13.

95. Ibid., pp. 8, 20.

96. Bale, *Image*, 1: sigs. H7-verso, 14. Bale argues here that there had been seven seal-openings in the Old Testament period, as well in post-Ascension Church history, and that the twenty-four elders of Revelation 5:8 represented the Old Testament faithful as well as the New.

97. See above, Chapter 2. For this theme in *Image*, see 1: sig. G8. For the idea of the Church's invisibility, as seen in the works of Wyclif and of the sixteenth-century English reformers, see Woodhouse, op. cit., pp. 5-6, 15-16, and passim.

98. See his exegesis of Revelation 12:6 and 20:8-9, in *Image*, 2: sigs. e3-e5; and 3: Hh6-verso to Ii5.

99. Ibid., 3: sigs. Gg3 ff.

100. See, e.g., ibid., 2: sig. h7: Bale argues that the elect before Christ ate of the same spiritual meat, and drank from the same spiritual rock (in the wilderness) as those who came after the Incarnation. The spiritual eating and drinking were crucial.

101. Ibid., 2: sig. r6.

102. Ibid., 2: sigs. i6-verso to i7.

103. Ibid., 1: sig. L8-verso.

104. Ibid., 2: sig. p3: "Sittinge in the temple of God which is with in man, with suche wicked lawes as they made under the name of God and of Christe, they terryble vexed, tormented, and cruciated the weake consciences of men, leavinge them commonlye in most peinefull desperacion."

105. See e.g., ibid., 3: Gg4-Gg6 and passim.

106. Cf. Knappen, op. cit., pp. 60-71.

107. Bale, *Image*, 2: sig. k3 to k3-verso.

IV / The English Past

1. Antwerp? Stephen Mierdman? 1545? (STC 1296.5); London, Mierdman for Richard Jugge, 1548 (STC 1297); London, Mierdman

for John Day and William Seres, c. 1550 (STC 1298); and London, John Wyer, 1550 (STC 1299). A fifth edition appeared from the press of Thomas East in 1570 (STC 1301). For Stephen Mierdman as the printer of various books attributed to Jugge, Day, Seres, and others, see Colin Clair, "On the Printing of Certain Reformation Books," *The Library*, 5th ser., 18 (1963): 275-287.

2.   See William Lamont, *Godly Rule* (London, 1969) and also the trenchant critique of this book by Bernard Capp: "*Godly Rule* and the Millennium," *Past and Present* 52 (August 1971): 106-117, and "The Millennium and Eschatology in England," *Past and Present* 57 (November 1972): 156-162. See also Christopher Hill, *Antichrist in Seventeenth-century England* (London, 1971), passim, and Ernest L. Tuveson, *Millennium and Utopia* (New York, 1964), pp. 22-70.

3.   John Bale, *The first two partes of the Actes or unchast examples of the Englysh votaryes* (London, 1560), 2: sig. I7. Subsequent references will be to this edition of 1560.

4.   For this tradition see V. H. Galbraith, *Historical Research in Medieval England* (London, 1951); C. L. Kingsford, *English Historical Writing in the Fifteenth Century* (Oxford, 1913); F. J. Levy, *Tudor Historical Thought* (San Marino, California, 1967), pp. 9-32; and C. A. Patrides, *The Grand Design of God* (London, 1972), pp. 36-39.

5.   For humanist history in England, see esp. Levy, op. cit., pp. 33-78.

6.   *L & P*, 17:177. It is not clear from the proclamation what the offending author's book was, though it is most likely to have been an edition of Bale's *A Christen Exhortacyon unto Customable Swearers* (Antwerp [C. van Endhoven's widow], c. 1542). This book has been at times wrongly attributed to Miles Coverdale (viz. Davies, p. 214 n. 4) but its *incipit* matches that of the work called *Contra iurandi consuetudinem*, which Bale claims as his own in the *Catalogus*, 1:704. For the printer see Wouter Nijhoff, *L'Art Typographique dans les Pays-Bas II*, (The Hague, 1902), under "Christophorus Ruremundensis," 4, plate 9, which type matches that of *Christen Exhortacyon*. Nijhoff (p. 23) notes that after 1535 the printer Johannes Hoochstraten was also using van Endhoven's types occasionally, so it is possible that Hoochstraten was the one who published Bale's first pamphlet.

7.   Bale, *Christen Exhortacyon*. Cf. H. G. Russell, "Lollard

Opposition to Oaths by Creatures," *American Historical Review* 51 (1946): 680, who feels that Bale probably picked up this theme on the Continent. But since he was so preoccupied with Lollardy in the early 1540s, with his study of *Fasciculi Zizaniorum*, it is quite possible that Wycliffite ideas moved Bale to write this pamphlet.

8. John Bale and William Turner, *The epistle exhortatorye of an Englyshe Christyane* ("Basyle," [i.e., Antwerp, A. Goinus], 1544), sigs. D5-D6. Bale never claimed this little tract as one of his own works, but his friend John Foxe later attributed it to him (J. Foxe, *Actes and Monuments*, [London, 1563], p. 574) and the historical themes in the pamphlet mark it unmistakably as one of Bale's.

9. M. M. Knappen, *Tudor Puritanism* (Chicago, 1965), pp. 59-65.

10. John Bale, *A brefe Chronycle concernynge . . . syr Iohan Oldcastell*, (n.p. [Antwerp, A. Goinus], 1544).

11. See below, Chapter 5.

12. John Bale, *A mysterye of inyquyte* ("Geneva" [i.e., Antwerp, A. Goinus], 1545). Viz. fols. 33 and 58 for some of these themes— Boniface III, Sylvester II, and so on.

13. The printer, Stephen Mierdman, moved from Antwerp to London sometime between 1546 and 1549, and may have printed the tract there: see Clair, loc. cit., pp. 275-276.

14. The first edition of *The Actes of Englysh votaryes* had a Wesel colophon, but it was clearly from Mierdman's press: ibid. Bale was used to disguising his actual location with false colophons, though in this case perhaps he was simply announcing, with a certain bravado, his impending move.

15. Honor McCusker, "Some Ornamental Initials used by Plateanus of Wesel," *The Library*, 4th ser., 16 (1936): 452-454. Miss McCusker shows that van der Straten printed all ten of Bale's works from 1546 to 1548. Davies (pp. 250-258) thinks that some of these books may have come from the press of Johann von Kempen at Marburg, but STC agrees with Miss McCusker (STC 848, 850, 1279, 1287, 1295, 1296, 1305, 14717, 15180, and 17320).

16. Some copies of the *Summarium* bear an Ipswich colophon, but this was probably a device to evade English restrictions on imported books.

17. W. K. Jordan, *Edward VI: The Young King* (Cambridge, Massachusetts, 1968), pp. 125-166.

18. McCusker, pp. 29-54.

19. Winthrop Hudson, *John Ponet* (Chicago, 1942), p. 50. For Bale's collation, see Hampshire County Record Office, Winchester, Reg. Ponet, fol. 12-verso.

20. See his *An Expostulation or complaynte agaynste the Blasphemyes of a franticke papyst of Hamshyre* (London, 1552). The title supplies an accurate impression of the pamphlet's contents.

21. See below, Chapter 5.

22. For the printer of these books, and the location of his press, see Leslie P. Fairfield, "The Mysterious Press of 'Michael Wood' (1553-1554)," *The Library*, 5th ser., 27 (1972): 222 n. 10.

23. William Whittingham (?), *A Brief Discourse of the Troubles at Frankfort*, Edward Arber (London, 1908), p. 36. For the suggested attribution of this book to Thomas Wood, see Patrick Collinson, "The Authorship of *A Brieff Discours...*," *Journal of Ecclesiastical History* 9 (1958): 188-208.

24. McCusker, p. 25.

25. British Museum MS. Harley 417, fol. 113: a letter of Grindal to Foxe, 10 May 1556, sends greetings to Bale. Another letter in the British Museum would seem at first sight to upset this chronology— Add. MS. 29546, fol. 25, from John Ponet to "my verey lovinge freend Mr. Bale ... at ffranckford" and dated simply 6 July. Internal evidence shows that the year must have been 1556, just before Ponet's death. Ponet says, "My furst book is ready and loe I send you one.... Yf your counsell can helpe me to utter some copies ye shew me a pleasure, for my second book must lye still till this be utterid." The two books must have been Ponet's *Apologie* against Thomas Martin, and his *Shorte Treatise of Politike Power*, both published in 1556. Viz. Hudson, op. cit., pp. 80 ff. The only likely explanation for Ponet's mistake about Bale's whereabouts is that in fact he did not know that Bale had already left Frankfort.

26. Christina H. Garrett, *The Marian Exiles* (Cambridge, 1966), pp. 78, 156-157.

27. Inner Temple Library, London, MS. Petyt 538/47, fol. 380: cited in Patrick Collinson, *The Elizabethan Puritan Movement* (Berkeley, California, 1967), p. 33, n. 9.

28. Theodor Vetter, *Literarische Beziehungen zwischen England und der Schweiz im Reformationszeitalter* (Zurich, 1901), p. 39.

29. British Museum MS. Cotton Titus D.X, fol. 178-verso.

30. J. Le Neve, *Fasti Ecclesiae Anglicanae*, T. D. Hardy, ed. (Oxford, 1854), 1:60.

31. See below, Chapter 6.

32. John Bale, *A Declaration of Edmonde Bonners articles* (London, 1561). A note on sig. A3 indicates that Bale had written this at Basel in 1554. Since Bonner's articles were published in September of 1554 (ibid., fol. 68—signatures B through V bear foliation numbers) and since Bale is known to have been in Frankfort the same month, he must have written this pamphlet while on a visit to Basel later that year.

33. For other details relating to Bale's life during the years 1540 to 1560, see Davies, pp. 213-230, and McCusker, pp. 14-28.

34. See above, n. 3.

35. John Bale, *A dysclosynge or openynge of the Manne of synne* ("Zurich" [i.e., Antwerp], 1543), fols. 96-verso to 97.

36. Ibid., fol. 37-verso.

37. Bale and Turner, *Epistle exhortatorye*, fol. 11.

38. Bale, *A mysterye of inyquyte*, fol. 10-verso; for some reason Bale later changed his mind or was unable to publish what he planned to call "The battayle of John wycleff:" see Bodleian Library MS. e Musaeo 86, fol. 1-verso.

39. Bale and Turner, *Epistle exhortatorye*, fols. 13-15.

40. Bale, *The first two partes of the Actes*, 1: sig. A7-verso.

41. For the importance of this myth in Elizabethan England, see Carol Z. Wiener, "The Beleaguered Isle. A Study of Elizabethan and Early Jacobean Anti-Catholicism," *Past and Present* 51 (1971): pp. 27-62: a useful antidote to William Haller's (nevertheless valuable) *Foxe's Book of Martyrs and the Elect Nation* (London, 1967).

42. Bale, *The first two partes of the Actes*, 1: sigs. A5-verso-A6.

43. Ibid., 1: sig. C1.

44. Ibid., 1: sig. D6-verso.

45. Ibid., 1: sig. D8.

46.   In fact, Theodore had been consecrated in 668; Bale clearly fudged the date to make it coincide with the number of the beast in Revelation 13. Though he referred to Bede for support on this point, Bede in fact had given the date of Theodore's consecration correctly as 668. Viz. Bede, *Venerabilis Baedae opera historica*, C. Plummer, ed. (Oxford, 1896), 1:203.

47.   Bale, *The first two partes of the Actes*, 1: sigs. K4-verso, M3-verso.

48.   Ibid., 2: sigs. D8-verso, K3, M1-M2, Q2, and passim.

49.   Ibid., 2: sigs. S2-verso ff.

50.   For a slightly longer summary of *The Actes of Englysh votaryes*, see Glanmor Williams, *Reformation Views of Church History* (Richmond, Virginia, 1970), pp. 39-40.

51.   *Summarium*, fols. 245-246.

52.   Levy, op. cit., p. 94.

53.   Cf. by contrast McCusker, p. 123, who sees him as essentially an antiquary, and a propagandist only by accident.

54.   Cf. the structure of Johann Trithemius's *Liber de Scriptoribus Ecclesiasticis* (Basel, 1494).

55.   For Bale's population of early Britain, see T. D. Kendrick, *British Antiquity* (London, 1950), esp. pp. 69-72; cf. Annius (Nanni) of Viterbo, *Commentarii* (Rome, 1498), sigs. P3 and R1-verso ff.

56.   *Summarium*, fol. 110-verso: "*Istum ideo in hac tertia Centuria primum posui, ut ab eo discant prima facie lectores, quales illi sint qui per eam etatem sequantur, paucissimis exceptis.*"

57.   Ibid., fol. 42, re Theodore of Tarsus: "*Nostre salutis anno .666. qui in Apocalypsi Ioannis & numerus Bestie & numerus hominis est . . . . Quod vero tunc venerit cum magne illius Bestie caractere, apud Cestrensem, Capgravium & alios Anglicarum rerum fide dignos scriptores perspicuum est. Non enim ante id tempus tam potenter operabatur Antichristi spiritus, iniquitatis sue mysterium.*" See also fol. 65-verso, about the monks at Floriacum: "*Unde prodiit impostor ille pessimus Gerebertus, seu Sylvester papa secundus, qui post mille annos a Christi nativitate de abysso diabolum soluit, ut palam Antichristus suam in sanctos exerceret tyrannidem.*"

58.   This was what Bale had done for the Carmelite Order in the second, biographical section of *Anglorum Heliades*: British Museum MS. Harley 3838, fols. 54-112.

59.   Viz. Bale's comments in his dedication of the *Catalogus* to Otto Henry, Count Palatine of the Rhine: *Catalogus*, sigs. a3-verso-a4.

60.   Cf. ibid., p. 142, re Sylvester II: *"diaboli ope adiutus, Romani papatus sedem accepit: eius vicarius factus, quem e puteo Tartareo suis praestigiis ac necromantiis soluit, Apoc. 20. . . ."*

61.   Another edition appeared in 1559—virtually the same as the first—and references hereafter will be to the later one. Both editions draw on the *Catalogus* for practically their whole content. Exceptions are as follows: the forty-page introduction, then pp. 338-344, pp. 435-436, pp. 492-495, pp. 517-519, pp. 521-525. It is necessary to distinguish very clearly between the Latin editions of *Acta Romanorum Pontificum* (Basel, 1558-1559), and their English translation, *The Pageant of Popes* (London, 1574), edited by John Studley. This latter contains copious additions by Studley (e.g. fols. 1-14 on Saint Peter, which represent a massive expansion of pp. 2-4 in *Acta*), and must be used only with great care as an expression of Bale's thought. Cf. Levy, op. cit., p. 92, where the difference between the Latin and the English editions is not recognized.

62.   And which he had repeated in the *Summarium*: fols. 245-246.

63.   Bale, *Acta*, sigs. '3-'4. The first twenty leaves of the edition lack pagination.

64.   Cf. Public Record Office, London, SP 1/111, fol. 187 ("The answer of John Bale pryst"): "ye wurde of god, (whych schuld onlye grownde goodnes in ye ceremonyes)." Viz. also Bale and Turner, *Epistle exhortatorye*, fols. 7-verso to 8: "so long as the blasphemouse beggeryes of the blodye Bishoppes of Rome are not plucked up by the rootes / as were the unsaverye sacrifyces of Baal and of Bel; and so broken in peces with the brasen serpent idolatrouslye abused / the lawes of Gods true worshyppynes (which are in the Byble prescrybed) set up in theyr stede / so longe (I saye) is it all in vayne to banishe the Pope out of Englande; but he wyll styll dwell there in the secrete consciences of menne. . . ."

65.   On this point see *inter alia* Levy, op. cit., pp. 79-83, 105-109; Williams, op. cit., pp. 15-20; and John M. Headley, *Luther's View of Church History* (New Haven, Connecticut, 1963), pp. 163-181.

66.   Viz. John E. Booty, *John Jewel as Apologist of the Church of England* (London, 1963), pp. 130-137.

67.   *Summarium*, sig. A3: *"Neque enim temere ulla doctrina*

admittenda est, cuius testimonium non extet in primae ecclesiae doctoribus."

68. See the letters of 24 September and 15 November in William Whittingham (?), op. cit., pp. 36-37.

69. Inner Temple Library, London, MS. Petyt 538/47, fol. 380. The letter continues at length, arguing that the 1552 Communion service was not in the least "popishe," and attacking this new "Church of the Purytie." The letter is dated "Ano 1556"; it is a transcript, not in Bale's hand.

70. Robert Barnes, *Vitae Pontificum Romanorum* (Wittenberg, 1536), sig. C7; cf. Bartolomeo Platina, *De Vita & Moribus summorum Pontificum* (Cologne, 1529), p. 29.

71. Bale, *Acta*, p. 17: *"aperta blasphemia est."*

72. Ibid., p. 11: *"Quod ille per quatuor temporum ieiunia, Dei populum iudaizare fecerit, fabulam esse credo."* Cf. Barnes, op. cit., sig. C2-verso.

73. Bale, *Acta*, p. 21: *"Plaustra decretorum ac mendaciorum, Carsulanus, Platina, Stella, & alii Paparum adulatores, his Christi martyribus, sed falso, tribuunt: ut suarum caeremoniarum, ne dicam blasphemiarum, institutio diabolica, eorum autoritate, comprobetur."*

74. Ibid., p. 27: *"Horum decreta sunt in libris inserta consiliorum: sed ex his pleraque tam sunt levicula, tam nugatoria, tam aliena prorsus a sacris litteris, ut credibile sit, ab aliis longo post tempore fuisse conficta. Sin autem vera sunt, & ab illis emanarunt, tunc sane, quod vaticinando Paulus dicebat. . . ."* I.e., what Paul said in II Thessalonians 2:8 about the "lawless one" had come true even in the early Church.

75. There was one exception: ibid., p. 37, concerning Pope John I—some historians (viz. Barnes, op. cit., sig. F3) had reported that John had adorned various altars with silver. Bale decided that this must be a fable, since John had also encouraged the Emperor Theodoric to resist Arianism. John therefore had been an anachronism in this age, a good pope, and would not have wasted silver on popish altars. One need scarcely observe that this was no less an *a priori* judgment than Bale's conclusions regarding the first-age popes, and based on no more evidence.

76. Cf. Levy, op. cit., p. 89. Levy notes Barnes's "totally uncritical use of sources," but neglects to add that Bale's methodology was no

different. For comments on *Acta Romanorum Pontificum*, see also Williams op. cit., pp. 41-42.

77. Bale, *Concernynge . . . Oldecastell*, fol. 5 to 5-verso.

78. Antwerp, S. Mierdman, 1546 (STC 1270); London, T. Raynalde, 1548 (STC 1271); and London, S. Mierdman for A. Vele, 1551 (STC 1271.5).

79. Viz. *The Olde Faythe of Great Brittaygne*, c. 1549: see Levy, op. cit., p. 97.

80. For different aspects of English anti-Catholic sentiment, see Haller, op. cit. especially chapter 6; Wiener, loc. cit., passim; D. M. Loades, *The Oxford Martyrs* (London, 1970); and William S. Maltby, *The Black Legend in England* (Durham, North Carolina, 1971).

81. For a critique of Haller's reading of Foxe, see V. Norskov Olsen, *John Foxe and the Elizabethan Church* (Berkeley, California, 1973), pp. 36-47.

82. Haller, op. cit., p. 62.

83. Ibid., p. 80.

84. John Bale, *The laboryouse Journey & serche of Johan Leylande* (London, 1549), sig. B6.

85. *Summarium*, fol. 246-verso: "*naturalis et officiosus erga patriam amor.*"

86. John Bale, *The vocacyon of Johan Bale*, ("Rome" [i.e. Wesel], 1553), fol. 47-verso.

87. Bale, *Manne of synne*, fol. 11.

88. Bale, *Expostulation agaynste blasphemyes*, sigs. A5-verso to A6.

89. John Bale, *King Johan*, Barry B. Adams, ed., (San Marino, California, 1969), p. 147. For the dating of revised conclusion, see p. 196, notes to lines 2680-81.

90. Bale elsewhere followed exegetical tradition in identifying Constantine as one of the figures meant by the angel ascending from the rising of the sun, sealing the elect: see Bale, *Expostulation agaynst blasphemyes*, sigs. A5-verso to A6.

91. Haller, op. cit., p. 80.

92. A. L. Rowse, *The England of Elizabeth* (New York, 1961), chapter 2.

93. Bale, *Journey of Johan Leylande*, sig. C5-verso.

94. *Summarium*, sigs. A2-verso to A3-verso, and fols. 245-246.

95. Bale, *Vocacyon*, fol. 47-verso.

96. For this tradition see Marjorie Reeves, *The Influence of Prophecy in the Later Middle Ages* (Oxford, 1969), pp. 295-392.

97. Cf. Lamont, op. cit., pp. 31-35, who argues unconvincingly for Sibylline influence on John Foxe.

98. For Bale's praise of Constantine, who had the added virtue of being half British, see *Catalogus*, 1:32-33.

99. E.g., *Acta*, p. 28: *"mitrati pontifices erant, canonibus ac decretis suis, Antichristo magno sedem parantes."*

100. On the significance of Constantine's reign, Bale agreed with the later English commentators John Napier and Thomas Brightman, and disagreed with Foxe. See Olsen, op. cit., pp. 74-79, and also below, chapter 6.

101. John Bale, *The Image of bothe churches* (London, 1548) 3: sig. li3-verso.

102. Bale, *Manne of synne*, fol. 7-verso.

103. Bale, *Image*, 3: sig. Gg7-verso.

104. Ibid., 2: sig. k7.

105. Tuveson, op. cit., especially pp. 22-55; for the distinction between the Calvinist and Lutheran attitudes toward eschatology, see Roland Bainton, *The Reformation of the Sixteenth Century* (Boston, Mass., 1956), pp. 114-115.

106. Kendrick, op. cit., esp. pp. 69-72.

107. Bale, *The first two partes of the Actes*, 1: sigs. L4, L7-verso to L8. Cf. Polydore Vergil, *Historiae Anglicae Libri XXVI* (Basel, 1534), p. 82; and Ranulf Higden, *Polychronicon* (London, 1482), fol. 309.

108. Bale, *Englysh votaryes* (Wesel, 1546), fol. 44-verso; cf. John Capgrave, *Nova Legenda Angliae* (London, 1516), fol. 282: Capgrave had said that the school taught *"metrice artis astronomie & arithmetice ecclesiastice disciplina inter sacrorum arcium volumina. . . ."*

109. Bale, *Englysh votaryes*, fols. 43-verso to 44-verso; cf. Capgrave, op. cit., fols. 281-verso to 282, where Theodore's consecration is correctly assigned to 668.

110. For simply one example among many, compare Bale's description in the *Summarium* of Archbishop John Peckham O.F.M. with the

source which Bale gives, Trevet's *Annales: "Equus ad Antichristi usum ferocissimus. . . . animo semper superbus & arrogans, eloquio, incessu, ac gestu pompaticus, ut eum Trevetus depingit" (Summarium,* fol. 121). Compare Trevet: *"Ordinis sui zelator erat precipuus, carminum dictator egregius, gestus affatus pompatici, mentis benigne, et animi admodum liberalis"* (Nicholas Trevet, *Annales sex regum Angliae,* Thomas Hog, ed., [London, 1845], p. 300).

111. Bodleian Library MS. Selden supra 64, published as John Bale, *Index Britanniae Scriptorum,* eds. R. L. Poole and Mary Bateson (Oxford, 1902).

112. Ibid., pp. xx-xxi. The book was a gift to Bale from Dr. Thomas Gibson, who had originally intended to use it for a collection of medicinal recipes (see Bodleian Library MS. Selden supra 64, fol. 25). For further notes on the dating of the MS. see Davies, p. 243; and Willy Bang's review of the Poole-Bateson edition, in *Englische Studien* 34 (1904): 110-113.

113. Including an autobiographical note on Bale's Carmelite period: *"Illud vite institutum, in quod per inscitiam etatis fuerat, vel delapsus, vel pertractus, nequaquam probabat, subinde dictitans nihil non facere ad prescriptum humanum, potius quam ad Christi regulam, nihil eo iniquius esse. . . ."* (Bale, *Index,* pp. 180-181). Needless to say, this was wishful thinking.

114. Trinity College, Cambridge, MS. R.7.15. Leland's work in toto was published as *Commentarii de Scriptoribus Britannicis,* ed. Anthony Hall (Oxford, 1709).

115. Trinity College, Cambridge, MS. R.7.15, fol. 1: *"Opus Johannis Lelandi, de illustribus viris anglice nationis, a Joanne Baleo Anglo ossoriensi apud hibernos episcopo, epitomatum, ac plerisque in locis emendatum et auctum."* For the dating of the MS. see Davies, p. 243, except that Davies' *terminus a quo* (1549) is perhaps too early.

116. Trinity College, Cambridge, MS. R.7.15, fol. 2-verso: *"Unum fortassis displicebit, nec mihi interim placet, quod sine discrimine doctrinarum ac spirituum exploratione pleraque sint hic pertractata, et iniqua pro sanctis admissa."*

117. Ibid., fol. 37 to 37-verso: *"Claruit Wolstanus, anno Christi 1000. Sathane abyssum egredienti, monachi sedes parant. . . . Claruit Oswaldus, anno verbi incarnati 1010. Sol his diebus obscuratur. Scripture enim negliguntur."*

118. Ibid., fol. 122: "*Perpende preposterum Lelandi iudicium hoc loco. Barbarissimum sophistam, theologum illustrum vocat, pios doctores lernas, et papistarum commenta frigidissima, immo iniquissima gladium evangelium.*"

119. The whole MS. is in Bale's most mature hand, with the continental ticked "u" which he adopted about 1543: see Davies, p. 246. The latest date is that of a letter to Bale from Robert Roll, 4 November 1559. Davies would seem to have missed that, as he dates the MS. "1549?-1557": ibid., p. 243.

120. John Baconthorpe's *Liber Sententiarum* and Philip Ribot's *Liber de Institutione et peculiaribus gestis religiosorum Carmelitarum.*

121. *Nota magnum Antichristum.* See British Museum MS. Cotton Titus D.X, fols. 133-verso to 134-verso.

122. See the letters reprinted in McCusker, pp. 68-71.

123. On this point, see Rainer Pineas, "William Tyndale's Influence on John Bale's Polemical Use of History," *Archiv fuer Reformationsgeschichte* 53 (1962): 79-96.

124. Donald R. Kelley, *Foundations of Modern Historical Scholarship* (New York, 1970), pp. 4-5.

125. See Patrides, op. cit., for this theme.

126. Bale of course had an indirect hand in Parker's project, as he made available to the archbishop in the early 1560s his vast knowledge of the medieval chronicles. See Bale's letter to Parker of July 1560, printed in McCusker, pp. 58 ff.

127. *Summarium*, fol. 246-verso.

128. For the search for a "useful" past in sixteenth-century England, see *inter alia* F. S. Fussner, *Tudor History and the Historians* (New York, 1970), pp. 245-250.

V / *The New English Saints*

1. Helen C. White, *Tudor Books of Saints and Martyrs* (Madison, Wisconsin, 1963), pp. 80-82. Chapter 3 as a whole discusses the attack on the saint-cult which Cromwell orchestrated.

2. In spite of the considerable scholarly literature on Bale, treat-

ment of his contribution to Protestant hagiography has not been extensive. William Haller, in *Foxe's Book of Martyrs and the Elect Nation* (London, 1967), deals with Bale's influence on Foxe's sense of history, but speaks only briefly about the former's contribution to the Protestant martyrology (see pp. 60-61, and also pp. 110-139). Other briefer references to Bale's importance in the formation of Protestant hagiography may be found in M. E. Aston, "Lollardy and the Reformation: Survival or Revival," *History* 49 (1964): 164 ff.; A. G. Dickens, *The English Reformation* (London, 1964), pp. 169-170; W. K. Jordan, *Edward VI: The Young King* (Cambridge, Massachusetts, 1968), pp. 27, 30, 147, 152; and Rainer Pineas, "William Tyndale's Influence on John Bale's Polemical Use of History," *Archiv fuer Reformationsgeschichte* 53 (1962): 79-96.

3. For this purpose, as it was felt by Continental Protestant hagiographers of Bale's generation, see Donald R. Kelley, "Martyrs, Myths and Massacre: The Background of St. Bartholemew," *American Historical Review* 77 (1972): esp. pp. 1326-1327.

4. For early hagiography in general, see White, op. cit., chapter 1, and also René Aigran, *L'Hagiographie: ses sources, ses méthodes, son histoire* (Paris, 1953), esp. pp. 132 ff.

5. PRO SP 1/111, fol. 184.

6. In *King Johan* Bale did, to be sure, present his hero's beliefs in Protestant hues—see John Bale, *King Johan*, Barry B. Adams, ed., (San Marino, California, 1969), pp. 81-82. But what might pass scrutiny in a popular verse-play would hardly do in a more serious saint's life, especially when the gap between Bale's portrait of the monarch and the reality was so great.

7. For a thorough discussion of this MS. (Bodleian Library MS. e Musaeo 86), see J. Crompton, *"Fasciculi Zizaniorum," Journal of Ecclesiastical History* 12 (1961): pp. 35-45, 155-166. The MS. has been published as Thomas Netter of Walden, *Fasciculi Zizaniorum*, ed. W. W. Shirley (London, 1858), in which Oldcastle's examination is found on pp. 433-450. Another version of his examination—virtually identical to the one in *Fasciculi Zizaniorum*—may be found in David Wilkins, *Concilia Magnae Britanniae et Hiberniae* (London, 1737), 3:353-357.

8. Bale filled in certain blank leaves of the MS. with his own notes (Bodleian Library MS. e Musaeo 86, fols. 98-verso to 103-verso) and dated these notes "1543."

212 / JOHN BALE

9. Another fifteenth-century account of Oldcastle is found in Thomas Walsingham, *Historia Anglicana*, H. T. Riley, ed. (London, 1864), 2:297-299. This account is short and would have been of little use to Bale alongside the material in *Fasciculi Zizaniorum*—even assuming that Bale in exile would have had access to the Walsingham chronicle. The argument that Bale used Walsingham heavily is not convincing; cf. L. M. Oliver, "Sir John Oldcastle: Legend or Literature?" *The Library*, 5th ser., 1 (1946-1947): 179 ff.

10. Sir Thomas More thought that it had been George Constantine: see his *The confutacyon of Tyndales answere* (London, 1532), sig. Aa 4-verso. But Bale assumed that Tyndale had edited the tract; and later on Foxe reprinted the material from a copy in Tyndale's handwriting: see J. F. Mozley, *William Tyndale* (London, 1937), p. 346, and A. M. E. Hume, "A Study of the Writings of the English Protestant Exiles, 1525-1535" (Ph,D. diss., University of London, 1961), pp. 273-275.

11. This is the argument of Pineas: loc. cit., pp. 90-92.

12. See K. B. McFarlane, *Wycliffe and English Non-Conformity* (Harmondsworth, Middlesex, 1972), pp. 144-168; and W. T. Waugh, "Sir John Oldcastle," *English Historical Review* 20 (1905): 434 ff. and 637 ff.

13. Bale, *A brefe Chronycle*, fols. 54-verso, 2-verso.

14. Polydore Vergil's *Anglicae Historiae Libri XXVI* had been published at Basel in 1534. Bale of course had other bones to pick with Polydore as well, especially over the Italian's coolness toward the historicity of the Arthurian legends. See Haller, op. cit., pp. 62-63; T. D. Kendrick, *British Antiquity* (London, 1950), pp. 78-98; and Fritz Levy, *Tudor Historical Thought* (San Marino, California, 1967), pp. 96-97.

15. Bale, *A brefe Chronycle*, fol. 6; cf. Vergil, op. cit., pp. 435-436.

16. Bale seems in fact to have invented out of whole cloth an interview between Oldcastle and Henry V, emphasizing the former's wholesome loyalty to his monarch. In this short passage (Bale, *A brefe Chronycle*, fols. 13-verso to 14), Oldcastle assures Henry of his total obedience, but adds that of course he opposes the pope with all his heart. This passage appears in none of the sources which Bale used, and indeed would be anachronistic if it did.

17. Ibid., fols. 7-8. In point of fact Bale was wrong about the

Praemunire legislation. Oldcastle's wife's grandfather, the Lord Cobham (whose title Oldcastle had assumed upon marriage), had been the one involved in that. Oldcastle himself evidently did not sit in Parliament until 1404: see Waugh, loc. cit., p. 437.

18. William Tyndale (?), ed., *The examinacion of syr Ihon Oldcastell*, sig. H3-verso; Bale, *A brefe Chronycle*, fol. 16-verso.

19. Tyndale (?), *Examinacion*, sig. H4-verso; Bale, *A brefe Chronycle*, fol. 18.

20. For Bale's rather erratic eucharistic thought, see C. W. Dugmore, *The Mass and the English Reformers* (London, 1958), pp. 234-236.

21. The scattered bits of biographical data concerning Anne Askew have recently been summarized in Derek Wilson, *A Tudor Tapestry* (London, 1972), especially pp. 159-167, 180-224, and 229-234. For the atmosphere at court at the end of Henry VIII's reign, see also L. B. Smith, *Henry VIII: The Mask of Royalty* (London, 1971), pp. 240 ff.

22. Both volumes have a "Marburg" colophon, but for the actual printer and place, see Honor McCusker, "Some Ornamental Initials Used by Plateanus of Wesel," *The Library*, 4th ser., 16 (1936): 452 ff.

23. John Bale, *The first examinacyon of Anne Askewe* (Wesel, 1546), fol. 5; John Bale, *The lattre examinacyon of Anne Askewe* (Wesel, 1547), fols. 11, 43-verso to 44.

24. Bale, *The lattre examinacyon*, fol. 8.

25. Bale, *The first examinacyon*, fols. 7-9. Bale did not repudiate the notion of the miraculous entirely—what Weber called *die Entzauberung der Welt* was hardly completed for Bale in his metamorphosis from Carmelite to Protestant. But he preferred to attribute miracles to God directly, and not to the saints as channels of supernatural power. Bale did accept the story that a thunder-clap had signalled Anne's execution, and he felt obliged to show that this phenomenon had indicated God's displeasure with Anne's executioners, and not with Anne herself: Bale, *The lattre examinacyon*, fols. 67-68.

26. Stephen Gardiner, *The Letters of Stephen Gardiner*, ed. J. A. Muller (New York, 1933), p. 278.

27.   Bale, *The lattre examinacyon*, fols. 45, 47. It should be noted that no evidence has surfaced to support Anne's claim that Rich and Wriothesley racked her with their own hands. The only other contemporary reference to the episode (a letter of the London merchant Ottwell Johnson) says merely that "she hath been racked since her condemnation (as men say) which is a strange thing, in my understanding." See H. Ellis, ed., *Original Letters, Illustrative of English History*, 2nd ser. 2 (1827): 176; cited in Wilson, op. cit., pp. 223-224.

28.   One minute factor confirming a part of Anne's account is found in the recollections of John Louthe. The latter records a discussion between Anne and the Lord Mayor of London concerning the putative fate of a mouse who might inadvertently eat consecrated bread: see J. G. Nichols, ed., *Narratives of the Days of the Reformation* (London, 1859), p. 41. Anne also mentions the incident in her account: Bale, *The first examinacyon*, fol. 8.

29.   Bale, *The lattre examinacyon*, fol. 11-verso.

30.   See e.g., ibid., fol. 25.

31.   For instance, John Bale, *A dysclosynge or openynge of the Manne of synne*, ("Zurich," [i.e. Antwerp], 1543), fol. 60-verso: "a mutuall pertycypacyon of christes bodye and blood. . . ." See also John Bale, *The Image of bothe churches* (London, 1548), 2: sig. h3: "mutual perticipacion of Christes body and bloud. . . ."

32.   Bale, *The first examinacyon*, fol. 38.

33.   Guildhall, London, MS. 9531/12, fol. 101; printed in John Foxe, *Actes and Monuments* (London, 1563), pp. 672-673.

34.   One would still give a good deal to know what Gardiner's specific objections were, but no one else seems to have criticized the pamphlet's accuracy on matters of fact.

35.   Editions came from the London presses of N. Hill (probably), W. Hill, John Day, and W. Copland, respectively (STC nos. 851, 852, 853, and 853.5). For the figure of 700 or so as the maximum number of copies in an edition, see H. S. Bennett, *English Books and Readers, 1475 to 1557* (Cambridge, 1952), p. 228.

36.   See W. K. Jordan, ed., *The Chronicle and Political Papers of King Edward VI* (Ithaca, New York, 1966), p. 179.

37.   John Bale, *The vocacyon of Johan Bale to the bishoprick of Ossorie in Irelande* ("Rome," i.e., Wesel [Joos Lambrecht], 1553),

fols. 15-verso to 42. The colophon to the pamphlet claims that it was printed "in Rome / before the castell of S. Angell / at ye signe of S. Peter / in Decembre / Anno D. 1553" (ibid., sig. G7; sigs. A1-G1 are numbered consecutively 1-49, but sigs. G2-G8 bear no numbering). There is no reason to question the date, but the place given is obviously a bit of bravado. The woodcut on the title page offers a clue, however, to the whereabouts of the press: it was a cut which had previously been used by one Joos Lambrecht (see Davies, p. 268). As of late 1553, Lambrecht's press was located at Wesel; see P. Bockmuehl, "Wo ist die erste Ausgabe des Werkes von Johannes Anastasius Velanus: 'Der Leeken Wechwyser' im Jahre 1554 gedrukt?" *Theologische Arbeiten* (Neue Folge) 13: 115-116. (Katharine Pantzer of the Houghton Library, Harvard University, was kind enough to supply this reference.) So it seems likely that Bale headed for Wesel, his former home in exile, in late 1553. One bibliographical puzzle remains, however, concerning the printer of *The vocacyon*. At the end of the work, on sig. G8-verso, one finds a printer's device which later appeared on books (printed on the Continent and in London) from the press of Hugh Singleton: the printer's rebus within a border, under which appears the motto "God is my helper" (R. B. McKerrow, *Printers' and Publishers' Devices in England and Scotland, 1485-1640* [London, 1913], no. 127). Miss Christina Garrett has suggested that Singleton spent some time at Wesel during the early reign of Queen Mary—which could fit the date of *The vocacyon*. So probably Singleton and Lambrecht collaborated in printing the work at Wesel. For Singleton's movements, see Christina H. Garrett, *"The Resurrection of the Masse,* by Hugh Hilarie—or John Bale?" *The Library*, 4th ser., 21 (1941): 154-155.

38. For the development of autobiography in England, see especially Paul Delany, *British Autobiography in the Seventeenth Century* (London, 1969), pp. 6-39; James Osborne, ed., *The Autobiography of Thomas Whythorne* (Oxford, 1961); Wayne Shumaker, *English Autobiography* (Berkeley, California, 1954); Donald Stauffer, *English Biography before 1700* (Cambridge, Massachusetts, 1930); and Owen Watkins, *The Puritan Experience* (London, 1972), pp. 1-35.

39. For the tradition of *res gestate* see especially Delany, pp. 107-157, and Shumaker, pp. 56-58.

40. Bale, *The vocacyon*, fol. 37 to 37-verso.

41. Ibid., fol. 2.

42. Ibid., fol. 43.

43. Ibid., fol. 3.

44. Ibid., fol. 2-verso.

45. Ibid., fols. 4-verso to 7-verso.

46. See Delany, op. cit., pp. 29-31.

47. Cf. Watkins, op. cit., pp. 9-14.

48. G. R. Owst, *Literature and Pulpit in Medieval England* (New York, 1966), p. 235: "In a word, then, our medieval pulpit satire adequately explains alike the coarseness and the acerbity of both Humanist and Reformer."

49. Bale, *The vocacyon,* fol. 36. For similar forays against clerical vice, see fols. 4-verso, 18, and 45.

50. Ibid., fols. 11-verso to 15-verso.

51. G. R. Owst, *Preaching in Medieval England* (New York, 1965), p. 58.

52. See Bodleian Library MS. Selden supra 41, fol. 195 to 195-verso; British Museum MS. Harley 3838 (*Anglorum Heliades*), fols. 111-verso to 112-verso; and *Summarium*, fol. 242. Bale of course published one more autobiographical sketch after he had written *The vocacyon*—in the *Catalogus*, 1: 702.

53. See John Bale, *The Laboryouse Journey & serche of Johan Leylande* (London, 1549).

54. Bodleian Library MS. Selden supra 41, fol. 95: *"me inter ceteros intersero, omnium minimus, ut sciant posteri inter hos me non semper ociosum fuisse."*

55. James Cancellar, *The pathe of Obedience* (London: John Waylande, c. 1556), sigs. D3-D7. Pollard and Redgrave in the old edition of STC suggested "1553?" as the date of the pamphlet, but sig. B8 mentions the executions of Cranmer, Ridley, and Latimer, so the tract must have postdated March 1556. Bale's rebuttal of Cancellar (written in Canterbury in 1561) is still in MS.: Lambeth Palace Library MS. 2001, "A Returne of James Cancellers raylynge boke upon hys owne heade, called the pathe of obedyence."

VI / The Last Years

1.   J. Le Neve, *Fasti Ecclesiae Anglicanae*, T. D. Hardy, ed. (Oxford, 1854), 1: 60.

2.   Bale's stipend may be deduced from entries in the Chapter Library, Canterbury, Treasurer of the Chapter's Miscellaneous Accounts, vol. 40 (case f2, shelf 5.4) under, for example, the year 1561-1562. Bale received £4.6.8 as a flat fee per quarter, plus 15d. for each day on which he attended services. In 1561-1562 this worked out to £40.2.11.

3.   Quoted in McCusker, p. 31. A full transcript of the letter may be found in Cambridge Antiquarian Society, *Antiquarian Communications* 3 (1879): 157-173.

4.   See McCusker, pp. 30-31; and Davies, p. 229.

5.   Chapter Library, Canterbury, Consistory Court Depositions, vol. X.10.7, fols. 36-39. The dialogue is actually drawn from four depositions (by Barnes, Hall, Pilkington, and Poole) and one cannot be sure that the conversation went exactly as reproduced here. The gist of the matter is not likely to have been much different, however.

6.   Bale would supply an interesting link between the late medieval friars and the Elizabethan preachers who, in Professor Morgan's view, assumed their role: Irvonwy Morgan, *The Godly Preachers of the Elizabethan Church* (London, 1965), pp. 1-10, 138-174. For an alternate reading of Bale's character—which sees his temperament as essentially scholarly rather than partisan—see McCusker, pp. 123-128. This interpretation hardly seems confirmed by the sources.

7.   See John Bale, *King Johan*, J. H. P. Pafford, ed. (Oxford, 1931), p. xxii.

8.   John Bale, *A Comedy concernynge thre lawes* (Wesel, c. 1548), sig. G1-verso: "Lete Idolatry be decked lyke an olde wytche ... and hypocresy lyke a graye fryre." The play was reprinted at London in 1562 as *A Newe Comedy or Enterlude, concernyng thre lawes* (London [Thomas Colwell], 1562).

9.   For the incident, see Chapter Library, Canterbury, Consistory Court Depositions, vol. X.10.7, fols. 136-141, and vol. X.10.8, fol. 2-verso.

10.   For the various stages of the case, see Chapter Library, Canterbury, Consistory Court Act Books Y.2.22, fols. 112, 128-verso; and Y.2.25, fols. 9, 12-verso, 22-verso, 36.

11. The date of Bale's death may be computed from the notation in Chapter Library, Canterbury, Treasurer of the Chapter's Miscellaneous Accounts, vol. 40 (case f.2, shelf 5.4) under 1563-1564, fol. 3-verso: "to Mr. Bales widow for 47 dayes that her husband lyved, of this quarter." The quarter in question ran from Michaelmas to Christmas, so if Bale had lived for forty-seven days in this period he probably died on the night of 15 November. His successor, Andrew Peerson, was paid for twenty-four days in this quarter, so he must have taken up residence on 2 December. He had been admitted on 30 November: see Le Neve, op. cit., 1:60.

12. Bale's burial in the Cathedral nave is revealed in Chapter Library, Canterbury, MS. precis of wills (Tyler Collection), no. 167: "Rich'd Beseley of the Cathedral Church of Xst in Cant'y. Preacher of the Gospel wills to be bur. in the Body of the said Church with the consent of the Dean and Chapter near unto the bodies of John Bale and Rob't Pownall his companions in Exile." (I am indebted for this reference to Dr. William Urry, former Chapter Librarian.) For Dorothy Bale's annuity, see Chapter Library, Canterbury, Treasurer of the Chapter's Miscellaneous Accounts, vol. 40, under 1564, fol. 41 and passim; under 1569, fol. 50.

13. For the most recent summary of their work, see May McKisack, *Medieval History in the Tudor Age* (Oxford, 1971), pp. 1-25.

14. See McCusker, pp. 58-66, for an accessible version of most of the letter.

15. Ibid., pp. 68-70 for these letters.

16. Ibid., p. 61.

17. References are scattered throughout the work; see e.g. Matthias Flacius Illyricus, *Ecclesiastica historia* (Basel, 1559-1574), cent. 11, cols. 374, 414, 519, 610, 613, etc.

18. Viz. ibid., cent. 7, col. 595: "*Cum mysterium iniquitatis in urbe Roma (Apocalypsim decimo septimo) ad fastigium properaret, & Phocae praesidio Maleficius supra omnes ecclesias esset elevatus*" . . . etc.

19. For comments on the *Centuries*, see Pontien Polman, *L'Elément Historique dans la Controverse Réligieuse du XVIe Siècle* (Gembloux, 1932), pp. 216 ff.; and Wilhelm Preger, *Matthias Flacius Illyricus* (Nieuwkoop, 1964), 2:413-477. Professor Haller is surely mistaken in suggesting that Flacius, for his part, influenced Bale (William Haller,

Foxe's Book of Martyrs and the Elect Nation [London, 1967], pp. 64-65). Bale's thought had taken shape a decade before Flacius's historical works began to appear.

20.   Haller op. cit., pp. 58-71; Fritz Levy, *Tudor Historical Thought* (San Marino, California, 1967), pp. 88-97, 104; and Glanmor Williams, *Reformation Views of Church History* (Richmond, Virginia, 1970), p. 51.

21.   John Foxe, *Actes and Monuments* (London, 1563), p. 7.

22.   Foxe did wisely excise the better part of Bale's commentary on Oldcastle and Askew, but he did accept willingly Bale's argument about the Oldcastle fracas at St. Giles' Fields in 1414—that is, that the story was a papist lie. Acknowledging that Walden, Fabyan, Polydore Vergil, and others had mentioned the abortive coup, Foxe nevertheless asserted (a bit weakly) that those writers had failed to treat the incident "in al poyntes rightli" (Ibid., p. 275). His account follows Bale's closely. Here is evidently one instance in which Foxe allowed his Protestant assumptions (and his friendship for Bale) to overcome any urge he might have had to probe into the sources too deeply. When attacked later for his version of the Oldcastle story, Foxe fortified the same position elaborately, though still with more rhetoric than proof: *Actes and Monuments* (London, 1576), 1:547-565. Bale's image of Oldcastle, the Protestant saint, was too attractive to renounce.

23.   See V. N. Olsen, *John Foxe and the Elizabethan Church* (Berkeley, California, 1973), pp. 197-219.

24.   John Bale, *The Image of bothe churches* (Wesel, 1548), 2: sigs. e4, h4-verso.

25.   Olsen, op. cit., pp. 69-73.

26.   Bale, *Image*, 3: sigs. Gg4-verso to Gg5.

27.   See Foxe, *Actes and Monuments* (1563), p. 9; and *Actes and Monuments* (1570), sig. iii-verso: cited in Olsen, op. cit., pp. 69, 113.

28.   John Bale, *Acta Romanorum Pontificum* (Basel, 1559), p. 28: "*mitrati pontifices erant, canonibus ac decretis suis, Antichristo magno sedem parantes.*"

29.   For Bale's view, see, e.g., *Catalogus*, 1:32-33; for Foxe's, see Olsen, op. cit., pp. 72-84, 183-185.

30.   Ibid., pp. 75-80.

31.   Bale, *Image*, 2: sigs. h3-verso to h4.

32. See, e.g., John Bale, *A dysclosynge or openynge of the Manne of synne* (Antwerp, 1543), fol. 11.

33. The distinction between premillennial (or chiliastic) and post-millennial views of the Apocalypse is the crucial one in studying English attitudes toward the Book of Revelation in the sixteenth and seventeenth centuries. The characterization of millenarian thought in sixteenth- and seventeenth-century England as either "centripetal" (Bale, Foxe, et al.) or "centrifugal" (Brightman, et al.) in William M. Lamont, *Godly Rule* (London, 1969), is misleading on several counts—chiefly because it assumes that Foxe and the other magisterial postmillenarians expected some sort of golden age on earth, which they manifestly did not. For a cogent summary of the flaws in Lamont's study, see Bernard Capp, "The Millennium and Eschatology in England," *Past and Present* 57 (November 1972): 156-162.

34. See Christopher Hill, *Antichrist in Seventeenth-Century England* (London, 1971), pp. 1-77.

Appendix I

1. Davies, pp. 244-246; see also W. W. Greg, ed., *English Literary Autographs, 1550-1650,* 2 (Oxford, 1928), plate 31.

2. Davies, pp. 240-241.

3. McCusker, pp. 97-110.

4. McCusker, p. 105: she refers to fol. 32-verso, which was evidently a misprint for fol. 82-verso.

5. Davies, p. 245.

6. McCusker, pp. 98-99.

7. Davies, p. 240.

8. McCusker, p. 103.

9. Davies, pp. 240-241.

10. Davies, p. 241.

11. Davies, pp. 209-213.

12. Davies p. 206; McCusker pp. 100-101.

13. Davies, p. 206; McCusker, p. 100.

14. Davies, p. 243 and McCusker, p. 104.

15. Davies, p. 243; McCusker, p. 102.

Bibliography

I. Sources in Manuscript

    A. *Cambridge*

       Cambridge University Library. MS. Ff.6.28.

       Cambridge University Library. Ely Diocesan Records AG 1/7.

       Trinity College. MS. R.7.15.

    B. *Canterbury*

       Chapter Library. Consistory Court Act Books Y.2.22, Y.2.25.

       Chapter Library. Consistory Court Depositions. Volumes X.10.7, X.10.8.

       Chapter Library. Treasurer of the Chapter's Miscellaneous Accounts. Volume XL (Case f.2, shelf 5.4).

       Chapter Library.Tyler Collection. MS. precis of wills.

    C. *London*

       British Museum. Add. MS. 29546.

       British Museum. MS. Cotton Cleopatra E.iv.

       British Museum. MS. Cotton Cleopatra E.v.

       British Museum. MS. Cotton Titus D.x.

       British Museum. MS. Harley 417.

       British Museum. MS. Harley 1819.

       British Museum. MS. Harley 3838.

       Greater London Record Office. Vicar General's Book, DL/C/330.

       Guildhall. MS. 9531/12.

       Inner Temple Library. MS. Petyt 538/47.

Lambeth Palace Library. MS. 2001.

Public Record Office, SP 1/111, 1/114, 1/115, 1/116.

D. *Oxford*

Bodleian Library. MS. Bodley 73.

Bodleian Library. MS. e Musaeo 86.

Bodleian Library. MS. Selden supra 41.

Bodleian Library. MS. Selden supra 64 (published as Bale, John. *Index Britanniae Scriptorum.* Edited by R. L. Poole and Mary Bateson. Oxford, 1902).

Bodleian Library. MS. Selden supra 72.

E. *Norwich*

Norwich and Norfolk Record Office. REG/10, book xv.

F. *Winchester*

Hampshire County Record Office. Register of Bishop John Ponet.

G. *York*

Borthwick Institute. Archbishops' Registers R.I.28 (Archbishop Lee).

Borthwick Institute. Chancery and Audience Court R.VII.3.

II. Primary Sources in Print

A. Works written or edited by John Bale, to which reference is made in the text above.

Acta Romanorum Pontificum. Basel, 1558, 1559.

The Actes of Englysh votaryes. "Wesel" (i.e. Antwerp), 1546; London, 1548, 1551.

The Apology of Johan Bale agaynste a ranke Papyst. London, n.d. (c. 1550).

A brefe chronycle concernynge the Examinacyon and death of the blessed martyr of Christ syr Johan Oldecastell. N.p. (i.e., Antwerp), 1544.

A Christen Exhortacyon unto Customable Swearers. Antwerp, n.d. (c. 1542).

A Comedy concernynge thre lawes. N.p., n.d. (Wesel, c. 1548).

A Declaration of Edmonde Bonners articles. London, 1561.

The Dramatic Works of John Bale. Edited by John S. Farmer. London, 1907.

A dysclosynge or openynge of the Manne of synne. "Zurik," (i.e. Antwerp), 1543.

The epistle exhortatorye of an Englysh Christyane. "Basyle" (i.e., Antwerp), 1544. (With William Turner.)

An Expostulation or complaynte agaynste the Blasphemyes of a franticke papyst of Hamshyre. London, n.d. (c. 1552).

The first examinacyon of Anne Askewe. "Marpurg" (i.e., Wesel), 1546.

The first two partes of the Actes or unchast examples of the Englysh votaryes. London, 1560.

Illustrium Maioris Britanniae Scriptorum . . . Summarium. "Ipswich," (i.e., Wesel), 1548.

The Image of bothe churches. N.p., n.d. (Antwerp, c. 1545); London, n.d. (1548); London, n.d. (ca. 1550); London, 1550; London, n.d. (1570).

King John. Edited by J. H. P. Pafford, Oxford, 1931; edited by Barry B. Adams, San Marino, California, 1969.

The laboryouse Journey & serche of Johan Leylande. London, 1549.

The lattre examinacyon of Anne Askewe. "Marpurg" (i.e., Wesel), 1547.

A mysterye of inyquyte. "Geneva" (i.e., Antwerp), 1545.

The Pageant of Popes. Edited and translated by John Studley. London, 1574.

Scriptorum Illustrium maioris Brytannie . . . Catalogus. Basel, 1557-1559.

A treatyse made by Johan Lambert. N.P., n.d. (Wesel, c. 1548).

The vocacyon of Johan Bale to the bishoprick of Ossorie in Irelande. "Rome" (i.e., Wesel), 1553.

B.   Other primary sources in print, to which reference is made in footnotes to the text above.

Abbas Joachim Magnus Propheta Venice, n.d. (c. 1516).

Annius of Viterbo. *Commentarii.* Rome, 1498.

Anonymous. *The Olde Faythe of Great Brittaygne.* London, n.d. (c. 1549).

Baptista Mantuanus. *Eclogues.* Edited by W. P. Mustard. Baltimore, Maryland, 1911.

Barnes, Robert. *A supplicacion unto the most gracyous prynce H. the .viii.* London, 1534.

———. *Vitae Pontificum Romanorum.* Wittenberg, 1536.

Bede. *Venerabilis Baedae opera Historica.* Edited by C. Plummer. Vol. 1. Oxford, 1896.

Cancellar, James. *The pathe of Obedience.* London, n.d. (c. 1556).

Capgrave, John. *Nova Legenda Angliae.* London, 1516.

Carion, Johann. *Cronica.* Halle, 1537.

The Chronicle and Political Papers of King Edward VI. Edited by Wilbur K. Jordan. Ithaca, New York, 1966.

Concilia Magnae Britanniae et Hiberniae. Edited by David Wilkins. 4 vols. London, 1737.

The County of Suffolk. Edited by W. A. Copinger. Vol. 2. London, 1904.

Documents Illustrative of English Church History. Edited by H. Gee and W. J. Hardy. London, 1910.

Dokumente zu Luthers Entwicklung. Edited by Otto Scheel. Tuebingen, 1929.

Erasmus, Desiderius. *A Playne and godly exposytion or declaration of the commune Crede and of the .x. commaundmentes.* London, 1533.

———. *Ten Colloquies.* New York, 1957.

Faculty Office Registers. Edited by D. S. Chambers. Oxford, 1966.

Fish, Simon. *A supplicacyon for the beggers.* Antwerp, n.d. (c. 1528).

Flacius Illyricus, Matthias. *Ecclesiastica Historia.* Basel, 1559-1574.

Foxe, John. *Actes and Monuments*. London, 1563, 1570, 1576; edited by J. Pratt, London, 1870; edited by George Townsend, New York, 1965.

Gardiner, Stephen. *The Letters of Stephen Gardiner*. Edited by J. A. Muller. New York, 1933.

Grace Book Γ. Edited by W. G. Searle. Cambridge, 1908.

Joye, George. *An Apology made by George Joye*. Edited by Edward Arber. Birmingham, 1883.

Lambert, Francis. *Exegeseos . . . in sanctam Divi Ioannis Apocalypsim Libri VII*. Marburg, 1528.

Leland, John. *Commentarii de Scriptoribus Britannicis*. Edited by Anthony Hall. Oxford, 1709.

Letters and Papers, Foreign and Domestic, of the Reign of Henry VIII. Edited by J. S. Brewer et al. 21 vols. London, 1862-1910.

Meyer, Sebastian. *In Apocalypsim Ioannis Apostoli . . . Commentarius*. Zurich, 1539.

More, Thomas. *The confutacyon of Tyndales answere*. London, 1532.

Narratives of the Days of the Reformation. Edited by J. G. Nichols. London, 1859.

Original Letters, Illustrative of English History. Edited by Henry Ellis. 11 vols. in 3 ser. London, 1824-46.

Platina, Bartolomeo. *De Vita et Moribus summorum Pontificum*. Cologne, 1529.

Pollard, A. W., Redgrave, G. R., et al. *A Short-Title Catalogue*, London, 1926.

Roy, William (or Barlowe, Jerome?). *A proper dyaloge betwene a Gentillman and an Husbandman*. Antwerp, n.d. (c. 1529).

Suffolk in 1524—Return for a Subsidy Granted in 1523. Edited by S. H. A. Hervey. Woodbridge, Suffolk, 1910.

Trevet, Nicholas. *Annales sex Regum Angliae*. Edited by Thomas Hog. London, 1845.

Trithemius, Johann. *Liber de Scriptoribus Ecclesiasticis*. Basel, 1494.

Turner, William. *The Huntyng & fyndyng out of the Romishe Foxe.* "Basyl" (i.e. Bonn), 1543.

Tyndale, William, ed. *The examinacion of syr Ihon Old-castell.* "Marburg" (i.e., Antwerp), 1530.

_____ et al. *The Whole workes of W. Tyndall, John Frith, and Doct. Barnes.* London, 1573.

Valor Ecclesiasticus. Edited by J. Caley and J. Hunter. 6 vols. London, 1810-1834.

Vergil, Polydore. *Historiae Anglicae Libri XXVI.* Basel, 1534.

Walsingham, Thomas. *Historia Anglicana.* Edited by H. T. Riley. London, 1864.

von Watt, Joachim. *Vom Alten und Neuen Gott.* N.p., 1521; translated by William Turner. London, 1534.

Wyclif, John. *Polemical Works in Latin.* Edited by Rudolf Buddensieg. Vol. 2. London, 1883.

III. Secondary sources to which reference is made in footnotes to the text above

Aigran, René. *L'Hagiographie.* Paris, 1953.

Aston, M. E. "John Wyclif's Reformation Reputation." *Past and Present* 30 (1965): 22-51.

_____ . "Lollardy and the Reformation: Survival or Revival?" *History* 49 (1964): 149-170.

Auerbach, Erich. *Mimesis.* Garden City, New York, 1957.

_____ . *Scenes from the Drama of European Literature.* New York, 1959.

Bailey, D. S. *Thomas Becon.* Edinburgh, 1952.

Bainton, Roland. *The Reformation of the Sixteenth Century.* Boston, Massachusetts, 1956.

Baker, Herschel. *The Race of Time.* Toronto, 1967.

Bang, Willy. Review of *Index Britanniae Scriptorum* by John Bale, edited by R. L. Poole and Mary Bateson. Oxford, 1902. *Englische Studien* 34 (1904): 110-113.

Barke, Herbert. *Bales "Kynge Johan" und sein Verhaeltnis zur Zeitgenoessischen Geschichtsschreibung.* Berlin, 1937.

Bennett, H. S. *English Books and Readers, 1475 to 1557.* Cambridge, 1952.

Berkovitch, Sacvan, ed. *Typology in Early American Literature.* Amherst, Massachusetts, 1972.

Blatt, Thora. *The Plays of John Bale.* Copenhagen, 1968.

Blench, J. W. *Preaching in England in the Late Fifteenth and Sixteenth Centuries.* New York, 1964.

Bockmuehl, P. "Wo ist die erste Ausgabe des Werkes von Johannes Anastasius Velanus: 'Der Leeken Wechwyser' im Jahre 1554 gedrukt?" *Theologische Studien.* Neue Folge, 13 (1912): 110-128.

Booty, John. *John Jewel as Apologist of the Church of England.* London, 1963.

Burnet, G., and Pocock, N. *History of the Reformation of the Church of England.* 7 vol. Oxford, 1865.

Capp, Bernard. "The Millennium and Eschatology in England." *Past and Present* 57 (1972): 156-162.

————. "*Godly Rule* and the Millennium." *Past and Present* 52 (1971): 106-117.

Carroll, Eamon. "The Marian Theology of Arnold Bostius (1445-1499)." *Carmelus* 9 (1962): 197-236.

Cheney, C. R. *Handbook of Dates.* London, 1970.

Clair, Colin. "On the Printing of Certain Reformation Books." *The Library.* 5th ser., 18 (1963): 275-287.

Clebsch, William. *England's Earliest Protestants.* New Haven, Connecticut, 1964.

Cohn, Norman. *The Pursuit of the Millennium.* London, 1970.

Collinson, Patrick. "The Authorship of *A Brieff Discours. . . .*" *Journal of Ecclesiastical History* 9 (1958): 188-208.

————. *The Elizabethan Puritan Movement.* Berkeley, California, 1967.

Crompton, J. F. "*Fasciculi Zizaniorum.*" *Journal of Ecclesiastical History* 12 (1961): 35-45, 155-166.

Cullmann, Oscar. *Christ and Time.* London, 1951.

Daniélou, Jean. *From Shadows to Reality: Studies in the Biblical Typology of the Fathers.* Westminster, Maryland, 1960.

Davies, W. T. "A Bibliography of John Bale." *Oxford Bibliographical Society, Proceedings and Papers.* Vol. 5, part 4 (1940), pp. 203-279.

Delany, Paul. *British Autobiography in the Seventeenth Century.* London, 1969.

Delehaye, Hippolyte. *The Legends of the Saints.* South Bend, Indiana, 1961.

Dickens, A. G. *The English Reformation.* London, 1964.

_____. *Lollards and Protestants in the Diocese of York.* London, 1959.

_____. *Thomas Cromwell and the English Reformation.* New York, 1969.

Dictionary of National Biography. 22 vols. London, 1949-1950.

duBoulay, F. R. H. "The Quarrel between the Carmelite Friars and the Secular Clergy of London." *Journal of Ecclesiastical History* 6 (1955): 156-174.

Dugmore, C. W. *The Mass and the English Reformers.* London, 1958.

Egan, Keith J. "An Essay Towards a Historiography of the Origin of the Carmelite Province in England." *Carmelus* 19 (1972): 67-100.

_____. "Medieval Carmelite Houses, England and Wales." *Carmelus* 16 (1969): 142-226.

Eliade, Mircea. *The Myth of the Eternal Return.* Princeton, New Jersey, 1971.

Elton, Geoffrey R. *Policy and Police.* Cambridge, 1972.

Fairfield, Leslie P. "The Mysterious Press of 'Michael Wood' (1553-1554)." *The Library.* 5th ser., 27 (1972): 220-232.

_____. "*The vocacyon of Johan Bale* and Early English Autobiography." *Renaissance Quarterly* 24 (Autumn 1971): 327-340.

Farrer, Austin. *A Rebirth of Images.* Westminster, 1949.

Feret, H. M. *The Apocalypse of St. John.* Translated by Elizabethe Corathiel. London, 1958.

Flesseman-van Leer, E. "The Controversy about Scripture and Tradition between Thomas More and William Tyndale." *Nederlands Archief voor Kerkgeschiedenis* 43 (1959): 143-164.

Fussner, F. S. *Tudor History and the Historians.* New York, 1970.

Galbraith, V. H. *Historical Research in Medieval England.* London, 1951.

Garrett, Christina H. *The Marian Exiles.* Cambridge, 1966.

_____. "*The Resurrection of the Masse*, by Hugh Hilarie—or John Bale?" *The Library* 4th ser., 21 (1941): 143-159.

Gray, J. H., *The Queens' College.* London, 1899.

Greg, W. W., *English Literary Autographs, 1550-1650.* Vol. 2. Oxford, 1928.

Hale, J. R. *Renaissance Europe.* London, 1971.

Haller, William. *Foxe's Book of Martyrs and the Elect Nation.* London, 1967.

Hanning, Robert W. *The Vision of History in Early Britain.* New York, 1966.

Harris, Jesse. *John Bale.* Urbana, Illinois, 1940.

Headley, John M. *Luther's View of Church History.* New Haven, Connecticut, 1963.

Herford, C. H. *Studies in the Literary Relations of England and Germany in the Sixteenth Century.* London, 1886.

Hill, Christopher. *Antichrist in Seventeenth-Century England.* London, 1971.

Hudson, Winthrop. *John Ponet.* Chicago, 1942.

Hughes, Philip. *The Reformation in England.* 3 vols. in 1. New York, 1963.

Huizinga, Johann. *The Waning of the Middle Ages.* Garden City, New York, n.d.

Hume, Anthea. "A Study of the Writings of the English Protestant Exiles, 1525-1535." Ph.D. thesis, University of London, 1961.

Jacob, E. F. *The Fifteenth Century.* Oxford, 1961.

Janelle, Pierre. *L'Angleterre Catholique à la Veille du Schisme.* Paris, 1935.

Jordan, Wilbur K. *Edward VI: The Young King.* Cambridge, Massachusetts, 1968.

Kamlah, Wilhelm. *Apokalypse und Geschichtstheologie.* Berlin, 1935.

Kelley, Donald R. *Foundations of Modern Historical Scholarship.* New York, 1970.

_____ . "Martyrs, Myths and Massacre: The Background of St. Bartholomew." *American Historical Review* 77 (1972): 1323-1342.

Kendrick, T. D. *British Antiquity.* London, 1950.

Kingsford, C. L. *English Historical Writing in the Fifteenth Century.* Oxford, 1913.

Knappen, Marshall M. *Tudor Puritanism.* Chicago, 1965.

Knowles, M. David. *The Religious Orders in England.* 3 vols. Cambridge, 1960-1961.

Lamont, William. *Godly Rule.* London, 1969.

Laslett, Peter. *The World We Have Lost.* New York, 1965.

Leclercq, Jean. *The Love of Learning and the Desire for God.* New York, 1961.

LeNeve, J. *Fasti Ecclesiae Anglicanae.* Edited by T. D. Hardy. Vol. 1. Oxford, 1854.

Levy, Fritz J. *Tudor Historical Thought.* San Marino, California, 1967.

Little, A. G. "Corrodies at the Carmelite Friary of Lynn." *Journal of Ecclesiastical History* 9 (1958): 8-29.

Loades, D. M. *The Oxford Martyrs.* London, 1970.

Markus, R. A. *Saeculum: History and Society in the Theology of St. Augustine.* Cambridge, 1970.

Maltby, William. *The Black Legend in England.* Durham, North Carolina, 1971.

McCusker, Honor. *John Bale: Dramatist and Antiquary.* Bryn Mawr, Pennsylvania, 1942.

_____ . "Some Ornamental Initials Used by Plateanus of Wesel." *The Library.* 4th ser., 16 (1936): 452-454.

McFarlane, K. B. *Wycliffe and English Non-Conformity.* Harmondsworth, Middlesex, 1972.

McKerrow, R. B. *Printers' and Publishers' Devices in England and Scotland, 1485-1640.* London, 1913.

McKisack, May. *Medieval History in the Tudor Age*. Oxford, 1971.

Milburn, R. L. P. *Early Christian Interpretations of History*. London, 1954.

Moorman, John R. H. *The Grey Friars in Cambridge*. Cambridge, 1952.

Morgan, Irvonwy. *The Godly Preachers of the Elizabethan Church*. London, 1965.

Morison, Samuel Eliot. *The Founding of Harvard College*. Cambridge, Massachusetts, 1935.

Mozley, J. F. *William Tyndale*. London, 1937.

New, John F. H. *Anglican and Puritan: The Basis of Their Opposition*. Stanford, California, 1964.

Nijhoff, Wouter. *L'Art Typographique dans les Pays-Bas*. Vol. 2. The Hague, 1902.

Oliver, Leslie M. "Sir John Oldcastle—Legend or Literature?" *The Library*, 5th ser., 1 (1946-1947): 179 ff.

Olsen, V. N. *John Foxe and the Elizabethan Church*. Berkeley, California, 1973.

Osborne, James, ed. *The Autobiography of Thomas Whythorne*. Oxford, 1961.

Owst, G. R. *Literature and Pulpit in Medieval England*. New York, 1966.

_____ . *Preaching in Medieval England*. New York, 1965.

Oxley, James E. *The Reformation in Essex*. Manchester, 1965.

Patrides, C. A. *The Grand Design of God*. London, 1972.

Pineas, Rainer. "William Tyndale's Use of History as a Weapon of Religious Controversy." *Harvard Theological Review* 55 (1962): 121-144.

_____ . "William Tyndale's Influence on John Bale's Polemical Use of History." *Archiv fuer Reformationsgeschichte* 53 (1962): 79-96.

Polman, Pontien. *L'Elément Historique dans la Controverse Réligieuse du XVIe Siècle*. Gembloux, 1932.

Porter, H. C. "The Nose of Wax: Scripture and the Spirit from Erasmus to Milton." *Transactions of the Royal Historical Society*, 5th ser., 14 (1964): 155-174.

————. *Reformation and Reaction in Tudor Cambridge.* Cambridge, 1958.

Pound, J. F. "The Social and Trade Structure of Norwich, 1525-1575." *Past and Present* 34 (1966): 49-69.

Preger, Wilhelm. *Matthias Flacius Illyricus.* Niewkoop, 1964.

Preuss, Hans. *Die Vorstellung vom Antichrist im spaeteren Mittelalter.* Leipzig, 1906.

Reeves, Marjorie. *The Influence of Prophecy in the Later Middle Ages.* Oxford, 1969.

Rowse, A. L. *The England of Elizabeth.* New York, 1961.

Rupp, E. Gordon. *Studies in the Making of the English Protestant Tradition.* Cambridge, 1966.

Russell, H. G. "Lollard Opposition to Oaths by Creatures." *American Historical Review* 51 (1946): 668-684.

Scarisbrick, J. J. *Henry VIII.* London, 1968.

Shepherd, L. C. *The English Carmelites.* London, 1943.

Shumaker, Wayne. *English Autobiography.* Berkeley, California, 1954.

Smalley, Beryl. *The Study of the Bible in the Middle Ages.* South Bend, Indiana, 1964.

Smith, Lacey Baldwin. *Henry VIII: The Mask of Royalty.* London, 1971.

Stauffer, Donald. *English Biography before 1700.* Cambridge, Massachusetts, 1930.

Strype, John. *Annals of the Reformation.* Vol. 2, part 2. Oxford, 1824.

Thirsk, Joan, ed. *The Agrarian History of England and Wales, Vol. IV, 1500-1640.* Cambridge, 1967.

Thomas, Keith. *Religion and Decline of Magic.* New York, 1971.

Thompson, Craig R. *Universities in Tudor England.* Ithaca, New York, 1964.

Thompson J. A. F. *The Later Lollards,* Oxford, 1967.

Thompson, J. W. *A History of Historical Writing,* Vol. 1. New York, 1942.

Toon, Peter, ed. *Puritans, the Millennium and the Future of Israel.* Cambridge, 1970.

Toulmin, Stephen, and Goodfield, June. *The Discovery of Time*. New York, 1966.

Tuveson, Ernest Lee. *Millennium and Utopia*. New York, 1964.

Vetter, Theodor. *Literarische Beziehungen zwischen England und der Schweiz im Reformationszeitalter*. Zuerich, 1901.

Victoria County History, Cambridge. Vol. 2. London, 1948.

_____. *Essex*. Vol. 2. London, 1909.

Watkins, Owen. *The Puritan Experience*. London, 1972.

Waugh, W. T. "Sir John Oldcastle." *English Historical Review* 20 (1905): 434-455, 637-658.

Welch, Edwin. "Some Suffolk Lollards." *Proceedings of the Suffolk Archaeological Society* 29 (1962): 154-165.

White, Helen C. *Tudor Books of Saints and Martyrs*. Madison, Wisconsin, 1963.

Wiener, Carol Z. "The Beleaguered Isle: A Study of Elizabethan and Early Jacobean Anti-Catholicism." *Past and Present* 51 (1971): 27-62.

Williams, Glanmor. *Reformation Views of Church History*. Richmond, Virginia, 1970.

Wilson, Derek. *A Tudor Tapestry*. London, 1972.

Winters, Roy L. *Francis Lambert of Avignon*. Philadelphia, 1938.

Woodhouse, H. F. *The Doctrine of the Church in Anglican Theology, 1547-1603*. London, 1954.

Zimmerman, Benedict. "The White Friars at Ipswich." *Proceedings of the Suffolk Archaeological Society* 10 (1900): 196-204.

Index